T0330407

The Future of Futures

The Future of Futures
The Time of Money in Financing and Society

Elena Esposito

Università di Modena e Reggio Emilia, Italy

Edward Elgar
Cheltenham, UK • Northampton, MA, USA

Originally published in Italian as *Il futuro dei futures: Il tempo del denaro nella finanza e nella società* by Edizioni ETS, Pisa, Italy 2009.
© Elena Esposito
Translated by Elena Esposito, with assistance from Andrew K. Whitehead

Published by
Edward Elgar Publishing Limited
The Lypiatts
15 Lansdown Road
Cheltenham
Glos GL50 2JA
UK

Edward Elgar Publishing, Inc.
William Pratt House
9 Dewey Court
Northampton
Massachusetts 01060
USA

A catalogue record for this book
is available from the British Library

Library of Congress Control Number: 2010929039

MIX
Paper from
responsible sources
FSC® C018575

ISBN 978 1 84980 152 2

Typeset by Servis Filmsetting Ltd, Stockport, Cheshire
Printed and bound by MPG Books Group, UK

Praise for *The Future of Futures*

'This is a brilliant and timely book that shows how financing is centrally implicated in the very unpredictability and uncertainty it purports to master. With the incisiveness characteristic of her style and writing, Esposito reads economics in innovative ways that disclose the hidden premises by which financial instruments trade and consume the prospects of the future.'

– Jannis Kallinikos, London School of Economics, UK

'Elena Esposito's analysis of financial markets and of their recent decline is radically different from the analyses which can be found in economic journals or books. Financial operations are reduced to their basic dimensions: time and money. Under this perspective, what is sold on financial markets is the possibility for the creation of commitments in the course of time, the possibility for the combination of these commitments with one another, and the identification of chances for the achievement of profit opportunities through the creation of specific combinations. The author argues that the recent crisis of the financial system was caused by oversimplified visions of the future and of risk leading to the consequence that options were not available in the present because all possibilities had been used up by the future. This oversimplified vision of the future imploded, and trust with it. The state tried to reconstruct options for the future in order to open up new possibilities and chances for learning. The author does not deliver recipes on how to prevent severe crises of the financial system in the future. Yet, her concept facilitates understanding of how financial futures are opened up or closed and thus provides insights into basic principles on whose basis future opportunities can be kept open and trust can be maintained.

Innovative reforms of the financial system can only develop on the basis of unconventional analyses. Elena Esposito's book contains an analysis of this kind.'

– Alfred Kieser, Mannheim University, Germany

'Within the cacophony of voices trying to explain the recent financial crisis, Elena Esposito's voice sounds clear and deep. Steering away from simplistic condemnations and equally simplistic prescriptions for betterment, she connects the very invention of derivatives to that eternal human hope – of controlling the future. While the task is impossible, the attempts never stop, and the very process of attempting it brings some consolation. And while derivatives can be seen, claim sociologists of finance, as performative, that is shaping the future they promise to control, even this is far from certain. Esposito's fascinating and beautiful work is an important contribution to the sociology of finance, a subdiscipline of sociology that took on itself an extremely important task of explaining how the finance markets really work.'

– Barbara Czarniawska, University of Gothenburg, Sweden

'Elena Esposito's book is a fundamental analysis of time in economics. With economic rigour underpinned by sociological reasoning, she explains the futures market more clearly than is possible with economic analysis alone. Economic concepts are considered in terms of time – actors deal in the present with future risks by transferring these risks to the present situation. As a result, we get more options and more risks at the same time: at present. No equilibrium will balance these trades because of the asymmetry of time: our actual decisions deal with our imagination of the future, that is, with the future of the present, but the results will be realized in the presence of the future – different modalities of time. The book is a sound reflection on modelling time in economic theory, a "must" for economists.'
– Birger P. Priddat, Witten/Herdecke University, Germany

'The Future of Futures is an original and intellectually provocative book which forces the reader to think. Esposito's essay fulfils two rather different functions. On the one hand, it brings new and persuasive arguments to bear against the erroneous thesis that the present financial crisis is merely due to human mistakes and to some specific government failures. On the other hand, the book suggests that only by reconsidering the role of time in the economy is it possible to make full sense of the crisis and to reorient in a desired direction the future movements of money. It is a well-known fact that traditional economics has always adhered to a spatial conception of time, according to which time, like space, is perfectly reversible. Whence its inability both to understand how economies develop and to prescribe adequate policies. The author's proposal is to move steps ahead in the direction of an analysis of an economy in time, where both historical time and time as duration can find a place. Esposito's well-written, jargon-free book will capture the attention of anyone seriously interested in the future of our market systems.'
– Stefano Zamagni, University of Bologna and Johns Hopkins University, Bologna Center, Italy

Contents

Foreword

Bob Jessop

It is a great pleasure to write the foreword to Elena Esposito's innovative and timely book. This addresses so many complex issues, ranging from the foundations of social science and the defining features of modern societies to the rationality of financial irrationality and questions of crisis management, in such a closely and consistently integrated manner that it is impossible to summarize briefly. As such, it is not a book to be skimmed – nor, indeed, a book to be read just once. It is a book to be studied for its rich and wide-ranging insights, its demolition of received wisdoms, its creative critiques of economics as a discipline, its innovative conceptualizations, its reflections on the actuality and inactuality of time, and its brilliant exploration of the enigmas, paradoxes and contradictions of economic organization.

The general approach and its creative power will probably not surprise those familiar with, and favourably inclined towards, the sociological systems theory of Niklas Luhmann and his followers in the German-speaking world and elsewhere. And it should certainly not surprise readers who are familiar with the author's other work, which has developed this approach, applied it in several detailed sociological enquiries, and addressed important contemporary as well as historical issues. But the present work illustrates the power of the approach when applied with the author's intellectual capacities and craft skills to the increasingly complex, paradoxical and (ir)rational world of the economic system. In addition to providing an excellent and accessible introduction to the basic ideas of sociological systems theory, Elena Esposito develops them significantly in three main directions. First, she gives a provocative account of the complexities, interweaving and contingencies of time, temporality, memory and future-oriented actions, and shows how this transforms conventional understandings of economics as an activity and as a discipline. Second, based on these arguments, she develops innovative views on the nature of contemporary society as a *Risikogesellschaft* (interpreted here as 'society at risk', a better translation than the conventional term 'risk society'), the role of markets in dealing with uncertainty and risk, the significance of money and the monetization of social relations in this respect, and, relatedly, the significance of derivatives in creating as well as handling risk. And, third, she comments on the nature of the recent global economic crisis, its causes, its consequences, and the prospects for the re-regulation of the market economy and the steering of its effects on the political system in the light of her diagnosis of the peculiar features of the market economy and the ways in which it handles the problems of (future) time.

In short, this is a work that is theoretically rigorous, intellectually challenging (in the sense of provocative rather than difficult to read), descriptively and analytically powerful, and, while clearly highly topical, has profound implications for understanding past pasts as well as future presents. Those familiar with my own work will rightly surmise that there are also areas where I disagree with the author's analyses or would want to supplement them with further remarks on the contradictions (as well as paradoxes) of contemporary capitalism. But one learns far more from engaging with the work of serious scholars with whom one has productive disagreements than one does from reading the umpteenth iteration of a position that one shares. I recommend Elena Esposito's book in this spirit. Put your intellectual certainties at risk by engaging with it, observe your reactions to its insights, paradoxes and analyses, learn from its challenging, paradigm-busting arguments, and contribute thereby to the development of science and the critique of economics.

Introduction

The title of this book is deliberately ambiguous. However, the use of ambiguity is not merely a rhetorical device. In the course of this book, I hope to show that the ambiguity belongs to the analysed phenomena. It leads to both their difficulty and their fascinating appeal. Because of this ambiguity, the book and its title can be read in many different ways.

Why the future of futures? Futures stand here for derivatives as a whole, as options, swaps, forwards and others, all of which are financial instruments. These instruments – some new, others less so – deal with the future. They settle in the present the buying or selling of something (which may be anything) that will take place at a future date. That is, they are contracts that deal today with tomorrow's decisions. As we shall see, they allow the build-up of a very complex way of trading future constraints. In this way, we speak of the future of futures first in terms of how derivatives see and shape the future, as a technical and formalized way of dealing with time and its use, having consequences for society as a whole.

This is not to say that derivatives claim to foresee the true course of things. On the contrary, they are tools that react to the uncertainty and instability of the world, to the growth of risk and the resulting alarm. Derivatives turn to the future, a future that they know they don't know, and promise to protect against risks. They promise to deal in the present with the fear of the unpredictable future (which remains unpredictable). The resulting dilemma is that nobody knows if this works. Experience shows that the very attempt to protect against risks produces other risks, and that the future can actually come out differently as a result of the use of derivatives. The future of a world that uses derivatives, therefore, is different from that which would have come about if the derivatives had not existed. In this sense, the future of futures is to be understood as that future which results from the trade with futures, the future produced by futures, the future of our 'financialized' world.

There is yet a third meaning to the title, one that has become all the more urgent as a result of the financial crisis in 2008. What will happen to derivatives in the future? What will be the future of futures, if we have seen that the forms of management, their regulation and their theorizing are inadequate, and should be more thoroughly reviewed?

Here the subtitle, which presents the proposal of the book, comes into play. In order to understand these tools (and the state of finance in general), it is necessary to reconsider the role of time in the economy, that is, the time of money. Therefore we shall deal with time, with how the economy handles and regards time, and with how time changes according to the way it is used. Finally, we shall focus on the general meaning of time, that is, on how it varies depending on how it is used and how it is understood. While some clues are already available, and belong to the traditions of economics and of sociological theory, the experience of finance in the last decades could lead us to reconsider these more effectively.

It is clear that, today, financial markets deal primarily with the management of time in the form of risk, with the sale of risk and the play of influences, and with the links that exist between the way the present sees the future and the way the future actually turns out. What is sold on financial markets is the possibility of the creation of constraints in the course of time, the possibility of the combination of these constraints with one another, and the possibility of the achievement of profit opportunities. These are often based on the present use of the future, even if (or just because) the future remains unknown. Later, we shall see precisely how this happens. The point here is that, if one doesn't take the role of time into account, then all the movements of finance seem purely virtual, inconsistent, and often led by an incomprehensible irrationality (which is how financial markets are usually presented). Financial markets are presented as the realm of gambling and unreasonableness, despite the use of computers and of complex and formalized techniques. If we do not take the role of time into account, we shall be constantly surprised by the unforeseen movements of the markets, when in fact we should be able at least to expect these surprises, in so far as we produce them, at least in part, through our own behaviour.

Classical economists have pointed out that money, in its essence, is time. We do not need it in order to satisfy present needs (if we satisfied them, we would no longer have any money), but in order to assure ourselves in the present of the indistinct nebula of possible future needs. We do not know what we shall need tomorrow, but we would like to be equipped to get it, if and when it is required. To this end, if we are able to pay, we will. It is because the possible needs of the future have no limit that we need money, and why that money is never enough. Financial markets 'play' with these future possibilities, in that they intertwine and compensate, imagine and deny, and produce present profits out of the unpredictability of the future. As a matter of fact, financial markets do in a more daring way what money has always done. They deal with and trade in tomorrow's uncertainty today.

To understand financial markets, therefore, one should start from the time of money. Then it becomes clear how money works in general. Approaching economics from this point of view compels one to give up many assumptions about it (at least in its mainstream version), that have the great advantage that they can be formalized. Economic models rely on specific ideas about the markets' equilibrium, about the distribution of information, about the role of prices, about the meaning of chance, and about the rationality of operators, all of which overlook the role of time as a fundamental factor in economic behaviour. These ideas result in relatively stable and seemingly reliable models. In the last several decades, these assumptions have been heavily criticized, especially since the financial crisis, given that they have been shown not to work. It has become apparent that different instruments are needed. My proposal is that, by starting with time, one can see what has not worked and why, and try to reconstruct the movements of money in another way.

The crisis, with all its problems and difficulties, could thereby become an opportunity. The drama of the financial upheavals in the course of 2008 drew attention to the markets and to the esoteric tools they use. In turn, these have become a topic in the mass media, in politics, in public opinion and, of course, in economics. Money is fashionable. It is the central theme of our time, a theme that both involves and concerns everyone. One could also say that, in this sense, our time is 'the time of money', a time obsessed with money, seeking to find in its movements a clue to the general sense of society and its evolution. This rather new attention to the financial dynamic, given the urgency of the looming crisis and its threatening and as yet uncontrolled effects, could become an opportunity to approach and reflect on money in new and different ways that could overcome the crystallizations that have recently blocked it.

This is the time of money in finance. Both mysterious and urgent, it seems to get out of the technical sphere and affect society in general. We now move to the last reference of our title, the time of money in society. This involves very different areas, such as politics, media, organizations and families, all confronted with a new form of money and a new construction of time. The time of money could help us to understand what time has become in our society, a society obsessed with time, yet a society that understands time less and less. Here our discourse leaves the economic and financial sphere and concerns itself with what has become the 'risk society', a society no longer defined by its past or its traditions, but turned to the future. This orientation is adopted as a means of preparation for that future, but this produces further uncertainties.

The popularity of risk relies predominantly on the urgency of the future. Compared with other formulas, like those of industrial society, capitalistic society or modern society, with their respective 'post-' formulations (post-industrial, post-capitalistic or post-modern) that define the present by looking backwards, the risk society defines itself by looking forward. It sees the present as preparation for an unknown future, a future that might make us regret what we are either doing or not doing today. We are left to speculate about whether or not things will happen as we expect and predict them to, and to acknowledge that what seems prudent today could tomorrow cause damage and lead us to wish we had done otherwise. It is always possible that we could discover that the future for which we are prepared is quite different from the future that actually comes to be. Despite our ability to recognize this possibility, we still make decisions without ever being sure that they are the correct ones, precisely because the future remains uncertain. Risk, therefore, is a deadlock situation. We worry about that which cannot be avoided, and the more one thinks about it, the more one realizes that any and all decisions (and also, therefore, any and all non-decisions) are risky. In this sense, safety is an illusion.

The situation seems irresolvable, and the theory of risk has inherent difficulties in producing proposals. While it succeeds in denouncing what is wrong when one binds the future, it fails to indicate what could be construed as right. The risk society feels pressed by a future that seems already to have started, but remains the prisoner of a present that cannot know such a future. The real problem is time, in that, as long as we don't know how to handle the future (or, for that matter, what future it is that we are to handle), we cannot manage its risks.

The time of money, however, shows how the future can be produced by the very operations that try to anticipate it. This is something financial markets do continuously. They sell derivatives that set the conditions for the future in the present, and look forward to how things will continue once the future is accomplished. In buying an option, one generates a constraint that influences the course of time and contributes to the creation of what will become true in the future. The future is both bound and open at the same time, and markets deal with these constraints and their transformations. They deal with risk and its management. Understanding how these movements transpire, then, helps us to understand the functioning of time in our society because its mysteries and its circularities get translated into specific economic operations that produce (or destroy) wealth and have very tangible consequences. In studying the time of money, one studies the time of a society that defines itself with reference to a future that depends on it, both in the economy and in other spheres.

These are the issues and the presuppositions of this book. They are both numerous and interwoven. The organization of the volume is linear, and should allow readers to follow the discourse, even if they are interested in only one of the issues considered (such as financial problems, sociological problems, or the concept of time). To facilitate these different readings, a brief introduction is placed at the beginning of each chapter. This summarizes the various topics discussed and addressed in the different sections, and serves to highlight the general thread of the discussion presented. Thus it should prove easier to follow the line of discourse even when it addresses rather technical issues in one of the sections, given that one will know the point of the chapter and the means by which it develops without having to go into its technical elements.

The volume is divided into three parts, becoming gradually more specific. The first part deals with very general themes, which set the stage for later arguments. It starts by asking what the role of time in economics is, and by presenting all the criticisms that economists direct to themselves on this point (Chapter 1). It then introduces the sociological idea of a time that does not exist by itself, but is produced by the present to get an orientation towards the future (Chapter 2). This construction becomes more and more complex, because it interweaves both future and past perspectives of different observers and of different presents. The economy serves to manage this complexity because, if we have money, we can rely on the possibility of satisfying our needs in the future, even should others want the same goods. Chapter 3 reconstructs the meaning of economy in this view. Chapter 4 presents the role and the function of money, which stands for every other good and which links different presents and all members of society with one another. The circulation of money presupposes markets, which circulate information and allow operators to observe one another (Chapter 5) (a fundamental problem, hitherto treated by theory in a simplified and, therefore, highly controversial way). Financial markets exacerbate the mechanisms of the market and show how specific markets centred on risk have been produced, with a dynamic and structures that require much more abstract theoretical tools (Chapter 6).

The second part deals with the specifics of finance and the relationship of finance to the world. It asks whether the reality of finance is only virtual or whether it is a concrete production and circulation of wealth, and what the relationship between the paper economy and the real economy (Chapter 7) consists of. Chapter 8 presents and discusses derivatives, showing that they are contracts to sell and manage risks – instruments that have become necessary in an increasingly unstable and uncertain world. It deals with the problem of whether or not they are a new form of money, though much more abstract and flexible, aimed directly at the present management of a future that one knows is unknown (Chapter 9). The resulting trade of uncertainty requires complex and formalized tools, which allow operators to price and circulate risk. Chapter 10 discusses the

techniques of structured finance and their limits. These have led to unforeseeable situations and to a dramatic interlacement of time perspectives.

Part III deals with the financial crisis in 2008. In it, I try to describe the
financial crisis from the point of view of the management of time and its
shortcomings. This part goes into the details of the techniques used and
the measures taken to mitigate the consequences of the financial crisis.
Chapter 11 reconstructs the basis of the crisis, showing that it was a
matter of oversimplified visions of the future and of risk that referred to
the present. As a result, the present found out that it had no longer had
open possibilities, in that it had already used its own future. Chapter 12
presents the spread of the crisis as an implosion of the future and of trust.
This has led to a situation where, instead of overusing the future, one
refuses to build it up at all, and remains paralysed as a consequence. The
state attempted to regulate the situation (Chapter 13), adopting various
measures that proved more or less adequate depending on the image of
the future they used, that is, depending on their ability to recognize the
unpredictability of the time to come and the need to learn from it as it
comes to be the case.

At the end of the journey, no concrete answers are presented and, in
fact, for those who must decide, there are not even precise indications to
assure them of the right thing to do or the way in which to do it. Such a
claim would go against the general approach of the book, which starts
with the uncertainty and obscurity of the future. This obscurity, however,
does not mean that the role of the future in operations and decisions
must be bleak. On the contrary, by underlining the use of time in highly
technical and often impenetrable questions of contemporary finance, one
will be better able to understand an area of our society that has increasingly become all the more mysterious. Underlying all formalisms, there is
the matter of the present management of the future, which is mysterious
because we cannot know it, but which must not be seen as mysterious in
our operations (though we often do not even realize that this is the point).
If, as we want to maintain, time is money, then, by studying the time of
money, one will be better able to understand both the present and its way
of building the future. One will be better able to understand how, and in
what ways, the future remains unpredictable.

Note: Page numbers in the notes refer to Italian or German editions where
stated (It. edn or Ger. edn). Translations are the author's own.

PART I

The time of money

1.   Time in economics

Is it possible that the problems of economics that we are faced with at present, which have recently been criticized as a result of the crisis of the financial markets, have to do with the ways with which time is dealt? In section 1, we discuss the charges that are frequently made against the approach of economics, which is regarded as static and overly oriented to equilibrium. In addition, we discuss possible alternative approaches that consider the role and relevance of time. Time, in the form of future uncertainty and indeterminacy, is seen here as a key resource for economic behaviour, one that fosters creativity and a spirit of initiative. Time can also explain how traders are mutually oriented to each other.

Traditional economics, usually not taking the situations of circularity into account (section 2), has neglected the role of time. Traditional economics did not consider the cases where the behaviour of the operators changes the world to which they refer. These are the situations addressed by the latest trends, based on formulas such as imperfect information, asymmetric information and adverse selection. These are all cases where an uncertainty that is not eliminable arises, because the information that would allow for the uncertainty to be overcome is produced by the very behaviour of the operators who suffer from this same uncertainty. In order to valorize uncertainty and its role in the economy, one must make a complex concept of time the starting point. This complex concept of time is compatible with inconsistency and with a continuous production of surprises, with the role of expectations and with circular relationships in which the effect becomes its own cause (section 3). Many hints at this concept can be found in the economics tradition. However, it would be useful to combine these with the proposals of sociology.

1.   THE INDETERMINACY OF THE FUTURE

The turmoil of the economic crisis of 2008 not only affected the markets, but also affected the theories that tried to explain their behaviour. Several have criticized these theories as being inadequate not only with regard to their predictive abilities, but also with regard to their ability to understand the major movements that remain ongoing. The debate surrounding these accusations remains an open one. It is not universally agreed that the task of a theory must be, or even should be, one of prediction. In any case, a reflection on the underlying assumptions of economic thought has begun. The ideas of the market, the role of the state, the techniques of risk management, and even the very notion of risk, have all been subjected to reinterpretation.

It now remains to be seen how economics, which is by no means unfamiliar with criticism, will react to these charges. The most curious aspect of these criticisms is that they have traditionally been harshest when from economists themselves, who accuse their discipline of being purely abstract, obsessed with standardization, and, above all, ineffective in guiding the operators and in explaining what actually happens in the economy.[1] The fact that this criticism has arisen again, in almost identical form, several decades after its original formulation, suggests that the theory is profoundly resistant to revising some of its basic guidelines. It should be asked what exactly has prompted this rigidity, especially given the apparent schizophrenia of the system, since the constant self-production of criticism seems only to further stabilize the approach of the theory.

The debate remains open on all these points. In this work, we shall focus on one of the most controversial issues, namely, the way (or inability) to deal with time and with temporal relations within the economy. This issue has become urgent in connection with the current crisis and the increasingly fundamental role of finance and new techniques of risk management (the most innovative and disturbing aspect of this particular crisis). Given that financial markets are primarily working with time, and that the reckless management of the future gave rise to a situation in which society as a whole seems not to have an available future (as it has already been 'consumed' by speculations and games with risk), the need for reorientation and for updating the available theories seems all the more evident. This perception remains widespread, and can be understood as giving rise to the panic of both the markets and public opinion. But is this perception accurate? And what does it mean?

The issue of time has always been crucial in economics and, correspondingly, it has always been highly criticized. It is hardly novel to complain that economics, based on models of equilibrium and coordination, is a static construction and does not take the issue of time seriously, especially in the sense of historical change, innovation and surprise.[2] This has been a classic theme of the Austrian School, from von Mises to Hayek, who have not only pointed out that the equations of economic equilibrium systematically exclude time because they postulate an unrealistic and simultaneous interdependence of all variables, but have also claimed that this failure has led to an inability to deal adequately with money, competition, market imperfections and the role of knowledge and its limitations in general.[3] However, Keynes has stressed that economic decisions are always uncertain, because they are taken on the basis of an unchangeable past and are aimed at a 'perfidious future'.[4] Keynes saw the role of time as uncertainty and indeterminacy (an awareness that, according to some authors, has been lost in the simplification of what has been handed down as Keynesian theory), and not as a mere succession.[5]

The valorization of the uncertainty and indeterminacy of the future can be found in the works of scholars who, perhaps because of this valorization, were placed in a marginal (albeit prestigious) position in the development of economics. This statement applies primarily to Shackle, who constantly accused the mainstream approach of disregarding the role of time, considering it a nuisance and a troublesome complication, and failing to understand that time is a resource. According to Shackle, time is a resource in so far as economic practice actively exploits it and is always oriented towards a 'time-to-come' that serves to enhance creativity, imagination and novelty.[6]

What needs to be emphasized here is that time is not a marginal aspect, and is certainly not simply one aspect among others. How time is dealt with affects the way in which uncertainty (which is by now the key variable of economic behaviour) is understood and managed. Without taking time into account, one is unable to consider the most evident and deepest source of uncertainty, namely, the behaviour of other operators and how it is that individuals are oriented to each other. This orientation involves observing the other operators in the market. It is constantly changing and recursive, in that everyone refers to what other operators do. These operators, in turn, refer to the behaviour of the individuals observing them. This mirroring of perspectives, while difficult to systematize and formalize, is a key element of the information circulating in the economy. This moment of reflexivity has already been highlighted.[7] Shackle, for example, called for 'kaleidic theories' that could take the multiple perspectives of different individuals into account, perspectives that are always variable and often inconsistent with each other.[8] A theory that does not appreciate time, as we shall see, is not able to accomplish this task and is, therefore, destined to deal inadequately with these social dimensions.

2.   UNCERTAINTY AS A RESOURCE

The weakness of economic theory results from its lack of *circularity*. This lack prevents it from considering both the way in which the present depends on a future that depends on what the present expects from it, and also the fact that operators observe each other and the theory that describes their behaviour. Economic theory has failed to observe itself and its relationship with its object of study. These are not separated in the ideal relationship of an external observer with an independent object, a situation in which one observes something that is not affected by the ongoing observation from the outside. The observer and the object (made up largely of other observers who observe their being observed) are connected by a multiplicity of combinations and reciprocal influences that are increasingly difficult to ignore.[9]

One might ask why it is that economics remains so resistant. Sociology attributes this resistance to a particular 'relationship of loyalty and affirmation with its object',[10] similar to the relationship that binds pedagogy to education, theology to religion, political science to politics, and possibly epistemology to science. These are called 'reflection theories'. They are bound to orient effectively the behaviour in their specific field of study and are unwilling to discover uncertainties and paradoxes.[11] However, a discussion of this, beyond observing that the most pressing and controversial issues of economics derive from this very basic condition, exceeds the scope of this work. These issues constitute a radical challenge to the implicit assumptions of the discipline, as though the 'relationship of loyalty' to the object of study were now becoming dangerous rather than protective (we shall see later how the new meaning of risk tends to turn the alleged security into a threat). Circularity seems increasingly difficult to circumscribe.

Initially, we can see this difficulty in concepts that are already present in economics. We can refer to this circularity, but fail to address its role or origin directly. The key formula has been that of *imperfect information*, which is now widespread and presented as a real paradigm shift in economic thinking.[12] The turning point is not so much in signalling that the operators have access only to incomplete information, which we have known for some time, but in declaring that it cannot be otherwise: one never has all the necessary information; that would be impossible. However, this is not necessarily a bad thing. The imperfection of information is not due to a failure of the market or other disturbances. It is an inevitable and physiological condition of economic action. Imperfect information is not a defect, to be amended with improved transparency and better communication. It is the inevitable consequence of a condition where a significant part of the information is generated by the behaviour of the operators and evolution. Information cannot be known in advance, because it does not already exist. One must act in order to see what happens and how others react, generating the data one initially needed to decide. These data, moreover, will change immediately.

As has been stated here, the issue seems very simple. However, most of the questions that concern current economic thinking can be read in this key. There is much talk of *asymmetric information*, for example, cases in which information is chronically distributed in an uneven way, as in the market for life insurance or paradigmatically in the market for used cars (Akerlof's 'lemons'[13]). In the first case, this distribution favours customers, and in the second case it favours sellers. One party is unable to acquire the necessary information. It knows that the other party knows more (knows the true value of the car or the actual state of health of the individuals asking for insurance), and 'discounts' this knowledge from the value of the offer. The result is that the market for used cars is unable to discriminate between valid products and frauds (unless it refers to the trust in the seller, which remains an extra-economic factor) and ends by offering shoddy products (a market for life insurance for people over 65 years, for example, cannot even be produced). This phenomenon, known as *adverse selection*, is a typical case of information being primarily derived from the behaviour of the counterpart, and is often observed in this perspective. I must trust a person who knows that I must trust them, and eventually I no longer trust at all.

The problem can be understood as a condition of circular uncertainty, and is similar to those addressed by game theory. It differs from game theory in that game theory requires (quite unrealistically) a lack of communication between operators who know exactly what the result of every combination of strategies[14] will be (for example, in the prisoner's dilemma game, which is far more implausible than the more normal, but much more complex, conditions where the 'players' can talk to each other). In these more complex conditions, the players do not know everything (communication hides as much as it reveals), but the form of uncertainty changes. The lack of transparency, in this case, is not due to the fact that some information is kept secret, but due to the fact that some data do not exist at all. They arise only through the interaction between observers who depend on each other.[15] There is no calculus, however complex, that can formalize this condition. One can only watch the ongoing events and continually adjust one's guidelines.

This issue is well known and discussed. The consequence for economics (and our discourse) is a new assessment and valorization of uncertainty. Uncertainty has been recognized as inevitable. The search for information does not lead to its reduction but only to its amplification. If uncertainty is produced autonomously, by transactions and economic behaviour, it grows with the increase of available information. The awareness of a congenital lack of knowledge also increases,[16] while traders are bound to make decisions whose consequences they do not and cannot know.[17]

It is perhaps more realistic to adopt an approach that does not regard uncertainty and lack of knowledge as problems, but instead as resources – indeed as the key resources that motivate economic action, that are used, valorized and transformed.

For Keynes, as we have seen, ignorance of the future is essential and serves as the basis for the particular temporal relations of the economy.[18] Only in a world where the future is not only unknown but also unknowable can decisions be creative and innovative. According to Shackle, the world of economy 'feeds on uncertainty',[19] in so far as it is based on assumptions about future prices, which are then set in accordance with these assumptions and their effects. Determination is generated from indeterminacy and its exploitation. If the future were not indeterminate and unknowable, it would not be possible to use this uncertainty to set in motion a dynamic that ultimately produces the actual economic data, a movement in which 'uncertainty comes back on itself and creates its own source'.[20]

In this light, this feature of the economy can be understood as a condition of 'self-generated indeterminacy'.[21] Economic transactions make the future unpredictable, and use this unpredictability to generate structures, to create constraints and to limit arbitrariness. What is then realized (the prices and their movements, the opportunities and the failures) is not accidental, but stems from expectations of an unknown future and from present decisions. However, even if the future is indeterminate, it is not the case that 'anything goes'. Certain behaviours are rewarded and others are punished. There will be gains and losses, successes and disappointments. The 'structures of insecurity' give shape to the way in which the present leads to a future that can only appear indeterminate. The study of economics consists in observing how this occurs. In a simple way, and often without awareness of the theoretical implications, economic practices seem to reflect this condition. When one speaks of the 'economy of ignorance', for instance, where operators do not exchange goods, but uncertainty (in the sense of 'the mutual unconsciousness of what the future holds'[22]), this is precisely the case. We now need a theory that is able to take this into account.

3.   TEMPORAL INCONSISTENCY IN ECONOMIC BEHAVIOUR

Some hints to help us recognize such a theory are already available, hints that address the role of time in the economy (the issue that, as we have seen, is chronically overlooked by the mainstream theories).

There has been a great deal of discussion about the role of expectations in economic behaviour. Expectations are nothing more than a present reflection on an uncertain future and an attempt to build up an orientation. We do not know what will happen, but we can expect that something will happen, and this fact can serve as a guide in the face of uncertainty. It was the Austrian School that indicated the need for a 'general theory of expectations', explaining how doubts and uncertainties and hopes and fears work, and how economic dynamics are the reflection of these projections in the present of the uncertainty of the future and not the reflex of alleged objective data.[23] However, we are predominantly indebted to Keynes for our awareness of the role of expectations and an analysis of their temporal relations in economics.[24] He finds that operators have no other choice than to follow their expectations, which are based in part on existing facts, in part on future events that can be predicted only in an uncertain way. Expectations rely a little on the present, but, to an even greater extent, they rely on the future. However, the present, Keynes argues, is itself steeped in expectations, because the present data 'incorporate' past expectations, while expectations about the future are always mutable and change as the future becomes the present. In this sense, economic orientation is always a patchwork of both past and present projections, of uncertainties that bind themselves to produce the economic data to which we refer.

Therefore we need a more complex model of time than the linear one that is so often assumed. We need a model where time perpetually scrolls forward and transforms the unknown future into a known present. In this model, we know only the past, which increasingly expands and incorporates ever-growing portions of the future. This knowledge is not, however, enough to understand the present, and, in particular, the present of the economy, which is not so much determined by the past, but rather refers to the future (to a future that we can experience only in the form of our present imagination). We only have access to knowledge of what we expect today, not of what will actually be the case (which is usually different, often because of our very expectations). People are beginning to say that economics should be built on the basis of more complex and intertwined time relations,[25] where, for example, one knows that our ability to predict the future is based on knowledge of the past. This is not because the future will be similar to the past, but rather because we know that it will be different (not only from what we know, but also from what we can expect to change). From the past we can learn only that we cannot learn anything from the past.[26] In other words, we can expect only to be surprised, a fact that we should at least be aware of and able to consider.

One can observe a situation of 'temporal inconsistency' in the economy, a situation in which one discovers *ex post facto* the meaning of what one thought in a given present. We need models that admit the 'inconsistency of plans', not only when such plans are unsuccessful, but also and precisely when our predictions are correct. This can be understood as a form of 'non-consequential reasoning'. This reasoning tries to take into account the conclusions one would draw in the future should the projected events be accurate, and discovers new perspectives on the past when such things have changed.[27] Not only will the future be different from the past, but it will also be different from what we expect to be different. This is not because we are wrong in our expectations, but because our predictions are correct. The economy urgently requires this to be the case, because it is in the economic sphere that one has to deal with events that proceed in reverse from what is considered (this issue will be further discussed later on, albeit more or less naively) the 'natural course of time' (the harvesting of wheat depends on the land that provides it, but the value of the harvest is not a function of the land. The value of the land depends instead on the presumed value of the harvests[28]). The values are set according to the future, a future that will change according to these values. In this sense the present depends on the future, which, in turn, depends on the present that is oriented to it.

We shall have to deal with this circularity throughout this work, entan-gling the intertwining of perspectives that underlie what at first glance seems no more than a puzzle. In the words of Hicks,[29] we shall try to explain what kind of time lies behind the specific form of causality that operates in the economy, and does not correspond to the classical defi-nition of time where the cause precedes the effect. This kind of time can be understood in terms of 'retrospective causation', where the effect depends on a cause for which it is itself the cause. There is also 'contemporary cau-sation', where both A and A* are causes of B, but where the one cannot happen without the other. In order to accomplish this, we shall need a rather counter-intuitive notion of time, one that we shall try to build up throughout this work, starting with some ideas from sociological thought.

NOTES

1. The number of references could be multiplied at will. See, for example, Knight (1921) p. xxviii, It. edn: 'all of economic theory is purely abstract, formal and inconsistent'; Hicks (1979): 'Economic knowledge is so extremely imperfect . . . most of the "macro" magnitudes which figure so largely in economic discussion . . . are subject to errors and (what is worse) to ambiguities' (pp. 1–2); or the opinions of the highest reputed econo-mists gathered in Swedberg (1990) or in Motterlini and Piattelli Palmarini (2005).
2. See, for example, Rizzo (1979); Hicks (1979); Aglietta and Orléan (1982), p. 19; Stiglitz (2003), p. 580. But Voegelin (1925) had already said, within the framework of a critique of the current approaches, that 'Stationary economics is a contradictio in adjecto' (p. 189).

3. See Hayek (1937); O'Driscoll and Rizzo (1996).
4. Keynes (1936), pp. 147ff.; Davidson (1978), p. 7.
5. See Davidson (1978, 1996).
6. See Shackle (1972, 1988).
7. See Knight (1921), pp. 287ff. The discussed concept of 'reflexivity' used by George Soros to criticize the foundations of economics (and its alleged practical irrelevance) relies on awareness of the influence of the orientations of subjects on the data they refer to, either directly or through their influence on the orientation of other operators; see Soros (1987, 2008).
8. See Shackle (1972), pp. 76ff. and *passim*.
9. An increasingly widespread observation, at the basis, for example, of the so-called anthropological approach, that does not, however, radicalize the dependence of the world on the perspective of observation: see Abolafia (1998); Callon (1998).
10. 'Verhältnis der Loyalität und der Affirmation an ihren Gegenstand': Luhmann (1997), p. 965.
11. About economics as reflection theory of the economy, see Luhmann (1997), pp. 964ff., (1988a), pp. 79ff., 124ff.; Baecker (1988), pp. 52f.
12. See Stiglitz (1985, 2003).
13. See Akerlof (1970).
14. Once again the structuring role of time is disregarded: see. Shackle (1955), pp. 42–3.
15. Apart from the fact that some data (classically sincerity) are not communicable: the one who declares that he is sincere raises doubts about the intentions of that sincerity, as rhetoric has always known.
16. Economic problems are reducible to problems of information and without problems of information there are no economic problems – thus Clark and Juma (1987), p. 95. See also Piel (2003), p. 20: information is not the solution but the problem.
17. Again a classical issue in Shackle: see, for example (1955), p. 18.
18. A discussion of this can be found in Hicks (1979), pp. 80ff.
19. Shackle (1972), p. 164.
20. Ibid., p. 165.
21. Luhmann (1996b), p. 1.
22. Betti (2000), pp. 3 and 209, as a representative of very widespread trends.
23. See Hayek (1937), p. 34; Lachmann (1977), pp. 65ff.
24. See Keynes (1936), pp. 46ff., 147ff., 293f.
25. See Loasby (1999), p. 5.
26. As Koselleck writes in a very different context: see Koselleck (1979), pp. 38–76.
27. See Lachmann (1977), p. 122; Shiller (2000), p. 205 It. edn.
28. See Coumet (1970), p. 587.
29. See Hicks (1979), pp. 25f., 62ff.

2. Time binding

In this chapter, we shall present the idea of time in sociological systems theory. This idea of time will guide our entire analysis of money and financial markets. The chapter is very abstract, refers to a very complex theory, and involves various issues that we cannot present within the limits of this work. However, it should serve to clarify both how, and why, time can be thought of in a different and unusual way, not only in everyday life, but also in many scientific works, and especially in economics.

We begin with a fairly simple remark (presented in section 1): time in itself is never present in its entirety, because it concerns three dimensions (the past, the present and the future) that can never be directly experienced. The past is already gone, the future has not yet arrived, and the present goes by immediately. Nevertheless, time remains a key component of our relationship with the world. We live with expectations and memories, which we need in order to generate projects for the future and to rethink our past experiences. Because it does not exist and, therefore, does not resist our constructions, time gives us great freedom.

We must then understand why we use time and what advantages it grants us (section 2). We need time in order to orient ourselves in our activities and in the world. We arrange these activities in an order that connects the past with the future. In this sense, we can see present happenings as a result of past events and as preconditions for the future. This order helps to guide us. This orientation also has the advantage of being very flexible. We can always change the orientation at a later date, without contradicting ourselves (it is always one and the same time, but seen otherwise).

Time, therefore, changes over time, and in a very articulate way (section 3). It is always the difference between past and future, but this difference is always experienced from a different present. The flow of time is constantly making us switch from one present to another. The way in which the past and the future appear to us is always different. Today, my past includes what was present yesterday, and tomorrow my future will belong to the past. To understand how time works, we must take into account this reflexivity and the fact that the flow of time is always producing different pasts and different futures that bind each other. In this sense, expectations and projects condition the truth of every present.

Even if they are not 'there' in the present, it remains important to note that the past and the future are not built up in the same way (section 4). The past can no longer be changed, and the future depends on what we do today. We therefore have freedom and constraints: we can build up our future (successfully or not, the future remains uncertain), and we can reflect on and evaluate what we have done in the past.

The success of our projects depends on those of others, to which we must always refer (section 5). Society provides some tools that combine the uncertainty about the future with the uncertainty about the behaviour of others. Even if we do not know what will happen, norms will determine how it is that everyone must behave, and money assures us that we shall obtain the goods we need. These tools function because we know that others also respect them. We can count on the fact that others will recognize the norms and will accept the money when we decide to spend it.

In some cases, however, the uncertainty of the future becomes more urgent and difficult to control. The term 'risk' is used to indicate such cases (section 6). Risk has now become the fundamental feature of our society. We have to deal with risk when we not only do not know what will happen tomorrow, but also what either we or others will think of risk when it does occur, and what criteria we will therefore follow. However, at the same time, we know that the future depends on what we decide to do or not to do today – that is, whether or not to build an atomic plant, speculate on the stock exchange, continue studying, or look for a job. The future presents us with opportunities, but only if we are aware of them and want to construct them (given that we know they can just as easily become threats). The problem faced by our society is how to use the uncertainty of the future, to exploit it without being paralysed by it.

1. THE FUTURE AND THE PAST OF THE TEMPORARY PRESENT

In discussing uncertainty and related puzzles, we have seen that it would be convenient to change the prevailing attitudes towards them, to move from a tendentially negative attitude to a positive one. Instead of considering the indeterminacy and incompleteness of information as problems, we can try to valorize these as resources, opportunities for change, innovation and surprise. A similar change of attitude could be made towards time, whose significance in the economy increasingly appears to be enigmatic and elusive, circular and recursive, to the point that one has the impression of no longer knowing what it is. It is difficult to work in this way.

Luhmann therefore proposes that we stop asking what time is 'in itself' (a question that refers to an ontological rest and is not very useful).

To ask what time is remains a fairly empty question. What matters, for those referring to it,[1] is understanding how it works, how it is used in order to make decisions, to remember, to hope and to design. Time, as often assumed, does not exist. The past and the future are never given in the concreteness of actuality. What is, is always present. What matters, then, is to understand how time is constructed in every moment, to understand how we project a past and a future that 'are not there', are not actual, and are formed in a present that disappears in the very moment of its realization. The enigma of time is, first of all, a result of its intertwining of actuality and inactuality. Time exists only as an actual projection of spaces of inactuality (a past that is no longer, and a future that has not yet come).

But why do we do this? Why make the present dependent on a past and a future that are not actually there? Why do we constrain the instantaneous space of actuality with the bindings of a past that cannot be changed and a future that we do not know? Presumably, we do this because the past and the future, as inactual, grant us more freedom. The inactual offers advantages because it leaves us greater freedom in structuring our choices and our constraints. In order to take this situation into account, however, we need 'a completely different concept of time',[2] one that is able to valorize the capacity of systems to orient to more and more articulated spaces of inactuality as a resource, which allows for the building of constraints and ensures a form of continuity to the flow of time (a time that is built up in a present in which we do not have time, because it is instantly cancelled in the passage to another present).

This is a peculiarity of our culture, a peculiarity that distinguishes our culture from ancient divinatory cultures, for example, where the past and the future were always present and merged with current events. Our society (however historicized) knows neither the presence of the past nor the presence of the future. Ancestors, origins and fate are all excluded from being contemporaries in the present moment, in that they cannot directly influence or determine what is happening.[3] The past and the future are only present as recollection or expectation, as mediated forms of a present operation, and can, in fact, be different from what actually happened in the past or what will happen in the future. The space of contemporaneity is, therefore, very small, and is limited to the punctuality of a present that does not last, but nevertheless remains the only time (a timeless time) in which we live and coordinate with others. Regardless of the time construction of others, with their presents and futures, memories and projects, we all share the same present. We could even say that because the present disappears immediately, we are able to build up time as we choose, given that in another present (which immediately follows) we can review and change our projections of the past and future.

The enigma of time lies in the fact that it exists only as something that does not exist. Past and future are never given, but become actualized as horizons of inactuality for a present that does not last. Time, Luhmann says, is 'the unity of actuality and inactuality'.[4] In this sense, time is a paradox, where only the inactuality of the past and future is actual, and these exist only in their present projection (the actual is inactual and the inactual actual).

So stated, the situation appears even more incomprehensible. However, the paradox moves the focus from the world to the observer. It makes us understand that we do not have to deal with independent data, but with the operations of a system. Through this shift of focus, the paradox (which is still unresolved) is unfolded and loses its mysterious (and slightly threatening) aspects. With respect to time, the tangle of data and negations, existence and inactuality, can be untangled through the realization that time is produced by a system in order to organize its operations and make them more complex. This is why time both exists and also does not exist at the same time. It does not exist as an independent entity, but only as an actual projection of a system that uses references to the past and future in order to structure its present operations. Time does not exist in an absolute sense, only for the system.

2.   THE ORDER OF TIME

However, why do we use this construct of time? The mere actuality, that is, the immediate presence of the present, leaves us no freedom. Modal logic shows that, in the present, the possible and the necessary coincide, because what is could not be different[5] (it will be different in the future, it could be different in the past, it can be different for another observer, but, at the moment, it is what it is, and there are no spaces of variation). To generate a certain contingency, to vary, design, correct and learn, we require a dimension that allows us to separate from the actual data and compare them to other possibilities. This comparison can come about through reference to other observers, or through reference to other presents, to presently inactual actualities projected onto the horizons of the past and of the future. Systems theory explains the genesis of time on the basis of the enormous advantages it offers. Time allows the system to separate itself from its own operations and its situation, linking it with other (past and future) situations in a complex framework of connections where uniformities, influences and corrections can be found.[6]

Time is, therefore, seen as a structure of systems, a structure that gives an order to operations and connects them to one another (an order that, as we shall see, is not a simple sequence but includes recursions and circularities, intertwinements and overlays, and allows connections with what happens to earlier and later operations, not in a random way, and without being directly determined by the ongoing events). One talks then of *time binding*, of the production of restrictions. It is not time itself that is bound (what happens, happens, and one cannot determine the future), but time that binds, that creates links between different operations that constrain each other.[7]

The advantage of using time in this way is that it works even if the environment remains unknown or if one operates with insufficient information (a condition that, in the economy, as we have seen, seems to be chronic). The bindings that make the present a result of the past and prepare for what will become its future work, even if the future remains unknown and therefore liable to be surprising (and if the future comes to be other than predicted). In this case, one will correct (and, in fact almost always does), but at least one will have something to correct (not a random condition, but an order from which to start in order to learn and change one's own attitude). The future in which we project and plan remains an open future, but we can address this openness in a structured manner. Time, as we have seen, binds the system and not the world, and it is precisely this binding that is valuable. By referring to time, the system produces an order via the difference in relation to the environment and not against it.[8] It uses this difference to increase its flexibility and freedom.

It is for this reason that it is inappropriate to use causal concepts when dealing with time. Time is not the cause of anything. It does not exist directly in the world and cannot exert any impact upon it.[9] It is more appropriate to talk in terms of conditioning, where a present operation sets the premises for later operations, which will in turn do as they want, though at present one can have knowledge of the data from which they will have to start (in this sense, while they are open, they are not arbitrary). The open future combines with an order in time succession that is not at all random and remains even if one considers the fact that constraints are not unidirectional, always proceeding from the past to the future, but can instead be understood as multidirectional, proceeding from the future to the past. The present prepares the future through its actions, but the framework of expectations and projections orients the behaviour of the system in each present.

It is because the reality of the future fails to coincide with our imagination that we manage to avoid getting blocked by the aforementioned inconsistencies of time. When the present comes to be other than expected, we can retrospectively change our interpretation of past behaviour. One learns not only by acquiring new data, but also by changing the way in which previously known data are considered, thereby avoiding problems of identity. Time binding means, among other things, that the system remains the same, and recognizes itself as the same, even when it assumes contradictory attitudes, thereby changing what it had previously thought and wanted. This change is possible, given that it occurs in another present, linked to the first only by time and not by fixed and unchangeable identities. It is a binding that binds only to a limited extent, but, none-theless, always connects, allowing an order to be maintained even when almost everything changes.

3. PAST PRESENTS AND FUTURE PRESENTS

Temporal relativity should be a rather familiar notion. Our society lives in a 'historicized' world, one where each datum and each reference must be located in a historic period and linked to the 'spirit of the time'. This relativity, however, is rarely radicalized. One therefore continues to work under the impression that there is an autonomous time dimension, a time that serves as a stable reference and influences both concepts and attitudes. This is certainly connected with the fact that historicism is associated with chronology, the (again typically modern) idea of an abstract succession of dates that extends infinitely backwards and forwards, and remains completely determined (for instance, we know that there will be a 28 April 2127, even if we know nothing of what will happen on that day). But time is not a date or sequence of dates, and the radicalization of historicism should lead us to recognize that time (far from being a stable reference) constantly changes with the passing of time. Time actually renews itself in each present, in so far as what is happening always adds something new to the past, thereby changing its meaning, and modifying what we had originally expected the future to be, in that things that no one could have previously imagined before are made possible. The horizons of past and future regenerate themselves in each present.

This is the internal reflexivity of time,[10] which indicates that time is not a simple difference between past and future, but an intertwining of differ-ences that are indefinitely reproduced within the two horizons. The past and the future include a multiplicity of (past and future) presents, each with its own horizons of past and future that reconstruct the whole of time from their unique perspective. The present past (the way we look back today and consider what preceded us) is always different from the past present (the way we saw things then), in the same way as the present future (our current anticipation of the future) is always different from the future present (and indeed from all the presents that will become actual in the future and have their own perspective on the world).

In order to deal adequately with time and the resulting constraints (the bindings with which we are concerned), however, it is not enough to consider this multiplication of perspectives, perspectives that seem indeterminate and uncoupled from each other (as though time persisted untouched and univocal from one present to another). The situation is far more articulate and recursive than this. The different presents are connected by a complex network of reciprocal influences, which serve to constitute the real structure of the temporal dimension. What appears today as past also depends on how the past has prepared its future and, above all (given the obsession with the future in our society), the present observes itself as the past of the future presents that it tries to anticipate[11] (and that will presumably be different from these expectations). The present always tries to be the right past for the expected future.

Furthermore (and here we are entering the intertwining of conditionings that give way to the problems of uncertainty we want to deal with), the observers know that this is the case, and can distinguish between what is present today and what will be the past in the future. They can also observe themselves from this point of view. Observers know, for instance, that they will presumably think differently about present issues tomorrow, and may even be aware of the fact that, in recollection, their perspectives will look different from how they do now.[12] On an operational level (still with regard to the future), observers make decisions that affect what will be possible in the future, but must do so with the knowledge that they do not know the future. They do so with the knowledge that the freedom to decide differently once that future has become present (a present they will have contributed to and where they know how to intervene) will remain intact. As we shall see, many operations of the financial markets use this temporal structure.

With this approach, time becomes very complex, but remains fully operational. The puzzles of time solve themselves (eventually turning back into problems). Time (as both problem and solution at the same time) is produced by systems in order to generate a certain freedom of choice, to grant options. Time allows us to order our choices and proceed in a non-random way. It connects our choices with others. The world that we act upon and that is constrained by these choices, however, remains largely unknown. We always have limited information, both concerning the behaviour of others who are oriented to us and also concerning the future that will result from our choices. But this is the advantage of an order that is built upon time in the recursive form of the intertwining of constantly renewed horizons. Even if the world is unknown, one still has a known and acceptable orientation (in so far as one can even apply, as will be made explicit later in relation to the case of the economy, criteria of rationality and calculation procedures) that can always be revised in a future present. In this way, coherence can be maintained even when self-contradiction occurs.

From this point of view, the uncertainty and obscurity of the future, while initially presented as a problem, become a resource. Shackle has argued in countless formulations that they become the fundamental resource that allows for imagination and creativity given that decisions make sense only in conditions of 'bounded uncertainty'. In the face of a future that is unknown, but known to be bound to our decisions, they are subject to an open but not a random future.[13] Because the future is open, it leaves space for every determination, but comes about each and every time univocally, thereby excluding any arbitrariness. While this can seem quite abstract, it remains a condition that one can work with. One can speculate, with very concrete consequences in terms of gains and losses, about what is of concern. One makes decisions that determine an indeterminate future. One then uses the resulting constraints (e.g. selling security towards a future that remains uncertain and can, therefore, be other than predicted, or, conversely, selling contingency, even if things will come about univocally, or any number of other combinations). In any case, one can work with the difference between different presents (particularly the difference between present future and future present), knowing that each of them, when the prediction turns out to be true, becomes actual and determined and yet remains indeterminate on the horizons of the inactuality of another present (as a past that cannot be changed, but is remembered selectively and used when convenient, and especially as an unpredictable future).

4. THE STRUCTURE OF TIME

The two horizons of past and future, even if they are both inactual and depart from the same present, reflecting the one in the presents of the other, are not symmetrical, but their difference provides time with a structure that can be used. Neither the past nor the future 'are there', and their inactuality, as we have seen, gives the present the necessary distance to have a freedom of projection and a selectivity of remembrance. They are not, however, inactual in the same way. This is why time can bind itself and give structure to the observations of the systems. The past can no longer be changed, while the future depends on what we are doing at present (one cannot act upon the past, while one must act into the future).

We can, therefore, say that the future depends on the past, not because the past determines the future (as the future remains open and unpredictable), but because it sets the conditions from which the future will have to proceed (either confirming them or, more likely, deviating from them). The past, however, is not equally flexible (if it were that open, it would not be possible to settle any structure or form any binding). The reflexivity of time would immediately reflect on itself in an infinite game of cross-references with no holds, handles or limits. The past cannot be changed, and, thereby, provides an orientation. The future depends on the past (although in the form of discontinuity, and not that of continuity), not because knowledge of the past teaches us what will happen in the future, but because it teaches us how the future will be different.[14]

The structure of time relies on the game of reversibility and irreversibility that is constructed on the basis of the asymmetry of past and future, which remains even if memory continually transforms the image and evaluation of the past (that is, changes it). As we have seen, each present reconstructs time as a whole, and not only the future. Each present changes the image of a past that is seen as immutable (what changes is the image of what cannot be changed, the position from which one has to start in order to design the future, which is seen, contrarily, as open and modifiable). The schema of a given past that influences an indefinite future remains even if the form of this determination changes in the transition from one present to another. Time carries with it a 'contingency scheme',[15] a configuration of possibilities that condition each other but leave alternatives open. The past could have come about otherwise. However, things have transpired in this way and can no longer be changed, even if the way in which the resources made available by the past and their meaning in the memory can be changed. A defeat (a dismissal, a failure) can be reformulated as an opportunity (as having offered an opportunity for a different career, for example), but nonetheless remains the starting point for future endeavours.

The past, then, serves primarily as a means of selection. Everything could be possible, but only some possibilities come about, and these condition the possibilities that are made available for the future. The future is, therefore, both determined and indeterminate at the same time. One knows where one has to start from, but does not know how (although one may know that this will affect the meaning of the present that decides it and the meaning of the past that determines it). This is why the form of the determination appears different according to the direction one considers. Looking at the future, one sees an opening (the fact that one does not know what will happen), and looking at the past, one sees a closure (the fact that certain things are no longer possible today). At the same time, however, one can consider that the past does not determine the decision one has to make today (it leaves some freedom). One can also consider that this decision will restrict what will be possible in the future (it closes the future). The evaluation of possibilities depends on the present from which one starts.

Since the past and future are asymmetric, time can be built as a mirroring of possibilities that open and close (without thereby getting lost in arbitrariness), as a continuous mirroring where the future includes a future present from which I can look at my present as past, without sinking in the mirror and losing every orientation.[16] Time has an order and allows for the building of an order, where one does not move randomly from the future to the past (even if one knows that the future will probably be different from the past and that the past will probably be reviewed on the basis of experience). Time acquires a structure that remains, in so far as the future turns on the past (every past present brings along projections of possibilities and not the simple actuality of the given; that is, what one expected and not only what has been).

On an operational level, it is this structure that allows systems to use time, and, in particular, to exploit the ignorance of the future, the uncertainty and the imperfection of information. In making decisions, operators face a future they do not, and cannot, know, with flexible and revisable planning, ready to learn from the future experience (not only from disappointments when things go wrong). One makes a decision and introduces a conditioning for the future state of the system (for example, when one buys options, which refer to a future moment) and leaves it open to the future to decide what orientation to take when the consequences of the initial decision can be observed (one can decide later whether or not to exercise them). One introduces a conditioning, not a determination. One does not exclude possibilities, but rather offers opportunities that produce information that is used in new and as yet unpredictable ways.[17] One operates with an orientation to the openness of the future, not to its determination, ready to retrospectively establish the sense of what one decides today in accordance with the way a future present uses it to produce further conditionings (which remain largely unpredictable today). The opening of the future, in this sense, lies not only in the fact that one does not know which option will be realized, but also in the fact that one does not know what options and acts (today) would best accord with it. This opening turns ignorance into a resource.

The temporal integration of the system (the fact that the different presents all belong to the same time) is not given once and for all on the basis of the fact that the past precedes the future, but is instead continuously produced and revised as time progresses (the constraints introduced in the present are subsequently revised in the context of a control that evaluates and corrects them, but remembers their past sense). The future redescribes the past in accordance with how it remembers the way in which the past present had projected its future, and recognizes itself as the future of that past, as a different perspective inside the same time (selections have an order, and that, as we have already stated, is what time is needed for).

5. THE UNCERTAINTY OF THE FUTURE AND THE UNCERTAINTY OF OTHERS

If our reconstruction holds so far, then we must now deal with a concept of time that is much more multifaceted and open than what is usually assumed, one that sees time as a performance of a system (it is the system that builds time in order to orient its operations). The system, however, is not normally alone. We must therefore consider how constructions are affected and influenced by those of others. The more one is free to construct one's own temporality, the more one must take the equal and yet opposite freedoms of others into account. The uncertainty of the future is multiplied by the uncertainty of the behaviour of all other operators who are oriented to the same future, further increasing the complexity, but also offering the possibility of structuring it.[18] Time bindings have social costs, in that they constrain others and become intertwined with their constraints. However, they also have social support, in so far as the uncertainty appears less uncertain if others handle it in the same way.

How temporal contingency combines with social contingency can be seen, for example, in the modern phenomenon of fashion, born not by chance in the sixteenth to seventeenth centuries, when the idea of a motionless eternity began to be abandoned. This idea of eternity was understood to be fixed and identical for everyone, and therefore certain. All that one needed were the tools with which to contemplate it, as God can. For God, past, present and future are all accessible – that is, contemporary. Humanity, on the other hand, is limited, and must therefore be content to gain 'glimpses' of the inaccessible spaces of the past and the future through divination, prophecies and the reading of sacred texts.[19] Humanity is condemned to ignorance. The modern concept of time, however, which is built on the difference between past and future, generalizes ignorance. Nobody, not even God, can know a future that does not exist, because the future depends on the present and on the decisions that are undertaken in the present. In these conditions, it becomes necessary (and, for the first time, plausible) to use orientations that hold even if they are only transient. These orientations serve for the current situation, but were not appropriate in the past and will presumably not hold in the future. The strange thing is that we know this, but they seem to work nevertheless.

With regard to fashion, it is only in modern times that it has become not only acceptable, but also socially necessary, to orient to novelties, to forms that are not based on stability and tradition, but instead rely on variability and discontinuity.[20] In all fields, not just clothing, the seventeenth century showed a prevalence for criteria (philosophical, aesthetic, alimentary, lifestyle fashion) that were followed, even if one knew that they did not hold in the past and would not hold in the future. These worked nevertheless. They worked because of the intertwining of temporal contingency with social contingency. One does not know what one can expect for the future, but this same truth holds for everyone else, and the uncertainty is thereby generalized. In these conditions, it is more convenient to turn to criteria (such as the dictates of fashion), which serve to 'neutralize' temporal uncertainty with social uncertainty. The seeming nonsense of taking something that changes (and that we know changes) as a reference, and as the only stable reference, becomes empty when one sees that others do the same thing. This generates a transitional safety out of the combination of two dimensions of insecurity.[21]

The same happens with other forms of time binding, structuring temporal uncertainty based on social uncertainty (that is, on the non-transparency of others), and vice versa.[22] In the societies of the nineteenth and twentieth centuries, this concerned norms and scarcity governed by money.

Norms bind time in so far as they refuse to learn. They establish how it is that one must behave in order to immunize oneself from disappointments. The problem with the future is that we cannot know if we shall regard our present behaviour as correct, given that we shall be in a different and partly unforeseeable situation. Norms protect us from this uncertainty in that they establish that they will continue to hold even if someone goes against or violates them. They will not be amended – for example, if one sees someone crossing the road when the lights are red, one does not 'learn' that henceforth traffic lights work differently. This has the advantage of allowing one to know today how it is that one will judge in the future, and, in this sense, one does not have to worry that tomorrow (under conditions one does not know and with information one cannot predict) one will regret the choice made. The norm does not change. It holds across different moments, both for the individual and for others, who, at least ideally, confirm the same expectation (for example, they also know that one must not cross when the lights are red).

We shall discuss scarcity and money further in the next few chapters. Here, it is important to note that, in this case too, we are dealing with a form of time binding, in that the availability of money reassures future contingency (even if I do not know what I shall need in the future, I know that I shall need money to get it, and uncertainty loses [or should lose] its threatening side). The link with the social dimension lies in the circulation of money. The loss of liquidity of the one who buys (spends money) translates into increased liquidity by the one who sells (receives money). One can rely on the fact that others will accept the money one accumulates today (at least in so far as the monetary system works) in the future (even if no one knows or can foresee how they will use it).

The problem is that all forms of time binding have social costs, because they not only bind time, but they also bind the opportunities and perspectives of all other operators.[23] Norms, for example, discourage behaviours that could be advantageous in certain situations. For example, all children must go to school at the same age and follow the same pace, even if some of them could, in fact, go more quickly. Parents must follow the norm, and this reassures against possible doubts and future regrets, albeit only to a certain extent, given that in some cases one cannot avoid considering the possibility that, in the future, things will appear differently, either to oneself or to someone else, and will no longer neutralize the excluded possibilities (for instance, when qualifications lose their importance and work experience becomes more important).

Normally, the conditions of 'positivization' are enough to secure this reinforcement, both in law and in other cases of following norms. The possibility for changing the norms when the circumstances change always remains – for instance, if the majority in the government should change (as shown by the transitory nature of fashion, mentioned earlier). We follow an orientation even if we know that it can change (often because of this fact). However, as long as it holds, it must be respected. Sometimes, the reflexivity of time introduces a future contingency into the present that cannot be bound (typically in cases of possible disasters, where one cannot avoid anticipating the possible, albeit unlikely, future regret for something today). How can one accept the production of GMOs (even if it is legal) if one cannot dismiss the possibility that by now they produce unpredictable genetic damages? The fact that the law permits this production is not enough to reassure me; the law itself does not know what to do. The problem is always uncertainty, which assumes new and difficult forms to be managed.

In these cases, the norms tend to adopt an orientation towards consequences, consequences that, when taken literally, mean depriving the very meaning of normativity. The current constraint, which should neutralize future uncertainties, in that the only problem should be deviance, that the norm is violated, comes to depend on these same uncertainties (it could happen that one has reason to regret even if one followed the rule). This orientation leads to the blatant case of strict liability, where the law acknowledges that, if a behaviour causes damage one must pay a compensation, even if one followed all the norms in force (for example, the coffee seller must indemnify the customer who got burned with the hot liquid because they did not warn of the danger, even if there is no rule imposed to do so). Time binding comes back upon itself in that one cannot bind time simply because one anticipates the consequences of the binding.

Something similar happens with money. One accumulates money to protect oneself against possible future needs (I do not know what I shall need, but I know that I shall be able to buy it). This only works if money circulates, because then one knows that others will also accept it. The very social circulation of money, however, with the mechanism of credit and the corresponding complexity,[24] questions this reassurance. Speculation on financial markets shows this clearly. In order to accumulate money, it can, in fact, be most effective to spend it, activating the mechanism of multiplication that produces the further availability of money for the future. One who saves, then, in fact loses money (the money they could have earned) and, in the future, could be in the situation of not being able to buy what they could have afforded if they had invested (in this sense, the attempt to reassure towards an obscure future becomes something of a threat).

In these conditions, where the future sneaks in a future view of the actual present, the balance with which we are familiar tends to break down. The typical alliance between the social and the temporal dimension in modern society, where the uncertainty of the future is governed by reference to the uncertainty of the behaviour of others, which in turn is governed by referring to an unknown future, has seemed to work so far. The mechanism has apparently worked to the extent that these two levels have remained separate. Should these two dimensions of uncertainty begin to affect each other, the solution will begin to waver[25] (I do not know what others do, but I know that it [also] depends on my expectation. I do not know what will take place tomorrow, but I know that it [also] depends on the way others are trying to reassure themselves). In these conditions, we (also) need more complex forms of time management, which include the intertwining of social reflexivity and temporal reflexivity, and increasing rather than neutralizing them. On this level, we remain poorly equipped (for instance, we are still surprised by every new speculative bubble, and fail to understand the intertwining of expectations and reactions behind them).

6. THE RISK SOCIETY

The key word used to express the discomfort we are describing here in reference to time is *risk*: ecological risk, political risk, financial risk, up to a generalized condition of uncontrolled exposure to future contingency. Our society is labelled as a 'society at risk' (*Risikogesellschaft*), and this is taken as its defining feature.[26] Traditionally, as well as in contemporary understandings, risk is understood as a matter of time. It concerns the relationship of the present with an unknown future, and the opportunities and threats this relationship entails. The indefinite future is a space of promises and hopes, but it is also a space of possible damage and anguish. Risk comes into play when, beyond mere fate, one considers the way future events depend on present behaviour – that is, as opportunities to build or as possible failures (the two aspects are linked in that if we do not expose ourselves to possible damages, we cannot enjoy possible benefits. Whoever does not risk does not win[27]).

More or less explicitly, the question of risk always concerns the construction of the future, the awareness that future opportunities depend on present choices (which are always uncertain, because the future that one constructs remains obscure). We talk of risk when we have to decide what behaviour to adopt today, already knowing that in the future we shall either enjoy or regret our behaviour (when one adopts the perspective of a future present in the present, one may suffer a damage that can be attributed to the present decision). If I had not invested in actions x, which are now devalued, I would still have my money. The same is the case if things go well. If I had not invested my money, I would now have much less of it. If I had saved my money, I would now have suffered a loss. The paradox one has to face in the present is that the conditions of gain are at the same time conditions of loss, but one cannot know how things will be today, even if one knows in advance that one will attribute the outcome to one's decision.[28] I cannot even know what I shall think or what criteria I shall follow (which negates the familiar forms of time binding), because the risk assessment changes with time and with risk. If things go well or badly, one will be more or less inclined to accept risks – that is, a positive feedback that can lead to an uncontrolled accumulation of risks, as the dynamics of the financial markets demonstrate.

Thus, risk can never be avoided. I risk if I choose to take the opportunity and then things go wrong, but I also risk if I prefer to abstain, and then lose the gain. The world has nothing to say on the matter, because the issue refers to a future that does not yet exist and, as such, cannot offer either positive or negative hints. There are no norms or criteria of rationality that can guarantee that I shall not regret in the future because nothing says that, in this future that does not exist, I shall think the same way, favouring prudence or temerity at all costs, should things go badly. Experience is not cumulative, and one can always change one's mind about changing one's mind.

This requires a new form of temporal organization, one that supports the disappearance of the minimal constraints produced by the familiar mode of time binding; the minimal coherence that makes us think that in the future we shall still recognize the norm or appreciate the availability of money (that is, that minimal identity that connects the present future with a still unknown future present). Risk forces us to face a still more radical discontinuity, which separates the future from the present because we know that the first will be the result of the second. The future is not only unknown, but also unknowable, given that what we can predict are only its non-future aspects. Time itself, including the future assessment of our actual present, is generated in time, but does not exist alone. It is generated because the present decision produces a difference to what would result from the past if one had decided otherwise, and one always sees it from the perspective of the present.

Here the world can offer no reference. Only the (actual or expected) behaviour of others – that is, the reference to the social dimension – can fulfil this function. We are not alone (a circumstance that at first further increases the risks), and opportunities can be lost if they are seized by others. Norms can be ineffective because others do not respect them. In such circumstances, the one who follows them not only loses an advantage, but looks like a fool. The fact that we are not alone, however, is also a guarantee and can serve to curb the spread of reflexivity, not so much because others will do or think like us (recognizing the norm or accepting money), but rather because they will behave as a result of having observed what we have done and are doing (they build financial transactions starting from our investments; they violate the norms counting on the fact that we respect them). One can speculate on this fact, and build forms that allow for time to bind itself by exploiting the diversity and mutual non-transparency of observers (this would be a different form of time binding, one that multiplies social contingencies by temporal contingencies).

Decisions made under risk, the overwhelming mode of decision-making in our society, show how one can create bindings without assuming an alliance of the temporal and social dimensions (as was the case with norms and money). Instead, one starts by assuming the tension between them (without assuming that the uncertainty of others is bound by my uncertain decision, but is instead multiplied by my uncertainty). Yet there is a kind of order that arises, however recursive, circular and revisable. What multiplies is the diversity of perspectives that come into play and are accepted (the difference between present present and future present, and the difference between the perspective of the one who decides and that of those affected by the decision). Decision-makers collect their data and make their reflections, though a different observer sees things in a different way in so far as they are located in another situation and are not subject to the same constraints. They then observe the same decision in a divergent way, seeing what the decision-maker sees and what they failed to consider (for instance, that they believe a rational operation to be in play and that they are able to monitor the consequences ahead of time, while a different observer might discover that the very pretence of rationality has shortcomings and can lead to damage, or can exploit these shortcomings in order to make profits, either as a free rider or as a speculator).

The risks of the decision-maker, believed to be known and controlled, are, for the observer, uncontrollable and unpredictable dangers (for the observer and/or for others). There is no higher perspective from which to establish who is right, as there is no overarching temporal perspective that can coordinate the present and the future (but the two points of view would not exist if one had not decided something). The most effective way, one that our society is beginning to experiment with, is a form of time binding that produces determinacy and indeterminacy at the same time. It binds the future as much as is needed to be able to decide and know what to correct. The present decision does not claim to predict or determine the future, but only to create a constraint from which different perspectives (of other observers, of other presents, or both) can start to make other (probably different) decisions. The future does not exist by itself, and remains elusive if we do not do anything (from which we can deviate later). The present creates the future, not as an identity, but as a difference, and this even with regard to itself. One only discovers afterwards the meaning of what one has done, on the basis of the consequences and of the reactions it provoked (that is, enabling the different perspectives of the future and of other observers). These remain different, but on the basis of the decision, this difference can be used to compare and to correct, thereby building an identity that would not be there if one had not made the decision.

The meaning of the binding remains that minimal continuity, in terms of both mobility and flexibility, between the contingency of time and the contingency of observers. Differences are produced, in terms of what would have otherwise happened, and can be shared. The future and other observers remain unpredictable, but can still be observed, serving to generate data from which we can start in the future. This is the only form of control one can acquire, but it is enough to carry on the operations in a non-random way. We anticipate the reference to financial markets. With regard to derivatives markets, for instance, current investments are not bound to a price or decision (one is not obliged to buy or sell), but only set a constraint that will allow for later decisions to be made (whether or not to buy), depending on how others react to the constraint and the developments it generates. One buys contingency (i.e. the freedom to decide otherwise starting from the decision taken today). One builds the future without planning or determining it. One produces only the possibility that it becomes possible (without knowing or having to know how).

In this meaning of risk, the obscurity of the future is used to produce opportunities that arise because the future is indeterminate and nobody can know how it will come about. The uncertainty of the future, usually seen as the main problem that makes all risky situations puzzling (how do I decide if I know that I can never reach any security, and I fear that I shall have regrets?), now becomes a resource with which I can acquire future benefits (if I use it well). The (obviously paradoxical) challenge is to generate uncertainty and be prepared to react to it, to grasp the unforeseen developments of what we expect today in unpredictable ways. As we shall see, this highly abstract capacity is actually applied in the everyday practice of risky decisions and, in particular, in the very concrete production of wealth on financial markets.

NOTES

1. In sociological perspective primarily systems: first of all social systems and then the individuals relating to them – but the consequences for the concept of time do not change: it must not be considered as an 'absolute' matter, but relative to operators using time in their processes. See Luhmann (2000), p. 152.
2. Luhmann (1996a), p. 9.
3. Think only of the future of Oedipus, already fixed in the past independently of what he can do in the present.
4. Luhmann (2000), p. 160.
5. Thereby the risk of confusion between *necessitas consequentiae* and *necessitas consequentis*, as the Scholastics recognized.
6. Luhmann defines time as 'asymmetrization of self-reference in the perspective of an order of selections' (1984), p. 176.
7. The concept of 'time binding' goes back to Korzybski (1953), who referred to the ability of language to maintain the same sense by ever-different uses of words, namely to maintain identity in diversity.
8. See Luhmann (1996a), p. 4.
9. Again, only for our society. Until modern times, time was also *kairos*, 'the right moment', indicating what to say and to do and affecting the meaning of events: see Esposito (2002), pp. 174ff., 279f.
10. See Luhmann (1980), pp. 289ff.; Koselleck (1979).
11. Luhmann (2000), p. 161 speaks of 'anticipatory care of memory'.
12. Again Luhmann (1991), p. 49: 'one can already know today that the remembered present will not be equal to the now actual present'.
13. See Shackle (1990a), pp. 13, 22, 28–48.
14. The physics of non-equilibrium of the 1970s–1980s expressed similar ideas in talking of irreversibility of the 'time arrow': see Prigogine (1985a) and (1985b).
15. Luhmann (2000), p. 141.
16. Luhmann distinguishes function of memory (past) and function of oscillation (future): memory stays for the presence of the past in the system and oscillation for the presence of the future: see Luhmann (2000), pp. 163ff.

17. That is, not only in the sense of a branched decision tree, where the future has only the possibility to choose the bifurcation, not to build a different path, or even a different tree. See the later discussion on the methods for the pricing of derivatives: Chapter 8, section 3.
18. The sociological term is 'double contingency': see Luhmann (1984), pp. 148ff.
19. See Esposito (2002), pp. 73ff.
20. See, more extensively, Esposito (2004).
21. In the same way temporal contingency neutralizes social contingency: the paradox of autonomous individuals seeking their originality and self-determination and recognizing the same originality to the others – and then being like all the others. But they do it following – as all (or virtually all) others – the dictates of a fashion that changes constantly, i.e. realizing a compliance that immediately deviates from itself.
22. Here I follow Luhmann (1991), pp. 57ff., who speaks of 'symbiosis of future and society', i.e. of some indeterminacies in the temporal dimension and in the social dimension – of an alliance between the two indeterminacies, using the poor specification of both of them.
23. See Luhmann (1991), pp. 59ff.
24. We shall see this in more detail later: see Chapter 4.
25. To continue with our example: this is the problem of contemporary fashion, where one begins to see that the true original is the one who is out of fashion and succeeds in showing it (Prada), or where the search for novelty is directed backward (vintage) if the others also remember it. One talks then of anti-fashion or of the end of fashion, but they also become fashionable (and pass on).
26. The same situation is indicated in economic literature, since the very influential work of Frank Knight (1921), as uncertainty, while risk indicates a form of insecurity that can be controlled by planning and calculation – precisely the opposite of the sociological sense. The terminological difference can produce some confusion.
27. In Italian: 'chi non risica non rosica'.
28. This distinguishes risk from danger. One talks of risk when the possible future damage is attributed by the decision-makers to their own behaviour (as by reckless driving), while one talks of danger when the damage is attributed to the external circumstances or to the behaviour of others (e.g. to the rain or to the reckless driver, when one is not driving oneself). The danger can be controlled by caution or calculation – not in the sense that things will go well, which can never be known, but in the sense that one will not have to blame one's own behaviour. I know now that I shall not say that it was my fault, and this helps me decide. On the distinction between risk and danger, see Luhmann (1991), pp. 30ff.

3.   Economy is time: needs and scarcity

Risks are widespread in every aspect of our lives and they produce uncertainty. However, we can insure ourselves against these uncertainties. This gives us the impression that we are protected against them. Insurance, however, cannot guarantee that the things we fear will not come about, only that we shall be compensated should they arise. Insurance transforms diffuse dangers into economic risks. The economy has a very close relationship with risk (section 1). Money serves as a reassurance against an obscure future, because it guarantees that we shall be able to satisfy our future needs even if we do not know today what those future needs will be (and, indeed, we don't have to know). Money, therefore, is not needed in order to satisfy present needs, but to manage the uncertainty of the future. Its essence is time.

This temporal aspect of economic exchanges and credit was rejected in both antiquity and the Middle Ages (section 2). The idea that one could create wealth through the circulation of money was believed to go against the natural order of things. One who lends money, such as a usurer, for example, creates wealth by selling time. Time, however, does not belong to men, but to God. One who sells time, then, is committing a serious theft in that he/she is stealing from God.

In modern society, where it was accepted that the movement of money does not destroy the order of things, but only creates a different order that benefits everyone, this attitude changed. The reference to goods and needs became much more abstract. Ascribing monetary worth translates each value into a sum of money, in the sense that everything now has a price, even when one has no intention of selling. The whole world can be seen as capital – and money can stand for everything (section 3). There is no need to possess many objects, but only to have much money, because it is money that allows one to possess any object should it become necessary. Given that one cannot know what one will need in the future, one can never have enough money. However much one has, one always needs more in order to feel prepared for tomorrow. In this sense, money allows one to possess a little of the future.

1.   THE INFINITE NEEDS OF AN UNCERTAIN FUTURE

Risk is a very general condition of our society, one that inevitably derives from the increase in contingency – that is, of the possibility (and the need) to choose, whether in the family (based on love – that is, on the evanescent criteria of idiosyncratic individuals, who can fall in love with anyone), in education (which must prepare for indeterminacy, and always has less fixed contents to transmit), in politics free from ideology, or in science based on hypothetical and provisional truths. The economy, however, not only presents particularly evident and widespread risks, but seems to attract the risks produced in other areas of society into its orbit, transforming them into its own specific forms.

Every economic operation (each payment) is expressed in a sum of money, one that 'forgets' that the reasons and context that brought each of them about are always different. Every economic operation indirectly compares with possible alternative uses of the available money (each payment 'brings with it' the awareness that one could have bought something else, bought something better or not have bought anything at all). One knows that it is always possible that one will regret one's decisions. Each economic operation, in this view, involves risk taking. However, the economy translates risks coming from other areas into its own operations, because it offers the possibility for insuring (paying) against the worrying prospect of a future damage (from any source). One can make an insurance, which (as the term itself says) compensates risk with safety, albeit only an economic safety. If one is worried that one will become ill, suffer an accident, or hurt others, insurance provides no guarantee that the dreaded event will not transpire, only that one will receive a sum of money in the event that it does. The specific and concrete danger of damage, then, does not disappear at all. Instead, it turns into an economic risk. This risk is one of wasting money on the insurance policy should things go well, or the risk of not being insured should things go wrong.

With insurance, the danger does not turn into safety, but into risk, into the prospect of a future damage no longer attributed to the world (a natural disaster), but to one's own actual or non-actual behaviour (not being insured). One has the impression of being better equipped for a damage that has been translated into monetary terms. In view of a present facing the uncertainty of the future, this translation seems to act as a guarantee, one that has become so widespread that the most recent financial instruments have been founded on, and diffused as, more and more non-specific 'risk coverage' – that is, as more and more refined monetary processing of the uncertainty about the future. How the abstract availability of money, which in itself is notoriously of no use, can act as a guarantee against the threats of an obscure (and always unknown) future is the issue that we shall examine in the next pages.

This protection against a threatening future is indeed the basic feature of all economic operations, and is, in fact, the real function of the economy. While it is true that payments are always meant to satisfy needs, and are, therefore, generally considered to be the primary function of the economy,[1] a thorough examination of the concept of need appears extremely tricky, and is so heavily influenced by the economy itself that its function becomes implausible. It becomes a demand generated by the very economy that has to satisfy it.[2] What are the real needs, and how can they be determined? Where must the demarcation line between basic needs and induced needs, luxury needs and demonstrative needs, be drawn?

If needs were an anthropological given or an elementary requirement, they would be restricted to the lower strata of society and, therefore, more or less quickly satisfied (we do not have many basic needs). However, needs are never exhausted and therefore do not disappear. In this view, one cannot explain the spread of the needs that spare no member of society. One cannot even explain the fact that there is never enough money, however rich we are, because there is no limit to the abstract urgency of needs. This is due to money itself and not to the needs. Money, which one can spend as one sees fit (even in ways that one doesn't yet know), represents in its abstractness the generality of all possible needs. We need money now because we do not know what we may need in the future, and we are, therefore, always in need, not of goods, but of money. Rather than satisfy needs, the monetary economy seems to generate the needs upon which it operates. Without money, there would not be the needs that money serves to satisfy.

If needs are never exhausted and affect all members of society, then perhaps they have nothing to do with what we need today, but instead address the indeterminate horizon where uncertainty is never controlled, the open and unpredictable future, where we never know which needs may arise. We cannot know what we shall need, and we therefore need more and more money in order to deal with this uncertainty. The reference of money thereby becomes the uncertainty of the future, and not needs themselves. This becomes the true reference of the economy. The economy, one should say, is not concerned with material needs, but with time, the open, uncertain and recursive time that appears as risk and tends to merge into the economy. Eric Voegelin stated this almost a century ago: 'Time is the meaning of the economy'.[3] The point is to understand how the economy (this very economy that, as we said in Chapter 1, seems to show a particular blindness towards time, dynamics and related issues) produces and manages time.

Temporal uncertainty interweaves with social uncertainty to generate a condition of generalized risk that must somehow be managed. Concerns about the future are intensified through the awareness of not being alone, through the awareness that others also try to satisfy their needs – and one never knows if there will be sufficient goods for everyone. The function of the economy is to guarantee the future supply of goods under conditions of scarcity,[4] to ensure that we will be equipped to satisfy needs that we cannot yet know, while others will do the same and will be striving for the same resources. Money and its social use has as its primary meaning a non-specific reassurance against the indeterminacy of the future (relying on the indeterminacy of money, which does not have its own utility but stays for an undetermined range of possible utilities). One knows that one will have needs despite not knowing what these needs will be. This lack of knowledge becomes a guarantee when one faces it, not by accumulating resources (which may be unnecessary), but by accumulating money that will translate into different resources when necessary. Whatever these needs are, we shall be able to cope with them by means of money. The reference to others' competing for the same goods changes its significance. Because others are doing the same thing, I am warranted in believing that this money will serve to satisfy my needs. Money circulates, is accepted today by both myself and others, and will presumably be accepted in the future. This dependence on others turns into a guarantee against concerns about the uncertainty of the future.

2. SELLING TIME

The meaning of the economy is time – that is, the present social management of the obscurity of the future and the social use of time to protect against the threats of time. In the view of many observers, this is what distinguishes specifical economic trade from an interest in immediate bargaining, barter and exchange – that is, a system of promises that refers to the future, which in turn transforms mutual dependence into a general guarantee.[5] What is traded in economic transactions is not goods but time, as has been clear since antiquity. This was why societies oriented to stability and repetition (that is, to the neutralization of temporal contingency) tended to condemn economic acting and rejected it as an element of degeneration and, therefore, as a threat.

In the Aristotelian sense (that of Greek and Roman antiquity and the Middle Ages), the economy excludes what is for us and for modernity its essence and its specificity, the exchange and the creation of wealth. For Aristotle, the economy was not even an autonomous area but was subject to policy and ethics.[6] The economy was concerned with the means for unity in conditions of the *oikos* (the governance of the house), and included the relationship to slaves, children and spouses, as well as the forms of acquisition for the necessary goods. It was always oriented to the stability, symmetry, conservation and confirmation of a given order.[7] 'Natural' and, therefore, approved forms of acquisition were agriculture, hunting, fishing, piracy and war – all forms that assumed the constancy of the goods and a simple management of scarcity. What belongs to one person is subtracted from another. Exchange was admitted if it referred to necessary goods, to the given and to the present (mainly in the form of barter). However, it was considered suspect if money came into play and with it 'chrematistics', the art of gaining, which was rejected as contrary to nature. In short, the economy was good in so far as it remained attached to nature, to the present and to the available data, possibly circulating them in order to balance needs. It became suspect when it claimed to create wealth, increasing the availability of money in a way that altered the constancy of nature and the world, mainly because it referred to time.

Chrematistic forms of acquisition depend on human laws and conventions, and therefore affect the immediate natural data. Above all, they used these social agreements to generate wealth, and in ways that seemed suspicious. In antiquity, money was lent, but this was deemed acceptable in so far as the sum remained fixed, in so far as no mechanisms were activated for the creation of credit through the circulation of money. Money was not lent for the purpose of investment, but for the purpose of compensating for the ups and downs of production due to natural disasters, wars or other external factors.[8] If, on the contrary, the very management of money created wealth (that is, if there were hints of an investment), the refusal was sharp, because this altered the order of things in an incomprehensible and threatening way. This was the justification for the centuries-old condemnation of credit, which was associated with usury and considered even worse than theft[9] (which, as with piracy or war looting, could also be accepted, because it did not modify the range of goods at stake, but only their distribution, in ways corresponding to social relations of force).

The usurer, as the thief, sells something that does not belong to him against the will of the owner. Usury appeared even worse because its aim is to sell something that belongs to God, something that, therefore, cannot be the object of profit. It aims to sell time, which is given free of charge to all men, but does not belong to them.[10] The gain of the usurer presupposes a mortgage on time that is unduly appropriated. The usurer, according to the Dominican Stefano Bourbon in the twelfth century, only sells 'the hope of money' – that is, time, which he does not and cannot own.[11] The sin is even more serious because the usurer sets himself in a position that is independent of God, His decisions and future events, since he is certain of his money regardless of how things and the weather may go, whatever crops or calamities may occur.[12]

Usury had to be condemned because it did not respect the natural order that God wanted to give to the world or time, and it claimed to generate wealth without effort (without work or action). It claimed to generate money from money – that is, from time. This accusation was directed at usury, but concerned economic life as a whole (trade and markets). Even if less striking, for the merchant, the opportunity for profit and the texture of his activity relied on time – as creation of reserves, search for opportunities and the favourable moment. The merchant also, then, did not operate in the natural time governed by God and by fate, but in a planned and programmed time, a time used and ruled by men.[13] Usury was a 'diabolic doubling of the economic function',[14] because it sold only the management of time. Every instance of economic traffic is involved in the same condemnation.[15]

This attitude changed over the course of the sixteenth and seventeenth centuries, when the interpretation of the economy gradually moved from agricultural work and the management of the house to trade and to the cities. The positive role of trade for the common good, and the legitimization of the quest for profit as motivation, began to be appreciated as an increasingly unstable orientation that depended on the exploitation of changing market situations rather than on the classical references to stability, quiet and perfection. People could make calculations of profitability rather than assessments of the quality of goods, and the approach broadened to include not only pure merchant trades, but also the production of goods in factories, and even agriculture, in the category of trade. The literature sets the turning point in coincidence with mercantilistic thought, which did away with the traditional idea of trade as an antisocial activity (because the advantage to one party is a loss to the other) and came to admit that exchange could be beneficial for both parties. The interest of the economy could thus be seen as the interest for society as a whole.[16]

If the idea that trade leads to the dissolution of society is discarded, then the quest for profit becomes a socially acceptable aim. This quest is even stylized as the source of a social order based on the market and its dynamic. This revaluation accepts, albeit almost unaware, the use and exploitation of temporal relations, the 'mortgage on the future' for present purposes that allows for the use of the insecurity of the future for the generation of present security. However, it loses sight of the role of time in the economy, as recurrent crises will force us to remember.

3. THE SCARCITY OF GOODS AND THE SCARCITY OF MONEY

The economy protects the present against the future, but only in the form of a capacity for payment, that is, only in the completely internal form of the availability of money. The economy, one could say, only reassures the future in the sense that it ensures that one will have money (a strange security, since money has no use). This safety, of course, lies in the fact that money stands for the abstract possibility of satisfying needs (needs that were themselves generated by the economy). This is the peculiar circularity of the economic management of time. The economy offers security with its own instruments (money), but affects the way one sees and understands the outside world (needs). The advantage lies in the fact that the uncertainty of the world is translated and handled in temporal terms (because, as we saw above, the non-actuality of time allows more freedom for movement and disposal). The future remains uncertain, but comes about in a form with which one can operate.

The mechanism works only if the world is translated into economic terms, if the possible goods that are the object of needs are transposed into sums of money. This is the manoeuvre that takes place in the seventeenth century and lies behind the turning point of mercantilism. The issue of the relationship with the future and with the scarcity of goods moves from property to money, from the availability of goods to the availability of money (with which one can buy goods). The protection comes about, not from the ownership of goods, but from the ownership of money. This reassurance, however, applies only if it is guaranteed that money will enable one to buy what one needs, whatever that may be. It requires that each object can be seen from the point of view of its ability to be liquidated. In this way, the object assumes a double existence: as goods and as potential sum of money.[17] This is the sense of monetization. Everything has a price, be it actual or hypothetical, and is part of capital. Cash is then only the circulating part of a general economic translation of other forms of value, because each object can now be considered from the point of view of its economic counterpart, even when one is not interested in selling it (or does not want to sell it at the moment).

For us, this condition is so widespread and normalized that we tend to lose sight of the improbability of this duplication, a kind of realization of a potential for the possession of things to be less important than their 'availability', in the sense of abstract possibilities for acquisition – one of the many forms of the increasing prevalence of the future on the present (and on the past) in modernity. The indeterminacy of the possible provides greater reassurance than the concreteness of actual possession. However, we must keep the limits of this spread of monetization in mind. It is true that everything can be translated into a sum of money, but this serves only as a reassurance on the economic level, and not with regard to other aspects. Things can still go wrong, or may have a different relevance.[18] Even though everything has a price, not everything can be bought, unlike at the beginning of monetization, when far more things could be bought than today. For instance, it used to be possible to buy the salvation of the soul, public offices, noble titles, women or friends.[19]

The issue of the economy is always a matter of scarcity[20] – that is, a way in which to manage the widespread condition of future uncertainty shared by others in the present. Scarcity is not a fact of nature, but a social condition generated by someone's access to limited goods. If the goods are given in finite quantities, then we all depend on each other. When someone secures access to goods, they exclude others from this advantage, creating (at least potentially) a conflict. It is in this way that scarcity arises. However, if money comes into play, then scarcity changes its form, from the real scarcity of an economy of subsistence to an abstract scarcity related to the hypothetical desires of people,[21] from the scarcity of goods to the scarcity of money.[22] This scarcity of money has the disturbing feature that it cannot be overcome. The availability of money always generates the need for new money (because the hypothetical needs have no end).

The advantage of this duplication of scarcity is its temporal projection. While it is true that the scarcity of money, referring to the indefinite future, can never be overcome, it is also true that it makes the social problem of the scarcity of goods manageable. If governed by money, someone's access to goods becomes the availability of money for others, and is therefore acceptable – that is, it becomes circulating money, which can be subject to rational calculations and profitability forecasts in the market. In its monetary translation, therefore, scarcity makes the darkness of the future manageable; the availability of money can be planned for. This planning is conducted with the support of others who do the same and rely on the fact that their money will be accepted in the future and will be used to purchase goods. The indeterminate danger of being exposed to future needs turns into the calculated risk of poorly managing one's money. The potential conflict is due to the fact that those who possess a commodity take it away from others, which turns into a problem concerning the distribution of money, which is governed by impenetrable (and therefore unassailable) entities such as the market and is endowed with a claim to rationality. The neutralization of the temporal uncertainty is met and supported by the neutralization of the social uncertainty, provided that the preliminary translation of goods into money has been carried out (the monetization of the economy).

In the modern monetized sense, the economy is not simply concerned with the acquisition of goods (in the 'static' Aristotelian sense), but is instead focused on the dynamic connection of the scarcity of goods (one can buy) and the scarcity of money (one must spend). It is for this reason that the economy is time, and, more specifically, future time.[23] It isn't a question of the technical problems of obtaining resources, but of the temporal problems of the distribution and the absorption of uncertainty. This is why the 'second scarcity' of money works differently from the simple scarcity of goods. Money by itself would not be scarce (one can print as much of it as one wants), but must be kept artificially scarce to warrant the exchangeability of goods. Only if money is scarce does the renunciation of a purchase have an economic significance with respect to other possible purchases, thereby protecting others who renounce these goods.

Money, even if it is as scarce as the goods, is not just a particular kind of good[24] requiring different theoretical tools, because (as became increasingly clear in the recent financial turmoil) it can become free from the assumption of constancy of sums and give rise to situations in which (in an entirely regulated and non-random way) spending money generates new wealth and the amount of money changes depending on how it is used (which does not hold for other goods). These are the circular relations that arise in the economic field and give rise to forms of retroactive causality that are difficult to manage. One must be capable of dealing with a wealth that is no longer measured by the availability of goods, but is concerned with the management of time and its contingency. We must examine how it is that money works.

NOTES

1. Also from a sociological perspective: think of Parsons (Parsons and Smelser, 1956) and the placement of the economic subsystem in the box of AGIL dedicated to adaptation, namely to the acquisition of energy in order to satisfy needs. See also Weber (1922).
2. See Luhmann (1988a), pp. 59f.and (1992), p. 39.
3. Voegelin (1925), p. 204.
4. Luhmann (1997), p. 758 and (1988a), pp. 64, 268.
5. See Appleby (1978). The issue has been dealt with in the debate on the significance of primitive economies and the role of the market, with reference to Polanyi (1957).
6. Aristotle, *Politics* 1250–80, *Nichomachean Ethics* 1160; Cicero, *De officiis*.
7. Reciprocity, still a fundamental condition of stabilization and of social order: see Luhmann (1997), pp. 649ff.
8. See Finley (1973), pp. 218ff. It. edn; Pribram (1983), p. 35 It. edn.
9. For example by Cato in the foreword to *De agricoltura*.
10. See Le Goff (1986), with many citations; Kaye (1998), pp. 19ff.; Pribram (1983), pp. 35ff. It. edn.
11. Quoted in Le Goff (1960), p. 4.
12. This was said by Roger Fenton in 1611, quoted in Appleby (1978) p. 71. It is the same

mechanism that we found behind the 'safety' of insurance, which allows indifference to the world through its translation into monetary terms: as we shall see later, the financial innovations of recent decades have led it to extremes.

13. The famous argument in Le Goff (1960).
14. Le Goff (1986), p. 51.
15. Reaffirmed by the Vienna Council in 1311, with the same arguments referring to time.
16. See Dumont (1977), pp. 55ff.; Appleby (1978), pp. 15ff.
17. See Luhmann (1988a), p. 201.
18. In sociological terms this translates (in Parsons's terms) into the difference between universalism and specification typical of all functional subsystems: not only the economy, but also law, science and politics deal with every aspect of the world and of society, but only from the point of view of money, legitimacy, truth, consequences for the government etc. – i.e. only from the point of view of their specific function. See Luhmann (1997), pp. 375ff.
19. See ibid, p. 723; and Luhmann (1988a), pp. 239f. That there was resistance to monetization is nothing but a confirmation of this trend: the late medieval difficulties in accepting that land and labour were subject to the laws of the market, but also the moral resistance to 'pricing the priceless', as in the case of life insurance, was not accepted in the USA until the second half of the nineteenth century: see Zelizer (1983). But this does not indicate that the power of the market has been overestimated (ibid., p. x), nor that money is not a generalized and anonymous medium (as maintained by Zelizer, 1997, 1998). Indeed, the development of idiosyncratic and personalized forms of relationship with money (where for example one uses the money won in a game or got as a gift differently from the money earned working, or develops special 'earmarkings' for specific social interactions) is only a consequence. Localism and personalization are the other side of universalism and anonymity. Precisely because there is a medium which is the same for everyone and is indifferent to the specificity of the objects, I can develop my personal use of it and can isolate specific objects (family property, mementoes etc.) that I decide not to sell – but the decision makes sense only if I know that they could be sold, and if I know that a different economic logic exists. The issue remains of course open as to which one of these logics can claim to be rational.
20. Walras himself defined the unity of economic science in terms of scarcity and the impossibility to overcome it, even in conditions of abundance: see Baecker (1988), p. 48.
21. See Appleby (1978), p. 98.
22. Luhmann (1988a), pp. 195ff.
23. Thus Fini (1998), p. 120.
24. A 'partial set inside the set of scarce goods': Luhmann (1988a), p. 199.

4. Money

Reassurance against risk, first of all, relies on money. Money has no inherent use; nevertheless, it has the strange feature of providing reassurance against uncertainty for any and every person. Whether metal or paper, money has no utility. So, why has it become so useful?

The reflection of economists has not offered a true theory of money (section 1), especially because it never really clarified its function or the source of its value, nor did it even clarify the true meaning of value. Does wealth lie in the goods themselves (in which case, money is only an abstract entity, a 'veil' superimposed on authentic values), or does money create wealth, bestowing value on things?

We need to clarify what money is needed for – that is, what its function is (section 2). Economics usually points out too many functions (measure of value, means of payment, means of exchange), without clearly distinguishing the main function and how it is connected with others. One can think that money serves to gain time, to delay the moment when one must decide how to use one's resources. This becomes important when the future is uncertain. With money, we can afford to wait in order to collect additional information and observe others. When the time comes, we shall be able to pay for what we need, or make the most convenient transactions.

Money works because we all accept and want it. Indeed, we always want more of it. Money expresses the connection between everyone and everyone else, because it refers to society as a whole as well as to all exchanges. If money were not accepted by all persons, at all times, and for all goods, it would be worthless (section 3). This is especially true for the modern form of money, diffused since the seventeenth century, which uncouples the value of the currency from precious metal and refers directly to the abstract movement of credit. It 'forgets' who paid and for what goods. Money succeeds in comparing very different goods and very different persons because it represents every possible future need (section 4). This explains the three classic functions of money.

Money translates each value into a number that corresponds to a price, and offers only this information to operators. What gets lost? Is it enough? (section 5). The issue is rather mysterious, because we have known for some time that prices do not correspond to the real value of goods, and that these prices change in seemingly irrational ways. In actuality, operators not only observe prices, but they also observe changes in prices, thereby obtaining additional information about what other operators know and observe. One is interested in precisely this when goods are scarce and there are many competitors. In order to obtain this information, people observe prices in markets.

1. THE MYSTERIES OF MONEY

Money has always elicited suspicion and mistrust. Luther's famous definition of money as the 'devil's dung'[1] is part of a long tradition that associates money with the devil. This is because money is incomprehensible and threatens both the established order and the harmony of things and the world. In the Middle Ages, it was taken for granted that money was 'a cabala difficult to understand',[2] not only because it was technical and therefore complicated, but also because it was the source of absurd paradoxes – for example, money that is lent out comes back to the source in the same amount, thereby multiplying the mass of circulating money. This happens in such a way that the quantity of money is simultaneously both the same and not the same. Puzzles of this kind can be found everywhere and, until the seventeenth century, a genuine theory of money was not available. In the seventeenth century, however, the contrast between the traditional contempt for money and the new discovery that 'everything can be bought with money'[3] became apparent. This instrument, money, elicited both excitement and uneasiness because it seemed capable, through the attribution of a value, of putting such different things as a working day, a load of exotic fabrics, family goods and the cost of a loan on equal footing and allowing for their comparison, ultimately dissolving many of the traditional social structures.[4]

The seventeenth century developed an analysis of money that started directly from the source of its value. Its value depended on the gold and the silver from which it was made, that is, on the amount of precious metals. Complications arose, however, from the practice of 'shearing' (the filing of coins to obtain gold or silver). The need for money was so high that even coins with a much lower content of metal than was declared were accepted.[5] The question also arose regarding whether money should be considered only in terms of its usefulness in the circulation of goods and the satisfaction of needs.[6] The issue was later solved, when both the correspondence between the intrinsic value (gold) and the commercial value of money, and the gold parity (and every other form of stable coverage of the circulating value, right up to the much-discussed cancellation of the Bretton Woods agreement in 1971) was overcome. The meaning and operating mode of money, however, have never been sufficiently clarified.

Economists themselves find that a real theory of money is needed. Neoclassical economic theory, they say, relies implicitly on the model of barter.[7] This model is actually set as the theory of a system that works without money, where goods are what really matters, and money becames an abstraction. One thinks of a 'real' system (the market) that operates by distributing goods, with the 'veil of money' laid on top of it. Economists should tear this veil and switch from the 'metaphysical' plan of flimsy entities to the genuine plan of the forces that produce wealth.[8] Money, in this view, emerges from the market as its consequence and does not have any power by itself. It cannot create any real wealth, only illusory wealth. According to critics, this approach completely overlooks the real power and true nature of money. It is not a metaphysical entity, but a very real and concrete given. It is not that money emerges from the market, but that the market and its power are consequences of the monetization of the economy.[9] Money may be abstract, but it is a 'real abstraction',[10] and we must explain it as such.

Money expresses the social aspect of the economy, the fact that each exchange refers to all other exchanges and that money has a value only because other members of society are also ready to accept it. Today, one speaks of 'embeddedness' in this respect, but the abstraction of money requires an accurate analysis of its mechanisms and of its mode of operation.

2. A MEDIUM TO DEFER DECISIONS

The weakness of economics is revealed in its ambiguous definition of the function of money and the standard distinction of the three tasks it performs: (1) measure of value; (2) means of payment; (3) means of exchange.[11] In fact, the relationship of the three functions is very vague. It is hard to understand which came first and whether it is possible to derive one from the others. Is there a primary function? What is it? How does it affect the other tasks of money?

From a historical perspective, it is likely that the first coins were produced in order to measure and compensate values – that is, as a 'substitute for gratitude'.[12] On this basis, a dynamic of exchanges was triggered. However, in a monetized economy, like that of modern times, the movements of money are autonomous from a point-to-point correspondence with external goods, and the movements of money must be explained in a more abstract way. Modern money cannot be defined as referring to the value of goods, because it has no inherent value apart from its use. It must be spent (or at least able to be spent); otherwise, it is worth nothing. It must circulate, because it has a value only if it is spent. Here we find its social reference. It has a value only in so far as it has a value for others.

Today, the fundamental function seems to be that of an abstract means of payment and of 'credit-money'. It is difficult to explain money on the basis of the other uses. It is not plausible that the idea that money can be used for any transaction, at any time, and with unknown people could emerge from the concreteness of a myriad of deals, which are always individual, personalized and local.[13] It is difficult to envisage any continuity between the initial uses of money and its modern use in the market economy or even in the financial economy. It is far more plausible that there has been a leap due to a different and more abstract function, which includes the three 'classic' functions. But what can this function be?

The big advantage of money – and here we come back to time – is that it leaves completely open the moment when one must spend it. Because it is abstract and indeterminate, its value remains, even if one waits before spending it. It remains available even when one defers the decision in view of other situations, other partners or different conditions. The meaning and function of money lies in this temporal delay, in the possibility that is offered by money for using time to increase decision and choice options.[14] This was Keynes's opinion, for example. He explicitly stated that the importance of money lies in its being 'a link between the present and the future',[15] which becomes necessary when the future is unknown and hence 'perfidious' and threatening.

This function of money is only necessary in a modern economy, which (like any other part of society) faces an unknown and indeterminate future, while knowing that it depends on present decisions. The future is therefore frightening, but can nonetheless – and, in fact, must – be acted upon. We do not know what will happen in the future. However, although our expectations may be false, the value of money nevertheless remains and we can use it in different conditions than we had initially expected. Money allows us to act even if we cannot control the consequences, because it allows us to postpone decisions or actions while retaining its value. We do not need to decide how we will spend the money today, and we can operate in such a way as to have money in the future, in order to be able to decide later. Only in a world of uncertainty can money have this function, since it acts as a 'bridge' between the (usually wrong) plans of the past, current expectations and expectations for a puzzling future.[16]

Shackle stated it explicitly. Money is not primarily a store of value: value changes and transforms. Nor is it a means of exchange: we do not know what to exchange or where to get it. It is, however, a 'medium of deferment and of search'.[17] This is its primary function; this performance is the starting point from which to explain its functioning. We need money in a world that is oriented towards an unknown future, because the sense of monetization lies in the possibility of postponing the choice to a later day, when one will have more information. The advantage of money is that it allows us to operationalize our lack of knowledge. This is possible because, having no value of its own, money remains entirely indeterminate. It does not bind future choices, apart from the simple fact that one will eventually have to make a choice – namely, to spend. When bartering, ignorance puts one at a disadvantage because one does not know if and where one will find the goods one is interested in. However, in a monetized economy, it does not have this effect because money allows one to use time to search for additional information about how to get these goods. Money, in other words, is a tool that deals with the uncertainty of the future in the present. As Hicks says, money has a value because it allows freedom, and can do so because it gives us time to think.[18]

3.   THE SOCIAL REFERENCE OF MONEY

How can this abstract entity with no value of its own drive the mass of goods and values that make up the very concrete wealth of modern society? How can it motivate everyone without having a specific object? We do not know what we or others want now, or may want in the future, but everyone wants money.[19] Very different performances are all compensated in the same way – with payment.

Sociology always answers this question in the same way. Money works because it represents a social relation, or because it *is* a social relation consisting of obligations and claims among the participants in the economy.[20] So argued Weber, who wrote that an exchange that makes use of money is always 'community acting', referring implicitly to the potential acting of others and ultimately to all participants.[21] Money is accepted only because one expects to use it in future transactions. This depends not only on the counterparty, but also on all potential others who could be interested in exchanging, whom one also expects to accept money. Every monetary transaction, even if timely and concrete, among people one knows and may trust, extends beyond this level and refers to the entire community, to all possible anonymous and indeterminate transactions, among unknown people and in still unknown moments. As Simmel observes,[22] money can fulfil this symbolic function and connect the punctuality of every single exchange with the totality of the goods and the people because it is completely devoid of value. As the history of money shows, every residue of intrinsic value becomes an obstacle to the primary function of money. Its value lies only in its ability to convert into other values. Its use as a means lies only in its ability to become an end. As a symbol for each value, this means that the absence of value becomes the last value and the last aim for which everybody strives. The concrete confidence in people and the relationships between different individuals turns into an abstract 'systemic confidence' in the functioning of the economy as a whole.

Money is able to motivate anyone, even to do things that would otherwise be irrational (as demonstrated by the widespread desire to have a job – that is, to labour). In this social 'homogenizing' function, combining a variety of individual and quite heterogeneous motivations without any conflict, money seems to assume the role formerly fulfilled by religious motivation, which was also valid for everyone. Monetary motivation, according to Burke, can be seen as 'a technical substitute for God', because God was the unitary instance that could collect the diversity of all motives.[23] In this sense, money (according to Simmel, among others) can be seen as 'the God of our time',[24] a secular and socialized God who addresses indifferently disparate motives and objects.

Within the economy, money is an 'established self-reference'[25] whose meaning lies in the reference to the system that inevitably accompanies every consideration on goods and commodities. In every transaction, the debtor is not the person who is paying, but the economy as a whole, which is guarantor of the circulation of both money and also the sense of the transaction. Modern money is a powerful agent of depersonalization, even if this fact remains unnoticed. In the form of money, the exchange becomes relatively independent of the debtor and their solvency. Once he/she has paid, money circulates by itself. It depends instead on the dynamics of the economy as a whole which establishes what this money will be worth and under what conditions. This is why every single economic operation has a global meaning and cannot be limited to the timely context in which it takes place.

It should be obvious that this condition comes at the end of a long process, which led to the specifically modern form of money, the one to which we refer in this work. This modern form is that of capitalism, a form of 'credit-money' in which money is uncoupled from any particular relation, from any specific goods and, especially, from any precise context. This brings about the unlikely condition where money has a value that exists irrespective of the person who pays, of the goods exchanged and of the relationship of the parties, depending instead on other 'systemic' variables.[26]

Once again, we must deal with a typically modern form, one that is characterized by the fact that processes become autonomous from external factors. In the economy, one deals with money and variations of capital, and not directly with the quality of the goods or the relations among persons (which are, of course, there, but only as environmental data[27]). This development started at the end of the fifteenth century, together with the discovery of double entry accounting, when economic processes began to be regarded as abstract entities that could be calculated and dealt with as such, without any reference to specific goods. Double entry accounting, for example, compensates revenues and expenditures as numbers, and does not take account of the quality or the characteristics of the goods.

Following from this, the creation of debts in the form of 'bill of exchange', without an effective exchange of goods, ensued. One talks of 'dry exchange' or exchange *per arte*, which underlines the fact that it is not something natural, and that it is clearly distinguishable from previous trades, when the economy was still located in a tangible and concrete world.[28] Only paper is exchanged. From here, it is just a small step to the dissociation of the 'bill' from each particular exchange relation, to depersonalized and generalized debt relations. Previously, even when money was involved, credit contracts corresponded to a specific social relationship between particular persons, established in front of a notary; they were usually verbal. The debt was not normally transferable and remained bound to the persons of the contractors and to the specific performances. Modern trade, regulated by the abstract form of 'credit money', comprises, on the contrary, pure promises of payment expressed by a sum, which can circulate freely in economic processes, be transferred to others and possibly transformed, and have as ultimate reference a public banking system guaranteeing the movement of money. A sum of money now equals an impersonal and non-specific credit that can be collected by any person in relation to any goods – as long as the economic system works as a whole.[29]

While the money at stake always seems to have been the same (the same or very similar coins) since the seventeenth century, the meaning of the medium has changed profoundly, to the point that the reference to the precious metal, even if maintained in various forms over several centuries, becomes purely symbolic. Economic exchange became a financial rather than a monetary relation, in the sense that the value is now autonomous from the intrinsic value of the cash. Instead, it now depends on general economic relations, on abstract exchange rates and not on the amount of precious metal. At this point, the function of the measure of value (one of the classic functions of money) becomes uncoupled from the function of means of payment, and the priorities invert. It is not the intrinsic value of money that allows it to intervene in payments, but the abstract circle of payments that sets the value of every good (completely independent from the inherent value of the currency, from the content of precious metal or from its convertibility into gold). Money is valuable, even if it is worth nothing as an object.

This is demonstrated by the creation of pure money of account, significantly referred to as 'imaginary money' (or *agio*), as with the 'lira tornese' in France, which never existed in the form of coins, but was used as an 'ideal' entity for the regulation of exchanges.[30] The detachment from the concreteness of goods and commodities could not be expressed more clearly. We now have to deal with imaginary entities, which work very well in the abstract circuit of the circulation of money. The realization of goods, when it comes down to it, remains an external fact. All money is first of all imaginary money. Even if a direct or indirect reference to precious metal remained until 1971, until the abandonment of the Bretton Woods agreement and of the abstract convertibility of any currency into gold through the dollar, the credibility of money has exclusively relied for centuries on the credibility of promises of payment at the level of the economy as a whole – that is, on the circulation of delayed credits or on the management of temporal relations.

4.   THE HOMOGENIZATION OF GOODS AND PERSONS

According to our assumptions, the first function of money is the management of the uncertainty of the future, the use of time to increase contingency. In other words, money functions to increase the opportunities available to the present decision. This is the function of 'deferment' emphasized by Shackle. Money allows one to make decisions without prejudice to future decisions, which serves to broaden their scope. If one has money, then one already knows today that one will be able to do what one prefers, in the context of economic opportunities, tomorrow, even if one does not yet know what one's preference will be. The safety of the future takes the form of payment capacity. The other functions of money, those that seem striking when one first sees them at work, should be understood as consequences related to the functioning of an abstract medium. It is, however, a social medium, and it becomes increasingly social the more complex and articulate it is. The function of time binding is fulfilled by mutual support (Luhmann speaks of symbiosis) between time dimension and social dimension, and, more specifically, between social uncertainty and temporal uncertainty, which, though open, remains controlled. Money, as sociologists have always said, is a social relation because it works only in reference to the society that guarantees and circulates it. It works because everyone knows that others know that it will be accepted. At the same time, money absorbs part of the social uncertainty. I do not know what others do even if I know that the availability of resources depends on their behaviour. However, if they spend money, I know that the circle of the economy will continue to produce money and opportunities of which I shall also take advantage.

The characteristics of money, particularly in its modern form, must be derived from its capacity for binding time. Bryan and Rafferty (2007), for example, find that money is able to perform the function of 'blending', to make extremely diverse goods comparable and convertible, because it fulfils the function of 'binding', because it binds the future to the present. It is monetization[31] that enables money to act as a measure of value and to compare and relate different goods (which can then be exchanged, if required). Money achieves a 'material homogenization' of goods and values that goes hand in hand with the social homogenizing discussed by Simmel. In fact, it is a precondition for it. The infinite variety of objects and performances (as different as livestock and ideas, land and work, books and houses) translates through the allocation of a price into the uniformity of a quantitative expression that allows for their comparison, 'forgetting' the characteristics of the object, the moment and the context. What remains is a number, which is always smaller or larger than any other number (hence comparable with it). This number can be divided at will or aggregated with other numbers, fragmented or added.[32]

Money can operate 'without memory', leaving behind all the concrete elements of the transaction, the motives and the people involved. A monetary sum has a value as a figure, no matter what function it performed, what goods were purchased, or which person undertook the transaction and spent the money as they liked, even if the money was used for purposes completely unacceptable to the person that the money originally came from. In the case of non-solvent individuals or companies, a certain ability to remember must then be retrieved artificially, with registers and similar devices. Money by itself does not care about its past. Monetization is what lies behind social homogenizing. Money motivates everyone because it is compatible with all motives, since it can be translated, with sovereign indifference, into any good or commodity. Money can absorb any desire and, thereby, become the object of non-specific desirability.

All goods, via monetization, become wares. All wares have a price, even when one is not willing to sell them. All wares, circulating or not, become part of the capital, which lives out its abstract existence. For example, it can increase or decrease according to how it is used, even if the goods remain the same. The financial markets are the most spectacular expression of this. This combination of generalization and quantification is the basis for the always surprising power of money. However, as Weber has observed, this is only possible thanks to the temporal reference. In monetary calculation, all goods and performances are considered in view of a sale or a purchase – not on the basis of their current utility, but in view of all future possibilities of use and evaluation.[33] The homogenizing of goods starts from the future, which is why it works so well. It not only concerns current wishes and needs, but also absorbs the vagueness of hypothetical needs and the uncertainty of tomorrow.

5. THE VALUE OF THE GOODS AND THE ABSTRACTION OF PRICES

If money translates all goods into a price, this means that people need only to orient themselves to prices in the economy. Indeed, mainstream economics starts from the assumption that the information available to operators is all contained in prices. Hayek, summing up a widespread belief, argues that in order to behave with competence in the economy, one needs only to know the prices, and can ignore any other knowledge about the way the goods are produced, used etc.[34]

Are prices enough?[35] It is true that prices indicate what needs to be done and that operators behave accordingly, and often with success, but suspicion that the information is somehow blind begins to spread. This can cause problems. Grossman compares the behaviour of operators who are oriented to prices to the behaviour of rats in a labyrinth, where prices are the walls. The operators bump against the walls, react and then move in the right direction, but they do not know where they are going or anything about the structure of the labyrinth.[36] Market price, according to Soros, provides a criterion of effectiveness, not a criterion of truth.[37]

The question is, of course, if and when truth is needed in the economy. The strength and effectiveness of a monetized economy, as we have seen, relies largely on the loss of information that characterizes prices, which can, in turn, afford to forget almost all the specific features of the goods and the context, the needs and desires one pays for, the origin of the money, ultimately reducing everything to an abstract quantitative expression. The economy can then focus only on economic variables without worrying about the environment.[38] On the other hand, the economy must refrain from operating with any direct information about the environment, including its own influence on it. An economy addressed only to itself, that is, addressed only to prices, cannot take account of the way its operations affect the environment, about which prices inform it (similar to the situation where the path of the rats modified the structure of the labyrinth, but they continued to bump against the walls without understanding it). How can we be certain of going in the right direction?

Blindness to the environment can influence the long-term effects on the natural environment (consumption of non-reproducible resources, pollution, so-called sustainability). It can also influence the way people regard the economy, the very circumstance that dictates that price allocation and transactions are facts of the world; prices will have to take this into account. Economics (under the label of information economics) is now aware of this fact, and tries to consider the circular relations that arise from it (the fact that 'the very activity of trading conveys information that affects the outcome of the activity').[39] In addition to the information 'contained' in the price, operators acquire significant information about what other operators know and what they expect the future direction of the market to be. An uninformed operator, for example, can use a price to learn something about the information available to informed operators, and can then act accordingly or speculate, changing the price accordingly. Prices not only provide information about external data, they also create the information with which the economy works.

This issue is expressed in economics by the difficult and problematic difference between *price* and *value*, where prices represent the information circulating in the system, and values refer to environmental data and events (always from the point of view of the economy). Prices are internal data; values indicate how the economy sees the outside from its point of view.[40] The economy would like to orient itself to values (to the world), but has access only to prices and must try to derive information about the 'real value' of goods and commodities from them. This occurs because the information that can be obtained from prices does not consist in the price itself. Grossman and Stiglitz maintain that the system of prices, even (and especially) in the case of an efficient market,[41] does not reveal all the information about the 'true value' of the assets, and does not contain the information one needs in order to obtain profits.[42] What is this value that the price should traditionally measure?

The fact that the issue is problematic has already been signalled by the scholastic debates on the 'paradox of value'. The fact that a pearl is worth far more than a mouse (even if the genus 'mouse' was created later and has a higher rank), and is more valuable than a piece of bread (even if the first is useless while the second is essential for survival),[43] are both examples of this paradox. The price of an asset, some scholars believed, should be determined by its 'intrinsic worth', independent of the passing of time. But how can one profit from transactions if there must be a strict equality between what one gives and what one receives?[44] As early as the seventeenth century, one could perceive that the idea of a value by itself, as both stable and objective, is quite abstract. Value exists only as one side of a distinction – that is, it exists only in opposition to a price. Values are not in the world, but the distinction between value and price is. Without money, without monetization and quantification (without prices), there is no point in talking about value. The right price does not exist, because there is no independent value that this price should correctly correspond to. Prices and values are only given together.

Prices, by nature, always change. The initial information that one obtains from them is not an absolute value, but a relative one – that is, a trend. What is observed first is the change in prices, which provides the elements to be considered (either to take advantage of opportunities or to protect from damage). This is inevitable if the problem is the management of scarcity, where there is a plurality of individuals competing for the same goods, projected into an uncertain future. One must first observe the observations of other operators, particularly their expectations. In Keynesian terms, one must be oriented to 'thoughts about thoughts', which can be derived from the expected values of economic variables.[45] Since these operators mutually observe each other, the orientation changes in accordance with the observation itself, and prices reflect this constant change. Prices vary, not because they are inaccurate and must adjust to better assess external values, but because the variation of prices is the very information one is looking for: the variation is the value to be measured.

As Simmel remarks, this explains the seemingly mysterious fact that the decrease in the price of a commodity often reduces the value of the goods themselves, which in turn further reduces the price.[46] A similar pattern occurs in instances of increase. This is not a novel thought. As early as the end of the seventeenth century, Nicholas Barber noted: 'Things have no value in themselves, it is opinion and fashion brings them into use and gives them a value'.[47] This comes about through money, which has no fixed value and varies disconcertingly. Even before the issue of the convertibility of money into precious metals came about, a fourteenth-century abbot lamented that 'on the point of currencies things are very obscure: they increase and decrease in value, and one doesn't know what to do; when you expect to earn, you find the contrary.'[48]

The modern economy operates on the basis of the abstraction of money, which circulates fluidly, is widespread, and is capable of expressing any value. It can do so because it forgets almost everything. It replaces external relevancies with the quantified expression of prices, which connect everything to everything else and any party to any other party in other transactions. The information that circulates in the economic system is translated into prices, with a brutal simplification that does not allow direct contact with the environment, but only mediated relations filtered by prices. The risk of this abstraction is compensated by the instability of prices which, in their continuous variation, permit and require the economic system to remain sensitive to environmental changes. Through trends in prices (upwards or downward, faster or slower[49]), the system perceives the information that prices themselves (being limited to quantified sums) cannot express –whether or not it is time to sell or if one should wait, what other operators think, and how they will presumably react to decisions. The complexity of the environment, which cannot be detected directly, is thus translated into the form of unstable prices that compensate for the lack of a direct mirroring of the environment with their variability. The value expressed by a price is always a selection, one that is contingent, may or may not be appropriate, and can change.[50]

Through prices, traders modulate their behaviour and experience its effects. One can never be certain that things will go well. From prices and changes in prices, one receives mere information, not direct indications for behaviour. The trader must decide each time how to use this information, and then acquire further information with which to confirm or change behaviour. Imperfect information, which from a sociological perspective is the only available form of information, carries with it the consequence that every economic decision is a risky decision, one with a cost, and one that we may later regret. The price, which reflects no objective external reality, is the only indication one can use, but it is not enough to make a decision. Enterprises and consumers require specific programmes that can serve to restrict the possibilities (that is, budgets),[51] and contexts from which they can locate the prices and related information. These contexts, as we shall see, take the form of markets.

NOTES

1. Luther (1883), n. 391.
2. Braudel (1967), p. 365.
3. Rice Vaughn in 1675, quoted in Appleby (1978), p. 199.
4. Luhmann (1988a), pp. 230ff. talks here of money as symbolic and diabolical medium at a time.
5. See, for example, Cipolla (1989).
6. See Appleby (1978), pp. 201ff.
7. See, for example, Hicks (1967); Aglietta and Orléan (1982), p. 13; Robinson (1971).
8. The criticism of this model can be found as early as in Keynes (1936), pp. 18ff. See also Robinson (1971), pp. 64ff., Smithin (2000). For a discussion of the illusion of neutrality of money see Ingham (2004), pp. 15ff.
9. See Ingham (2000), p. 17.
10. According to Sohn-Rethel (1990).
11. See for example, Hicks (1967); Bloch (1954), p. 35; but also Polanyi (1957), pp. 296–331 It. edn; Ingham (2004). Weber (1922), pp. 70ff. It. edn. defines money on the basis of its

dual nature of means of exchange and means of payment, which leads to the possibility of serving as a reference for future still indeterminate opportunities to use it.

12. See Luhmann (1997), p. 444 – within the framework of society governed by reciprocity, as described by Polanyi, who bases on this his thesis of a use of money independent from the market.
13. See Ingham (2004), p. 7.
14. The often mysterious entity of interest thus becomes understandable: interest measures and reveals this temporal relevance of money.
15. Keynes (1936), p. 293.
16. See Davidson (1978), p. 146; Goodhart (1989), pp. 55ff. It. edn; Moore (1979), pp. 123ff.
17. Shackle (1990a), p. 213 and (1972), p. 160.
18. Hicks (1974), p. 71 It. edn.
19. To the extent that, as Luhmann somewhat provocatively observed referring to the claims of trade unions, the 'categorical optative' of modern society is 'more money!'
20. A updated discussion can be found in Ingham (2004).
21. Weber (1922), vol. II, p. 314 It. edn.
22. Simmel (1889), p. 49 It. edn and (1900), pp. 219 and 338f. It. edn.
23. Burke (1969), pp. 92ff., 110ff.
24. Simmel (1889), p. 65 It. edn.
25. 'instituierte Selbstreferenz': Luhmann (1988a), p. 16.
26. Notwithstanding the arguments in Zelizer (1997), that can be seen as confirmation of the abstraction of money: personalization and individualized use of money presuppose that one normally uses it in an anonymous and generalized way.
27. In the technical terms of systems theory one talks of autopoietic closure: see Luhmannn (1997), pp. 92ff.
28. Here I follow Ingham (2004), pp. 119ff.
29. It is no coincidence that mercantilistic thought arises in the first half of the seventeenth century, underlining the autonomy of economic factors from their social and political 'entanglements' and emphasizing the 'trade cycle' ruled by specific skills and information: for a thorough discussion see Appleby (1978), pp. 26ff.
30. See Bloch (1954), pp. 57ff.; Braudel (1967), p. 359; Rotman (1987), p. 55 Ger. edn.
31. See above, Chapter 3, section 3.
32. A performance observed as early as the fourteenth century in the debate on the dual nature of money, that in exchanges serves as a 'medium for connecting' goods and services and makes them comparable, and in administration serves as a 'medium for dividing', which places all values along a continuous axis: see Kaye (1998), p. 174.
33. Weber (1922), vol. I, p. 75f. It. edn.
34. Hayek (1988), pp. 277–87.
35. A doubt that, like many others, has been raised by Shackle (1990), p. 189.
36. Grossman (1989), pp. 1–2.
37. Soros (1987), p. 369 It. edn.
38. Taking advantage of the benefits of closure, which characterizes many areas of modern society. On the functional differentiation of society in closed, autonomous, and primarily function-oriented systems, see Luhmann (1997), pp. 743ff.
39. This is the topic of Grossman (1989), p. 1.
40. See Luhmann (1988a), p. 55.
41. We shall came back to the concept of efficient markets later: see below, Chapter 5, section 1.
42. Grossman and Stiglitz (1989), p. 107: they speak of 'risky assets', but from this point of view all assets must be considered risky.
43. See Pribram (1983), p. 24f. It. edn.
44. Ibid., p. 29.
45. Quoted in Davidson (1978), p. 374.
46. Simmel (1889), p. 61 It. edn.

47. Quoted in Appleby (1978), p. 229.
48. Quoted in Bloch (1954), p. 51.
49. On financial markets, as we shall see, this speed of change is called volatility.
50. This would not be necessary if the price expressed only the 'intrinsic' value of the goods; the theory of correct price assumed that the price should remain fixed, apart from undue external influences.
51. See Luhmann (1988a), pp. 139, 249ff.

5.   The market

Although the market is the fundamental concept of the modern economy, it has no actual definition. Theories do not explain what it is, but how it works or, rather, how it should work, based on the dubious idea of a perfect market, where price expresses the balance between supply and demand in the most advantageous conditions for all participants (section 1). A market of this kind, which lends itself to the idea of maximal efficiency, is, curiously, governed by randomness – that is, by absolute unpredictability. If the movements of a market were reasoned, then they would be exploited and the market would no longer be balanced. The best working market, reportedly, cannot be observed by anyone and, in fact, cannot even be rational.

Much information circulates in the market, information that can be exploited for profit, and that mainly concerns the expectations and prospects of the operators. These expectations and prospects are in no way in equilibrium. They are also never complete, because they are continually reproduced by market operations (section 2). The more information produced, the more imperfect the market becomes.

The market works because its task is not to observe the world or the needs and state of production, but to observe observers, what they see, what they expect, and how they observe each other (section 3). The market works as a mirror, from which operators obtain the information they need in order to develop their strategies.

Competition ensues because no one has all the information. Everyone infers the information they need from the behaviour of others (who do the same). One can then decide how to use this information, knowing that one is observed. If one behaves rationally, then others can foresee this behaviour, and one will not gain any profit. Instead, one must develop a different rationality, a risk rationality that modulates to the expectations and observations of others, and both deviates from them and also confirms them. These expectations must be constantly reviewed as situations change (section 4).

One can also profit by using time, by circulating references and expectations, loans and debts, and by using far more money than is actually available, exploiting the uncertainty of the future in order to offer possibilities to present decisions. This is the task of banks and of credit management, which use risk to generate opportunities – namely, to produce the future (section 5).

1. THE EFFICIENT MARKET IS UNPREDICTABLE

Similar to what one finds when examining other basic notions, an examination of the modern concept of the economy reveals that it virtually coincides with the concept of the market economy. That is, the concept of market is so central that it sums up the definition of the economy as a whole. As we shall see, this is not at all fortuitous. In dealing with its central concept, economics lacks a genuine definition of the market – indeed it even lacks a convincing and shared market theory.[1] The market seems to be introduced as an assumption rather than as a concept, as something that must be presupposed in order to construct the theory, but cannot be clarified. 'The assumption postulates what should be explained.'[2] Sociological thought has developed and inserted into this gap a growing interest in markets, particularly emphasizing the role of an ambiguous conceptualization of 'culture' and an idea of 'embeddedness'. Market exchanges are part of social life and reflect assumptions, values and local practices that exceed the principles of economic rationality,[3] yet the concept of market remains undefined.

The notion has certainly evolved, beginning with a movement from the idea of a physical place (the 'marketplace'), where sellers and buyers actually meet, to the concept of an abstract arena of trade at a distance, oriented more to exchange than to production. In the modern market, coordination is achieved among anonymous and unknown operators, with a mechanism that sets prices among sellers and buyers and distributes them more or less uniformly in different places and among different people. This determination and diffusion of prices becomes the central pivot of the functioning of the economic system and the basis for the assessment of its rationality and fairness. The economy supposedly works because there is a market where prices express the balance between supply and demand and, after making the necessary adjustments, one is able to pay the same price for the same thing at every point of the market at any given time. This would be the perfect market, one that regulates and asserts itself. Should this perfect market not result, the attribution of some anomaly is made, an anomaly that must be studied, traced, and possibly eliminated, because the physiological functioning of economic processes should naturally lead to such perfection.

The idea of a perfect market justifies the brutal simplification and reduction of information expressed in prices. While it is true that people know only the prices, and hence very little about such things as the characteristics of the product, the seller, the history of production and trade that brought the product to the market, or what will happen to the product, it is also (supposedly) true that the market mechanism should serve to coordinate this dispersed and fragmented knowledge. This is Hayek's thesis; it expresses a widespread assumption that is maintained in most economic theories.[4] Operators possess only scattered, and often contradictory, fragments of knowledge. Nobody masters all the information that is required in order to decide in a competent and motivated way. The problem of the economy is not only how to allocate resources, but also how to distribute and use knowledge, given that everyone, with only limited data, must still make decisions. These decisions are based on people's orientation to prices. If prices were fixed by a tendentially perfect market, this market would use all the dispersed and diffused information in a coordinated way, and this limited knowledge would be sufficient to guarantee the optimal use for all knowledge and information.[5]

This abstract concept of the market, which allows us to conceive of the economy as a coordinated system of markets, developed at the end of the nineteenth century, and is the prerequisite of the theory of market efficiency (EMH: efficient market hypothesis), developed in the 1960s and widespread during the 1970s.[6] Market prices, particularly in financial markets, which are supposedly maximally efficient, always reflect the available information. If there are no information barriers, monopolies or other obstacles, and if investors behave rationally, any errors or irrationalities are automatically eliminated, because there will be someone who immediately exploits them for profit opportunities and, thus, deletes them. In an efficient market, it is impossible for someone to obtain greater profits than they should (that is, no investor can hope to 'beat the market' with an imaginative or particularly ingenious investment strategy), because the market automatically sets in and absorbs any inefficiencies. According to its supporters, this theory is confirmed by substantial empirical evidence, showing that, in the medium term, over-reactions and under-reactions of the markets compensate, bringing them back to a condition of equilibrium and substantial rationality.

A corollary of the theory of market efficiency, one that lies behind the idea that one cannot devise an effective long-term investment strategy (a strategy of success in the market), has spread under the term random walk hypothesis (RWH).[7] Roughly stated, this theory finds that, in an efficient market, where information is distributed evenly and without additional costs, changes in prices must be unpredictable – that is, they must follow a random walk. If all operators, actively moving in the quest for profit, have all the available information at the same time, then every possible opportunity for profit is immediately exploited and comes to find itself embedded in market prices. The only price changes that can come about are the unpredictable ones, which cannot be anticipated by anyone because they are not included in any of the available information. They must, therefore, be completely random. The more efficient the market is, the more its movements must be random and unpredictable. This seems a rather counter-intuitive conclusion, and reveals much about the implicit assumptions of economic theory.

The notion of randomness is a residual concept, informing not so much about the state of the world (where, as the natural sciences say, randomness does not actually exist[8]), but rather about the knowledge of the observer to whom it refers. What seems random is what could not be expected on the basis of the available information. It is presumably not random for another observer or for the same observer at another moment. Randomness, 'by itself', and without further specification (for whom, when), is not understandable. As has already been noted by many voices within economics itself, and as we have seen several times, the central role of randomness in a theory that claims to be rational shows, at the very least, that the current economic theory tends to ignore the multiplicity of perspectives and their reciprocal influences.

2. INFORMATION IN INCOMPLETE MARKETS

As we have seen, the assumption is that prices perfectly reflect all information. We have also seen, however, that prices can be, and are, used to obtain additional information that is not, and cannot be, contained in the prices themselves. Such information includes observing other observers, what they know and what they will supposedly do, market trends and variations that can be discerned and exploited. With regard to this additional information, markets cannot be efficient; at this level, their movements cannot be random. In fact, the contrary is often the case. One begins to wonder whether the functioning of markets can be usefully explained starting from the idea of complete information, or whether it would not be better to take the lack of information as the starting point for the motor of economic dynamics – that is, from ignorance rather than from information.[9]

Grossman and Stiglitz, for instance, claim that hypothetical informatively efficient markets are not possible, because there would be no reason for trade or exchange. If everyone knew everything and knew what others know, then there would be no opportunity for gain.[10] The degree to which

markets remain inefficient serves as a measure of the willingness of operators to engage in the gathering of information that allows them to take
advantage of gaps and imbalances for profit.[11] Information, far from being
evenly distributed and available to everyone, is the factor that enables
gain. It has its own tangible value in the market. It is not free, but requires
costs for its acquisition and updating. The main factor used by investors
and speculators in their activities involves the differences in the distribution of information. In short, information counts not so much for what
it says, but for the additional hints it allows for obtaining what others
know – that is, for the information beyond what prices explicitly transmit.
This information is not available to everyone, is costly, and is distributed
unequally.

Behavioural finance demonstrates that the behaviour of investors
cannot be explained on the basis of explicit information alone, but, nevertheless, should not be dismissed as irrational. What seem to be deviations
from rationality are, in fact, not random at all, but show regularities and
structures that can be studied; they show their own specific rationality.[12]
People often rely on information that may appear irrelevant if one refers
only to the alleged 'fundamentals' of the economy, including voices and
'rumours' circulating in the markets (noise), contexts and backgrounds of
the news that affect their reception (framing), and a widespread perception
of 'market sentiment'. These forms of information are far from balanced
and tend not to compensate in the way foreseen by the theory of efficient
markets. On the contrary, they often intensify and reinforce themselves
through a positive feedback mechanism, where investors buy in response
to an increase in prices and sell in response to their decrease – that is,
where investors make decisions based not on the explicit information
contained in prices (according to which they should buy at low prices
and sell at high prices), but in reference to the additional information
they read in prices, following trends and the perceived behaviour of other
investors. The market, in this case, does not behave like a filter, neutrally
transmitting information about the world, but becomes the real object of
observation. Investors turn their attention to the market and its dynamic,
neglecting goods and commodities.

The point (and herein lies the problem of the current market theory)
is that these behaviours do not happen by chance and do not follow a
'random' walk. They are predictable and can be observed, both by 'first-
order' operators who try to follow the trend, and by 'second-order' operators (the classical figure of the speculator) who exploit trends and operate
against them in order to gain profits. These second-order operators
observe what others expect and then alter these expectations through their
action. George Soros openly declares that this is the case, and attributes

his fabulous successes in financial markets to this mechanism. The market, he maintains, is not, and cannot be, always correct, since it is not simply an external circumstance but actively contributes to produce the information it should transmit.[13] Therefore the market can never be in equilibrium. Instead, it is in a condition of 'dynamic imbalance' that is neither efficient nor rational, and can be exploited in a non-random way. The market is not correct with regard to the world or to the future that some believe to read in it. However, it is correct with regard to itself. The market provides a framework in which the operators can recognize themselves and their inclinations. This, paradoxically, contradicts the hypothesis of market efficiency. Those who believe that markets are efficient make them more unstable, because they provide speculators with an opportunity to use their ability to read trends and operate against them.[14] If the market correctly anticipates future events, then it contradicts itself, given that these events fail to occur precisely because they have been anticipated. An alleged efficient market, then, follows a non-random walk and becomes predictable and, hence, inefficient.

A realistic study of the market should dispense with the idea of perfect and uniformly distributed information, and start from an explicit recognition of the imperfection of information instead. Knowledge is distributed in an asymmetrical way, so that one of the parties involved in the transaction often knows things that are ignored by the counterparty, who, however, knows that he/she does not know these things. We have already mentioned[15] the resulting processes of adverse selection, where one no longer reacts to the available information but to that which is lacking, bringing about a dynamic of growing lack of transparency. Someone who lends money would like to protect themselves from losses if the money is not returned. If, however, they increase the interest rate in order to compensate for the failed return, the percentage of insolvency may further increase. Those who could return the money tend not to apply for a loan that is no longer convenient; for those not returning the money, the increase in the rate is irrelevant.[16]

One talks about incomplete markets because informational imbalances do not allow for the offering of goods or commodities that would be required. In what way are these markets incomplete? The incompleteness is primarily informative. However, information can never be complete, since information, like randomness, does not exist as an independent thing in the world, something that can be traced, collected, retained or exchanged.[17] Information is always relative to an observer, for whom a given datum activates connections, produces consequences, motivates a certain behaviour or a decision. For another observer, or for the same observer at another time, the same datum is not informative, because they lack the prerequisites with which to evaluate it, because they are not interested, or because they already know it. The concept of information implicit in mainstream market theory is unsatisfactory, not because it incorrectly assumes perfect and instantaneous information, but because it thinks of information as a univocal given, or as goods that can be distributed homogeneously to different observers. Markets and their dynamics do not distribute pre-given information, but produce different information in different places and for different observers, which will inevitably be asymmetric because each observer has their own information and does what they want with it. One could try to study the movements of the market as processes of the production and coordination of information, but this leads to a significantly different approach.

3.   THE OBSERVATION OF OBSERVERS IN THE MIRROR OF THE MARKET

If one gives up the naturalistic idea of the market as a mechanism of neutral rationality, one must also give up the expectation of finding it more or less equal in all societies. It is a very specific and quite unlikely form of mutual observation of the observers and of bound observation of the future, which requires a series of unlikely assumptions. From Polanyi's research and the related debate, we know that the concept of the market cannot be simply identified with the presence of trade or the spread of money, given that many uses of money are independent of the presence of markets, and that one can make payments in the absence of a concept or generalized practice of trade.[18] One can speak about the market in a proper sense only when the prevailing view about the use of money is not the punctual purchase of goods, but profit, focusing not so much on the present situation, but on the orientation to the future through the exploitation of unstable and changing opportunities for gain. The essence of the market is the 'delay' that allows for the present anticipation of future transactions, translating these into gains or losses.[19] A prerequisite for the functioning of the market is, therefore, the abandonment of the traditional orientation to perfection and stability, and a turning towards variability and inconstancy.

In the transition to modern society and, more or less at the same time in different areas, forms such as fashion, democracy and the market became established. These work as 'formulas for legitimating transitoriness',[20] and act as references on the basis of their inherent instability. The time horizon of society as a whole now seems to be determined more by the economy with its mobile and open form of preparation of the future through the availability of money than by politics with its traditional orientation to wisdom.[21]

The recognition and autonomization of the market is usually dated to the seventeenth century, when the expansion of trade, international competition, monetary fluctuations and recurring discontinuities between supply and demand made economic processes more visible and more incomprehensible at the same time.[22] The existence of a market that is distributed in space and time becomes evident, and is clearly distinguished from the 'situated' form of a 'marketplace' that is restricted to specific places in limited hours and days. The market no longer appears as a place, but as a ubiquitous form of calculation and reasoning (it operates everywhere, without pause, even on Sundays), expressed in the quantitative terms of impersonal prices without memory. The use of money is thereby changed. It is no longer seen as a mere tool of exchange, but as a source of possibilities for profit, leading up, with monetization, to a 'permanent speculative attitude, submitting the world to the reflexive calculation of capital gains'.[23] This attitude, however, requires a detachment from the immediate context, with all its implicit assumptions shared by those people involved. From the vantage point of speculation and calculation, one also observes others as observers, who also calculate and potentially cheat. In the market (and, according to Agnew, on the stage of Elizabethan theatre), one experiences a new observation of operators as both actors and observers, and inaugurates a social dimension that is irretrievably divided into the two (distinct, yet real and viable sources of information) levels of the observation of the world and the observation of observers.[24]

In the market, one does not observe the world, but the observers (one does not observe the goods, but the operators, and only through them does one observe the goods and their characteristics). A monetized economy (as a market economy necessarily is) only has prices as sources of information, and only through prices can one access values and their oscillations. Goods are not directly at stake by themselves, with their features and their specificity, but only through their evaluation. Harrison White explicitly states that, in the market, operators (producers) do not observe qualities, but only payments and values, and proceed on the basis of these observations.[25] This means that the market is not a window through which one can observe the economy outside, because this outside is never accessible and, even if it were accessible, would not be significant. The market, according to White's fortunate metaphor, should be seen as a mirror, that, like the window, helps one to see, but only allows one to see oneself and what is around one. This is what observers observe when they observe the market. Producers observe other producers, their information, their choices and the prevailing trends, and consumers observe other consumers.[26] The mirror itself remains non-transparent, which is advantageous in so far as its opacity enables it to reflect and show what can be seen in the mirror. Even if this does not give one access to the outside world, the mirror is essential for seeing what would otherwise be inaccessible – that is, the observer and other observers.

This new reflexivity of the modern economy, which allows for the enormous leap in abstraction that is linked to second-order observation, requires the market, despite being hypothetical and always mobile, to be a means of modulation and control. Operators need information to guide their choices and their operations, and they retrieve this information from the market, which transforms the indeterminate and over-abundant complexity of the environment (the specificity of each asset, each context, each situation and the history of each transaction) into the determined and reduced complexity of prices and changes in prices, allowing anyone to know what others know and to infer what they will do. This is what is needed in order to operate in the modern economy.[27]

While it is true that one only sees oneself in the mirror, this observation is from a vantage point that would otherwise be inaccessible. Above all else, one sees oneself in a context – namely, the context of competitors whom one has to face in order to operate effectively. The success of everyone depends on what others are doing or will do, and it would be useful to have some information about these behaviours. Observing the market, operators develop their strategies – that is, how much to produce, how to promote the products – and consumers develop their strategies – that is, what to buy and when. For producers, the key competence is the ability to react to what is happening, and, above all else, to react to the supposed reaction of others (an almost simultaneous coordination among mutually dependent operators). This is precisely the information that one must be able to catch in the market (not prices as such, but what the offer of a particular price says about what others think of the future profits of the investment[28] – that is, the observation of others).

What is needed is not equilibrium, which would offer very little information, but a non-random imbalance between the information of various operators, which is interpreted and evaluated differently over time. The purpose of the market is not to anticipate the future but to combine the huge variety of present actions that will constitute an always uncertain future.[29] The purpose is the production of the future. In the market, one does not observe facts, but one tries to calculate possibilities through second-order observation, starting from the observations and the opportunities of other participants.

4. THE PARADOXES OF COMPETITION AND THE RATIONALITY OF RISK

The market produces the future while observing it. Operators react to present data in view of the future possibilities they can infer, knowing that others are both doing the same and also observing each other. The fundamental condition, and the fact that allows for the building up of structures, is somehow counter-intuitively the widespread and insuperable lack of knowledge of operators.[30] This explains the positive function of competition, which would make no sense in a hypothetical perfect market, where it would lead only to the paralysis or self-falsification of the market.[31] If everyone knew everything that all others know, profit opportunities would cancel themselves out because right decisions on the basis of the market would become wrong if others also made them. A perfectly transparent market would have no structures. Competition serves to discover data that could not otherwise be known, not only due to a lack of information, but also because these data are produced by the trends activated by the mutual observation of 'competitors' who always have imperfect information.[32] Each competitor reacts to the reaction of others, real or supposed, without knowing those others and without even having to meet them.[33]

Operators, who do not know everything, observe other operators in order to decide what to do. This circular observation produces what is called the prevailing inclination, market feeling or perceived trend, which does not reflect what people actually think, but only what people think that people think. This constitutes the shared reference to which everyone orients themselves. One does not know how things actually are; one knows only what to do. Behind this reference, there is no independent rationality. The provisional and revisable order that is generated does not guarantee that all circumstances have been correctly evaluated or that the most important needs of the economy have been satisfied.[34] Any combination of deficient knowledge does not produce greater knowledge, only an orientation that works as a criterion for decision.

Nevertheless, the effectiveness of competition tends to be confirmed in reverse, in the sense that the market often seems to behave in a way that corresponds to the perceived trends. Soros observes that this is not because expectations accurately anticipate future events, but because these events are governed by expectations.[35] The future that is produced by expectations tends to confirm these same expectations, but also to indicate that, in the market, expectations can falsify themselves. Competition, however, is not always a good thing. Competition can be helpful if rivals' strategies can be anticipated, but it becomes an obstacle if they behave unpredictably – that is, if they are irrational, speculative or simply creative.[36] The 'market logic' does not match the current idea of rationality, precisely because of the circularity of the mutual observation of operators. One who behaves rationally becomes transparent to the strategies of others (that is, predictable), and does not achieve the results their strategy, while rationally correct, aimed for. To be rational is, therefore, not advisable. In this view, the alleged perfect rationality is not only unrealizable, but also reductive. It would require that one also know the consequences of one's own actions, which cannot be known prior to being performed.[37] If observation is circular, then information will necessarily be incomplete, because it lacks the information produced by its own behaviour. In this way, rational behaviour becomes irrational.

The consequence, however, is not simply a call for irrationality, but for a sort of 'risk rationality' located at the level of second-order observation and offering non-random orientations. A risky strategy 'is correct when the strategy of the others is wrong and wrong when the strategy of the others is correct'.[38] The criterion will not be one of risk reduction and a search for stable references, but a continuous management of uncertainty, ready to modulate and correct itself according to the indications obtained by observing others and their orientations. For this kind of rationality, competition is an essential structure. Competition, in this sense, is not the source of operators' risks, but is what enables the structuring and management of the risk inherent in economic decisions.

Risk assessment changes its approach in order to account for the fact that it is not helpful to directly analyse the risk of investments in order to find out what to do. One must instead observe other observers, without knowing if they have carefully evaluated the circumstances. One must risk if others are willing to risk; otherwise, one misses opportunities. A willingness to take risks leads to increased risk. As we shall see, and as the financial crisis has shown clearly enough, at the level of the economy, this attitude can lead to an uncontrolled increase in risk-taking, alternating with the occasional uncontrolled risk aversion, to the point that suddenly everybody refuses risky investments (often independently of the actual performance of the economy). In the most advanced financial markets, a large amount of investment seems to be placed at this level, and is mainly guided by the transfer and management of risks with insurance, reinsurance, hedging and other coverages.

5.   THE CREATION OF MONEY BY SELLING TIME

In the market, the future is produced – that is, time is traded. The circulating wealth generated in the market – a market whose trends, as we have seen, do not depend on the world or on goods, but on the observation of observers – does not directly correspond to the quantity or quality of the available wares and commodities, but to how the uncertainty about future availability is managed. This very uncertainty can be the object that is traded. As had already been noticed in the eighteenth century,[39] the use of time can be isolated and the possibility for delaying payments and the pile-up of delays can become objects of economic transaction, and hence sources of wealth. With the mechanism of credit, which relies on a stable currency,[40] the means of payment can be multiplied beyond the circulating currency. The relative stability of money serves as a reference for an inter-twining of more and more articulated time relations – that is, for more and more developed dynamics. If money remains stable, then time becomes increasingly mobile and can be used in more imaginative ways.

The turning point came about when the key concept of markets changed from trade to credit.[41] One can even say that markets, in the modern sense, arise on the basis of this turning point. Only at this moment do money and the property of goods become clearly separated and transactions in the market come to concern money and its movements directly, with the property of the goods serving only as an external reference. In the market, it is a question of prices. Goods come into play only as references with which to fix prices. Those who have much money, not those who possess many goods, can then be considered rich. Goods can always be purchased if one has money. Therefore one normally needs money (or a translation of property into money) to begin with, and not vice versa. This insight can explain the miracle, or the paradox, of the creation of wealth in markets, and the production of money from money.

One can now also sell money, giving rise to the reflexive dynamics where one pays for money. This is the task of banks and other financial insti-tutions, which provide tools for multiplying the means of payment beyond the traditional correspondence of money with goods, beyond the necessary convertibility into precious metals, and even beyond the money that is actu-ally available.[42] Banks perform the 'miracle' of transforming debts into new money, accepting deposits (on which they pay interest) as the basis for grant-ing loans, and then circulating more money than is actually available. Only a small fraction of deposits is held as a reserve. Hence, if all creditors wanted to withdraw their money at the same time, the system would immediately col-lapse. The amount of money does not correspond to the quantity of goods, but expresses the fact that the system makes time available.[43] The possibility of using money we do not own for a certain period of time, and the possibility of spending money that we shall own in the future now, in the present, can both be explained in this way. This use of money generates costs, and credit comes into play to manage the circulation of delays and deferments, antici-pations and forecasts that are activated by money in the modern economy.

Banks and financial institutions take it upon themselves to manage the functioning of the economy. They manage the uncertainty about the future under conditions of scarcity – that is, under conditions where everyone's access to goods makes these goods unavailable for others. Banks face this uncertainty directly, and resolve it by guaranteeing that everyone will have the ability to pay, even when they do not have the money. They wager on the possibility of retrieving the money granted in the future, maybe through the use of this money itself. Banks bet on the time difference between present and future, creating the conditions for future payments in the present. They are playing time with the tools of time. This reflexive intervention on time takes the form of risk, of a present bet in the face of an uncertain future, influenced by present actions and expectations. Banks are compensated for this risk-taking, in so far as one pays for the management of insecurity, which takes a form that can be observed and worked with. The result is once again a multiplication of risks, which in our society concentrate and grow in the massive movements of financial markets.

NOTES

1. See Swedberg (1994), pp. 257ff. and (2003), pp. 104ff., many references to economic and sociological literature signalling this lack.
2. 'Die Annahme postuliert, was erklärt werden müsste': Baecker (1988), p. 23. See also Loasby (1999), pp. 107ff.
3. For an overview of positions and arguments of the 'sociology of markets', see Fligstein and Dauter (2007). On the idea of embeddedness, starting from Granovetter (1985), see, for example, Callon (1998).
4. See, for example, Hayek (1988).
5. Loasby (1999), p. 23 observes that, translated into theory, this approach should lead to the curious principle that one can control the economy without understanding it.
6. The standard reference is Fama (1970). The following debate is immense.
7. See Malkiel (1999); Lo and MacKinlay (1999).
8. See Schoffeniels (1975).
9. See Piel (2003), pp. 20ff.
10. On the contrary, argues Loasby (1999), p. 108, if one follows the model of a perfect decentralized economy, all markets should operate simultaneously and only once: when they reach a complete set of contracts in equilibrium, the markets should close forever.
11. See Grossman and Stiglitz (1980) and Grossman (1976). See also Smith (2002), p. 157.
12. See Shleifer (2000). From Kahneman et al. (1982) a flourishing research has developed that studies not only the various forms of irrationality of economic behaviour, which tends to vary with the context, with the overestimation of one's own skills and with an excess of confidence, but also the multifaceted ways an irrational decision may prove to be right, for reasons that the rationality model of classical economy cannot explain: a recent survey can be found in Motterlini (2006).
13. See Soros (1995), p. 375 It. edn.
14. See Soros (1987), pp. 353ff. It. edn; Lo and MacKinlay (1999), pp. 4ff.
15. See Stiglitz (1992), p. 43.
16. See ibid.

17. 'The environment contains no information. The environment is as it is': von Foerster (2003), p. 189.
18. See Polanyi (1957).
19. Agnew (1986), pp. 3–4.
20. 'Formel der Legitimation des Jeweiligen': Luhmann (1989b), p. 269.
21. Luhmann (1989a), p. 135.
22. See Dumont (1977), pp. 55ff.; Agnew (1986).
23. Agnew (1986), p. 46.
24. Heinz von Foerster (1981) distinguishes first-order observation (observation of objects) and second-order observation (observation of observers) – a distinction that has been adopted and developed by the theory of social systems: see Luhmann (1990a), pp. 76ff.
25. White (1981), p. 520.
26. Ibid.; (2002), pp. 27–34. This is in general the approach of 'field theory', studying how operators observe each other and develop their strategies from 'clues' caught in the supposed attitude of others: see also DiMaggio and Powell (1983) and Fligstein (2001).
27. This is why Luhmann says that the market is the internal environment of the economic system – the tool through which the system offers itself to the observation of internal operators as if it were something external: see Luhmann (1988a), p. 94.
28. Grossman (1989), p. 3. These are clearly variations and elaborations of the 'beauty contest' model in Keynes (1936), p. 156: evaluations where one tries to see not the world or how others observe the world (the prevailing opinion), but what the others deem to be the prevailing opinion.
29. See Lachmann (1977), pp. 122–4.
30. The market is essentially the seat of the 'eternal business of exploiting humanity's irremediable, built-in unknowledge of time-to-come': Shackle (1988), p. 8.
31. As Hayek (1978) argues, competition would be a ruinous adjustment method.
32. Hayek's classical argument. See Hayek (1948, 1978); O'Driscoll and Rizzo (1996), pp. 195ff.; Stiglitz (1986).
33. Sociologists have traditionally underlined this lack of interaction to describe competition on the markets as a pacific (Weber) or indirect (Simmel) conflict: see Swedberg (1994), pp. 265–76.
34. Cf. Hayek (1978), p. 201 It. edn. Therefore competition is taken as an example of the fact that the economy is driven by endogenous structures: see Stiglitz (1986), p. 401.
35. Soros (1987), p. 26 It. edn – a variant of market 'performativity' emphasized by sociological theory, assuming that the tools used by operators to act in the economic world depend on ideas about how economic activity should proceed: see Callon (1998).
36. See Stiglitz (1986), p. 425.
37. Shackle (1967).
38. Luhmann (1988a), p. 120. Luhmann (1991), p. 204 distinguishes risk rationality (*Risikorationalität*) and purpose rationality (*Zweckrationalität*): risk rationality assumes that the reachability of purposes is always uncertain, which can lead to doubt that they are desirable – even the purpose of purposes (*Zweckmässigkeit der Zwecke*) can be revised.
39. See Bloch (1954), pp. 102ff.
40. At least in the sense that it becomes independent of external factors such as those causing, until the eighteenth century, the variations in the value of money, for example tax needs of the sovereign, adjustments to the commercial value of precious metals, or the need to physically increase the means of payment. Variations (inflation/deflation) now depend only on the internal dynamics of the economy.
41. According to Nicholson (1994), p. 5, as early as the end of the seventeenth century.
42. This solved the chronic shortage of monetary means until the eighteenth century: see Bloch (1954), pp. 102ff.
43. See Luhmann (1988a), p. 148. Ingham (2004), p. 140 argues that banks create money overlapping payment delays with one another.

6. Financial markets

One can invest in and/or speculate on markets. Investments are generally assumed to generate concrete wealth, while speculations are only concerned with the internal movements of the economy, which are exploited for short-term earnings. Everyone must speculate, because everyone always has to deal with uncertain forecasts and what others do. All transactions that occur in financial markets have a speculative side (section 1).

Finance is becoming increasingly important in the economy as a whole. This importance is worrisome because finance is often seen as a kingdom of gambling and unreasonableness that cannot be controlled or even understood (section 2). More and more sophisticated financial techniques have been developed. These techniques do not make markets more efficient, but, on the contrary, produce new forms of irrationality. It seems that the most rational behaviour runs counter to the current idea of rationality and orients itself to what others think and do, thereby exploiting trends for one's own benefit.

The movements of markets always produce new uncertainty and new risks, to which one reacts by trying to protect oneself. Markets distribute risks, but this makes them even more dangerous given that no one feels responsible for them and one often loses sight of them. Hedging is observed and exploited by others, thereby producing new risks for both the single operator and for the market as a whole (section 3).

In the dynamics of financial markets, computers are essential. They accelerate processes to create a condition of virtual contemporaneity where effects are produced simultaneously with their causes. Media are also essential in that they create the information that everyone observes, allowing them to know what others know. These self-destabilizing markets are difficult to regulate, but, nevertheless, some regulation is required. Attempts to steer and reassure are immediately used to develop new strategies. However, the order that comes about is an order that is always different from that intended by those who decided on the measures (section 4).

1. INVESTMENT OR SPECULATION?

We always hear that financial markets are speculative and, therefore, continually produce risks that have an impact on the economy as a whole. The reasoning behind this, however, is convincing only if speculation and investment can be distinguished – that is, if one can draw a sufficiently clear dividing line between them. 'Normal' markets, then, would be those where prices react to actual changes in supply and demand, when markets translate data that are external to the movements of economic markets into amounts of money. Speculative markets, on the other hand, are those where prices react only to opinions about the future movement of prices, and are, therefore, self-referential markets, where economic movements reflect only economic movements (the mutual observations of operators and the observation of the future).[1] An investor is interested in acquiring and/or selling assets in the best conditions, and is willing to wait the necessary time to receive the benefits; a speculator is interested only in increasing his/her money by referring to the movements of money. The investor is turned towards the world, the speculator only to the economy.

This distinction, however, seems to be becoming more and more difficult, not only at the abstract level of reflection on the economy, but also in the concrete observation of economic operations. The dividing line between speculation and investment seems to have become vague even for experts.[2] One who operates on the markets tries to seize opportunities for profit, without distinguishing between medium- and long-term operations (investment) on the one hand and short-term operations (speculation) on the other. Even those without speculative intent cannot avoid using instruments like financial leverage and short-selling.

The distinction is also unconvincing on a theoretical level. Once again, Shackle observes this clearly.[3] In all cases where an operator hopes to gain, by buying now with the intention of selling later at a higher price, he/she is placing a bet on the expectations of him/herself and others. The value of an asset is not an inherent characteristic of the object, but reflects its place in the mutual observations of operators. Nobody invests according to the variation of the 'objective' value of the asset. The prospect of a future gain is always linked to the idea of using knowledge one does not yet have, and, in this sense, the prospect of gain is always an 'exploitation of ignorance'.

Speculation is indicative of a restless market, where today's assessments depend on suppositions about tomorrow's assessments (by both ourselves and others), on a steady regress of expectations on expectations, without fixed points and without a fundamental equilibrium. A suggestion that is convincing enough to attract many operators is sufficient to make the market move in one direction or another, with a trend that reinforces itself

until an opposite trend reverses the direction. 'A speculative market . . .
requires uncertainty.'[4] However, all markets actually behave in this way,
and all operators who are oriented to prices and their movements make a
bet on the future and on expectations – even if they think they are oriented
to goods and their value. Markets are inherently unsteady, and financial
markets remain the most evident and most volatile aspect of a general
feature of modern society – the presence of many different perspectives
that affect each other[5] (the fundamental role of second-order observation).

Operators know this very well. As early as 1818, Nathan Rothschild
said that when prices rise all purchases become speculative.[6] Over the
last few decades, this has become more evident as a consequence of the
instability of financial markets after the end of the Bretton Woods system
– that is, after the suspension of the convertibility of dollars into gold. All
monetary values become floating and directly reflect the values expected
in the future, greatly increasing the perception of uncertainty. Speculators
operate openly with this variability and the consequent uncertainty, and
those who would like to avoid risks must also engage in the same kind of
operations. Many operators use the tools offered by financial markets to
protect against possible future losses (to 'hedge' against risks), but these
very operations contribute to the restlessness of markets and can also be
targeted by speculators in order to bet on expectations and expectations
of expectations. These very operations, despite being meant to avoid
risks, contribute to the increase of the riskiness of the market as a whole.
Following the crisis of the European monetary market in 1993, it was even
discovered that the hedging carried out by enterprises had deeper effects
than the openly speculative activities of operators like George Soros.[7] In
the movements of the markets, investments for the purposes of hedging
are difficult to distinguish from those that are speculative, and they all
contribute to unpredictable and self-referential market movements, to the
little-controlled or regulated 'self-regulation of society to the probable'.[8]

2.   GAMBLING AND IRRATIONALITY

The result is often observed with concern. Financial markets are becoming
increasingly important, to the point that one talks about the domination
of finance in the global economic system.[9] In the present economy, the
central position is no longer occupied by industry and production, but by
the financial market with the various organizations involved: the stock
exchange, banks, various financial institutions, and the inscrutable cloud
of individual operators and informal institutions. There are fluctuations
in the cost of money and in the availability of liquidity, which affect the

periphery (labour markets, raw materials or products) in the form of variability and the uncertainty of the future.[10]

This has not always been the case. Until the modern age, the central
issue of the economy was the explanation of the exchange process and
of price-formation. The idea of investment was completely absent. When
one lent money, the sum remained fixed and there were no mechanisms
in place for the creation and management of credits. One did not expect
money to generate profit, but was instead concerned with production or
political purposes, without caring for regularities and trends or reflecting
long-term movements and price developments. The ups and downs of
wealth were attributed to natural disasters or political upheavals, famines,
wars or devastation, and not to internal economic factors like the relationship of supply and demand or cyclical crises.[11] The situation changed in
the seventeenth century, with the development of the Amsterdam stock
exchange, the first modern financial market with highly refined tools
and a reckless management of risk, and with the 'financial revolution'
in England.[12] The idea that intentions and expectations can have effects
on the world and allow for the spread of wealth developed into a well-
organized system of government loans for integrating and compensating
tax revenues. The traffic of credits exploded, and with this (as is always
the case) ensued a gigantic speculative traffic, parallel to credits and difficult to distinguish from them, with enormous risks and unscrupulous
operations.

Since its beginning, the rationality of the financial market has appeared
rather dubious. The spread of new monetary operations on money helped
to strengthen the traditional impression of credit as an incomprehensible
and tendentiously suspect 'cabala'. During the period when the enthusi-
asm for speculation spread in England and France, there was a parallel
diffusion of the passion for gambling, which was always dangerously near
to financial transactions. It is well known that John Law, the inventor of
the financial speculation that gave rise to the famous 'Mississippi bubble'
in France at the beginning of the eighteenth century, was first a gambler
and then applied the same techniques to business transactions.[13] Keynes
himself points out that, when the propensity to speculate spreads, the
development of the capital of a country threatens to become 'a by-product
of the activities of a casino'[14] – the same observation that constitutes the
foundation of Susan Strange's influential book.[15]

Just as gambling is difficult to master, so too is the functioning of
the stock exchange wrapped in a halo of mystery. Despite an enormous
use of resources and attention, the evolution of assets seems to follow
an unpredictable path for incomprehensible reasons – and Galbraith
would say without hesitation that 'nothing in economic life is so poorly

understood as the great speculative episode'.[16] The research on the stock market is often considered unreliable and is, therefore, not usually followed, while people tend to see the market itself as a sort of 'oracle, who pronounces mysterious and senseless sentences that we ask our leaders to interpret, and then we make the mistake of taking these interpretations as authoritative'.[17] The movement of markets seems to proceed in an erratic and irrational way, acquiring a structure only as a result of our efforts to find a logic in a trend that, by itself, has none. The theory runs after empirical developments that regularly precede and surprise it. In this sense, one can even think that the financial crisis should not have been avoided, because it is useful for the efficiency of markets, which are always uncertain and proceed by trial and error.[18]

This unpredictability could be a confirmation of the random walk hypothesis (RWH) – that is, indirectly of the efficient market hypothesis (EMH), where information is evenly distributed and simultaneously accessible to all operators. In actuality, the development of financial markets, with more and more refined tools, advanced technology and faster operations, seems not to be leading to the expected efficiency, which would be rational and distribute resources in the most effective way. On the contrary, it seems that when information is distributed better, a specific irrationality develops. Markets, while remaining essentially incomprehensible, become predictable in local and circumscribed (non-random) forms, contrary to the RWH (hence to the EMH). The financial market, which should meet the requirements of a perfect market better, behaves in a highly imperfect and apparently unsatisfactory way.

The alleged irrationalities of economic behaviour have been observed for some time, and have the interesting feature of showing regularities – that is, as not random and unpredictable, but rather following a kind of logic that goes against rational correctness.[19] These trends become much stronger in financial markets, where they take the well-known and much-studied form of phenomena like the return to the average (assets that lost or gained significantly tend to be normalized), 'size effects' (assets with low capitalization tend to perform better), calendar effects (around the weekend, during holidays and at the end of the month assets exhibit particular behaviour – for example, in buying assets on Friday and selling them on Monday, one often loses), and excessive reactions to profit announcements, among others. There are also cases of 'gregarious behaviour', where one tends to adapt to the behaviour of the majority, even when one recognizes that this behaviour is not rational. In financial markets, these deviations from logic are particularly puzzling, not only because such markets should supposedly be an arena of instrumental rationality, highly quantitative and possibly immune from falling into unreasonableness, but also because, once identified, they should immediately disappear. This, however, does not occur. One would expect investors, recognizing the phenomenon, to take advantage of it for profit, thereby compensating its effects. The irrationality of market behaviour not only questions the assumption of the rationality of operators, but also, and this is more serious, the hypothesis of the rationality of markets, namely their efficiency.

Phenomena like gregarious behaviour are even more serious because they also call the irrationality of the irrational behaviour into question. We have known for some time that in a situation where everyone is mad, it is wiser to be mad with others than wise alone,[20] and the observation of gregarious behaviour shows that one can even make profits by adopting this position. Apparently, investors behave rationally when they buy clearly overestimated assets, because they hope that the price will continue to rise, at least over the short term. They follow the strategy of the 'most foolish fool', trusting that there will be someone who buys at an even higher price. The rationality lies, not in estimating the real value of the asset or the situation of 'fundamentals', but only in time, in being able to choose the right moment to leave the race. This partly explains the lack of compensation of market inefficiencies. The alleged irrationalities would be opportunities for speculation, hints to observe others and their observations of the market, and hence not at all irrational, but expressions of another kind of rationality.

The famous speculative bubbles, pushed by an 'irrational euphoria'[21] beyond the scope of most standard economic explanations, seem to be driven by factors that, as Keynes says, despite being unreasonable, become legitimate when there is no solid basis for another kind of reasoning.[22] In these speculative explosions, the self-reference of markets comes to the fore, reversing the current rationality criteria. In a situation where the operators mainly observe the observations of other operators (who do the same), rational behaviour becomes irrational and vice versa. The action of the individual would be rational if others did not behave in the same way, which leads to 'cobweb' fluctuations that make the market completely unpredictable.[23] It then becomes rational to go against the stream, though one is then compelled to act against what should be the recognized rationality. Professional operators do not bother to act rationally, but predict the variations in current trends with a minimum of advance with respect to the general public, referring not to the value of assets, but only to the evaluations of the market. The first source of information is the media, not because they inform us about how things are,[24] but because they inform us about what everybody knows that others know,[25] and this is what one must bear in mind. At this level, there is no difference between 'objective' information, which changes expectations about fundamental variables, and pure 'noise', introduced by specific agents (noise traders) for purely speculative purposes.

The central factor is time, in the sense of choosing the right moment, and also in the sense of the general condition of being ignorant of the future, which affects all present observations and decisions. This is why, according to Shackle, the alleged rationality proves ineffective, without thereby giving way to pure irrationality. One follows criteria and builds expectations that are not arbitrary, but the result cannot be 'objective', and does not apply to all cases. One does not rely on fantasy, but on 'constrained imagination', based on what seems plausible at that time (following or deviating from it). Expectations operate according to their 'rules of the game', and these are not those of instrumental rationality.[26]

3.   THE RISKS OF THE OBSERVATION OF RISK

Financial markets are opaque mainly because their very movement creates uncertainty (an endogenous uncertainty that does not depend on a real instability of external conditions such as the so-called fundamentals). Markets, and hence prices, seem to be driven directly by the movement of prices, in a circular and reflexive trend that produces a constant irritation and makes any external evaluation very difficult. Expectations, which have always been the engine and reference of market orientation, are themselves driven by expectations, expectations about future prices that depend on current decisions to buy and to sell.[27] Referring to the future, expectations depend on themselves. As market observers say, 'the present is determined by the future and vice versa'.[28] Nobody can steer the movements of the market or control the future.

It may seem surprising that this endogenous uncertainty makes the market somewhat predictable, at least from the point of view of speculators who learn to observe trends (which are actual and fairly determined) instead of an unknowable future. For example, speculators can bet on the gregarious behaviour of less reckless operators and count on the positive feedback (or polarization) of investment (precisely what drags the market to disaster in the case of bubbles) – that is, on the fact that investors buy when prices rise and sell when prices fall. These 'trend-chasing' strategies, oriented only to prices and their movements, are based on short-term expectations, and are completely independent of long-term expectations about the movement of the markets (stronger oriented to fundamentals). These strategies count on the fact that less-informed operators tend to follow the choices of big investors who, however, reverse the trend of overestimated assets and return to more sober references at the appropriate time, generating enormous earnings. In these conditions, and in the short term, the very rational behaviour of more-informed speculators tends to destabilize prices and make the long-term movements of market trends completely irrational.[29]

Market development depends primarily on a prognosis of the development of markets (such as the views of experts), which guides the behaviour of operators.[30] This does not mean that things will always be good: MacKenzie showed that the history of the dizzying ascent and the very rapid collapse of the LTCM (Long Term [!] Capital Management) hedge fund can be connected with the widespread imitation it provoked – that is, to its own success,[31] which imposed times no longer compatible with the possibilities of the fund. This investment strategy could have been beneficial if there had been enough time, but had to be abandoned because of the consequences of an excess of imitation. The orientation to risk can be very risky because, when prices change, not only do the external factors change, but also the willingness to take more risks. When the market falls, one tends to sell to limit risk exposure,[32] and the opposite happens when the market rises. Even risk reacts to itself.

Whether one wants to avoid risks or to look for them, the dynamics of financial markets seem to lead to an overall rise in risk. This is primarily due to the fact that risk analysis is replaced by the observation of other observers, who have not always properly verified the external conditions. One tends to take risks if others are ready to risk, regardless of whether the investment itself is risky or not. The performance of markets, when one tries to reduce exposure to possible damage, is not one of reducing risks, but is instead one that distributes risk to multiple carriers with strategies of hedging, counter-hedging and other forms of insurance. In the end, a condition may arise in which the chain of decisions becomes so inscrutable that the overall risk (which has become very high and is no longer computable) cannot be attributed to any single decision-maker, but becomes a sort of widespread systemic risk.[33] Individual operators may also take calculated risks, but the resulting overall risk is greater than the sum of the knowingly considered risks, because a systemic risk is added that takes the form of an 'externality', an additional cost that is not calculated in the market.[34]

The theory of financial markets distinguishes between *non-systemic risk* (which should be eliminated by careful management of the investment portfolio, by diversification and hedging) and *systemic risk* (which derives from the endogenous uncertainty produced by the market operations themselves and cannot be eliminated).[35] Only systemic risk requires intuition and boldness of the investor in addition to the mastery of calculation and investment techniques, and only systemic risk should be compensated by the market. The profits of operators should reward their exposure to risk. Who risks more, earns more – if things go well. Systemic risk grows with the increase in number and complexity of financial transactions, including the completely 'hedged' ones, which are oriented only to protection against market contingencies.

The distinction between the two kinds of risk tends to become less and less clear. An increase in market risk produces unexpected changes even in specific risks, which in turn become more and more open and unpredictable.[36] When markets allow for the distribution of risks associated with financial activities among the investors, they lead all operators to take greater risks.[37] This happens either because one can speculate on hedging investments or because adverse risk operators venture into more reckless investments since hedging protects them against excessive losses.[38] When one protects against risks, one risks more, and everybody risks.

4.   THE UNCERTAINTIES OF THE REGULATION OF UNCERTAINTY

Can such adventurous markets be controlled? Is it possible to regulate financial operations in order to avoid the production of excessive damage? Since the renunciation of the Bretton Woods agreement in 1971, even the illusion of an order that binds market movements has been lost, and an unprecedented form of instability has arisen. Currency, which should provide some protection against the uncertainties of life and the future, seems to have become a source of further uncertainty.[39] Occasionally, the idea of a 'new financial order'[40] that is able to avoid crises with interventions or timely warnings re-emerges – but then one must recognize that warnings are completely ineffective because they are not followed, and often harmful because they contribute to the spread, rather than to the mitigation, of alarm among operators. Interventions, however, generally refer to the role of a 'lender of last resort'. This role can be filled by the Treasury, the Central Bank, the International Monetary Fund or others, and involves the task of restricting an excess of loan grants, which are often not sufficiently guaranteed. Conversely, these interventions also serve to encourage loans in periods of nervousness or fear. However, this kind of operation does not always work, and may even produce damages. If the markets know that they will be supported in cases of speculative excesses, they can count on this and produce their form of moral hazard,[41] increasing the risks and reducing caution and controls – the doubts about state interventions on troubled banks during the 2008 crisis demonstrate this fact. Some say that the regulatory authority should maintain a certain ambiguity in order to preserve the necessary uncertainty of markets.[42] If this were the case, however, it would be very difficult to understand how an order based on the guarantee of uncertainty would operate.

The awareness grows that we should give up the illusion of regulation because financial markets are no longer organized in a hierarchical way, with a vertex (Central Bank) that controls the operations as far as the periphery. Decisions and information are now distributed to a variety of operators, official and unofficial, which are regulated and over the counter, and even private individuals operate directly on markets, giving rise to a sort of diffused and non-transparent 'heterarchy', with flows going simultaneously in several different directions.[43] In these conditions, the only plausible form of regulation can be a self-regulation of markets based on their internal mechanisms.[44] Even the interventions of politics and/or law constitute additional elements of complexity and 'irritation', which are elaborated upon internally in a process that can be disturbed but not steered from the outside. This does not mean that politics or other external influences should refrain from intervening, as suggested by misunderstood liberal attitudes that have been sharply criticized after the giving up of the Bretton Woods system. Markets need external constraints in order to be able to build expectations. They need to be monitored in order to be able to grow in a controlled manner.[45] This control, however, is not the one exercised by the external authority. Markets, one could say, need external constraints in order to be able to control themselves. Even regulatory measures are used to develop strategies, to devise alternative plans starting from conditions shared by other operators, to risk or to predict the risks taken by others, in a situation where references are needed to know what others know, not to know what to do. From this complex of constraints an order emerges, but it is not the one imposed by the regulator, and it is constantly changing.[46]

A key role is certainly played by the spread of digitization and the use of computers. Many financial transactions are so complex that they could not be implemented without the support of computers, and the spread of telematics has created the possibility of giving investors direct access to financial transactions. There has also been an enormous acceleration in the speed of transactions, a form of virtual instantaneity, where one tries to react to operations almost simultaneously with their realization.[47] These operations act simultaneously on multiple planes, speculating both on the transaction and on its consequences for the movement of markets, thereby generating a complex recursive situation that completely escapes the familiar forms of causal control, which are constrained by the temporal difference between cause and effect (the first must precede the second).[48]

Some authors believe that in this time pattern lies the true significance of the globalization of financial markets, which anticipate a 'time world' where all contents must be understood in terms of processes.[49] Globalization would not be so much a spatial phenomenon characterized by the overcoming of boundaries and national territories, but instead a temporal phenomenon, linked with the virtual simultaneity of an interconnected universe that produces a 'global reflex system' located primarily on computer screens. This reality, built on the model of relations between mirrors that reflect each other, has no fixed content independent of the ongoing processes, but comes into being in the form of a carpet that is formed as it is unrolled.[50] The problem remains of what kind of orientation can be realized in this new mobile and evanescent reality – whether global structures can emerge or whether there can only be 'global microstructures' projecting local configurations and interactive structures on a general level.[51]

If operators refer to what others know first, and not to how things are or to what others actually think,[52] the media become very important, and increasingly attract the attention of operators. It was noted that the first speculative bubbles appeared roughly at the same time as the spread of newspapers (towards the middle of the seventeenth century), and that stock exchange crashes seem to be linked with communication technologies: in the 1920s, the advent of radio; in the 1950s, mass television; in the 1990s, the Internet.[53] Thus stated, the connection is a little too simple and automatic, because it has been pointed out that the stock exchange does not immediately react to media news, but seems to have its own time and its own priorities. However, the impression remains, as expressed by Hayek, that economic analysis tends to neglect the role of the press and other media.[54] Investors demand more than value, as is shown by the much-discussed emulation effects, and they very often demand trends that are disclosed directly by the media. For example, in the days immediately following the expiry of a tender offer or an initial public offering (which must be publicized by newspapers), the price of the stock tends to increase, because those excluded hurry to buy remaining stocks.[55] Assets seem to get an 'interest value' or a 'curiosity value' affecting their assessment.[56]

Media, on the other hand, give more and more space to financial news, which almost perfectly matches 'newsworthiness criteria', and distinguishes events that are particularly suited to become news in newspapers and on television. Somewhat like sport, there are always winners and losers. Numbers that are informational, regardless of their interpretation, are provided; changes and variations are presented; trends anticipated. There are heroes and conflicts.[57] Media, however, provide news in their own particular format, constrained by the limitations of space and attention, and by the inexorable law of novelty, inevitably leading to a simplification and a tendency to emphasize variations rather than constant data. Media give overemphasis to successes and market records, giving an impression of dynamism exceeding the real data. They also report the different views of operators and analysts, with an emphasis on the lack of agreement. Media focus on short-term data and often neglect long-term trends (they focus on the timely event rather than on the overall context), and rely on personal opinions rather than on insights or analyses.[58]

The consequence is that operators tend to focus on the interpretation of recent events and overlook basic macroeconomic trends. They give priority to immediate, unpredictable and dynamic news, to unconfirmed rumours, opinions and impressions, at the expense of long-term information regarding more complex events.[59] On the other hand, one must not think that media announcements have a direct effect on market movements. Even if operators pay exaggerated attention to the latest information, markets seem to react in a delayed way, often caring little for very important events and focusing instead on seemingly insignificant or minor news.[60] Apart from particularly explicit cases, markets seem to need time – not to interpret the news, but to see how the 'prevailing opinion' evaluates it. What counts, namely, is not the datum by itself, but the way in which it focuses the attention of the public, which becomes the relevant information reference, and this can usually be observed only afterwards.[61]

NOTES

1. The definition, among many others, comes from Strange (1986), p. 115 It.edn.
2. See, among others, Colombo et al. (2006), p. 43.
3. Here we follow Shackle (1972), pp. 12ff. and 46f. and (1988), p. 19.
4. Strange (1986), p. 115 It.edn.
5. See Shackle (1972), p. 79.
6. Quoted in Chancellor (2000), p. 97.
7. See Millman (1995), pp. 210–11 It. edn.
8. According to Oliver Wendell Holmes's definition of speculation, quoted in Chancellor (2000), p. 226.
9. Sassen (1996), p. 46.
10. Luhmann (1991), p. 192; (1996b), p. 4.
11. See Finley (1973), pp. 13ff., 218f. It. edn.
12. See Galbraith (1991); Chancellor (2000), p. 40; Agnew (1986), p. 158f.; Dickson (1967), p. 12.
13. See Chancellor (2000), pp. 49–50.
14. Keynes (1936), p. 159.
15. 'The Western financial system resembles more and more a huge casino': Strange (1986), p. 3 It. edn. The underlying attitude is already revealed by the title 'Casino capitalism'. See also, among others, Caranti (2003), who maintains that gambling is dignified by the calculus of probabilities, which changes it into a science like financial calculation – on the scientificity of the calculus of probabilities and related questions, see Esposito (2007).
16. Galbraith (1991), p. 103. See also Cesarini and Gualtieri (2000), p. 9.

17. Shiller (2000), p. 146 It. edn; see also p. 16.
18. As maintained by Allen and Gale (2003), p. 87.
19. The literature about this is now huge. For an overall picture see, for example, Motterlini and Piattelli Palmarini (2005) and Motterlini (2006).
20. The London banker John Martin said as early as 1720 that 'when all are insane we must somehow follow them' – quoted in Chancellor (2000), p. 93. The same argument can be found in Pascal (1670), n. 31: 'Les hommes sont si nécessairement fous que ce serait être fou par un autre tour de folie de n'être pas fou.' According to Strange (1998), generalized insanity is the defining feature of contemporary markets.
21. The expression used by Alan Greenspan in December 1996 to describe the behaviour of investors on the stock market. It is the starting point of Shiller (2000).
22. Keynes (1936), p. 154.
23. See Kindleberger (1978), pp. 34ff. It. edn.
24. Which is not their task: see Luhmann (1995), declaring in his title that the function of media is to create their own specific reality.
25. According to the famous 'beauty contest' in Keynes (1936), p. 156, where observation is at the 'third degree where we devote our intelligences to anticipating what average opinion expects the average opinion to be'.
26. See Shackle (1990a), pp. 6–13.
27. Gorge Soros declares it explicitly: see Soros (1987), p. 43 It. edn.
28. Chancellor (2000), p. 226. See also Demange and Laroque (2006), p. 216.
29. See Shleifer (2000), pp. 156f. Aglietta and Orléan (1982), p. 106 speak of 'convergence mimétique unanime' in the forms of self-validating speculation, where changes in prices are oriented only to changes in prices.
30. See Piel (2003), pp. 102–4; Eatwell and Taylor (2000), p. 117.
31. See MacKenzie (2005b).
32. See Grossman (1989), pp. 5–6.
33. Luhmann (1991), pp. 191–2.
34. See Eatwell and Taylor (2000), pp. 17 and 46.
35. See Hull (1997), p. 69; Manuli and Manuli (1999), p. 43. We shall discuss this again in Chapter 10, section 4.
36. See Eatwell and Taylor (2000), p. 188.
37. Demange and Laroque (2006), pp. 135f. See also Strange (1986), pp. 116ff. It. edn.
38. It is known that the crisis of 2008 was due largely to this kind of mechanism. We shall discuss it in Chapter 11, section 3.
39. Strange (1986), p. 107 It. edn.
40. Thus Shiller (2003). For a discussion on possibilities and limits of the regulation of markets see Eatwell and Taylor (2000).
41. 'Moral hazard' indicates that protection against risk can produce new risks, because one behaves differently than one would have done otherwise. The formula, dating from the seventeenth century, was introduced in the context of insurance, where people tend to take fewer precautions and expose themselves to greater risks when they know that the damage will be covered by insurance. In recent times, the problem of moral hazard is very much debated in relation to financial markets. We shall discuss it in detail in Part III.
42. See, for example, Kindleberger (1978), p. 171 It. edn.
43. See Luhmann (1991), pp. 211f. Heterarchy dissolves the hierarchical order – not because there is no longer a hierarchy but because there are many alternative hierarchies, that cannot be reduced to unity: see Luhmann (1997), pp. 312ff.
44. See Millman (1995), p. 17 It. edn; Betti (2000), p. 13.
45. This is for example the opinion of Soros (1987), pp. 96 and 129 It. edn.
46. In Chapter 13 we shall discuss the attempts to regulate the financial crisis of 2008 from this point of view.
47. See Sassen (1996), pp. 64–5 and (2005), p. 19; Chancellor (2000), p. 228; Luhmann (1990b), p. 117, fn. 49.

48. As we have seen in Chapter 1, and will see more specifically in the next few chapters.
49. Knorr Cetina (2005), p. 39. See also Sassen (2005), pp. 18f.
50. Knorr Cetina (2005), pp. 42 and 52.
51. See Knorr Cetina and Bruegger (2002).
52. Not the average opinion, but what operators think to be the average opinion: a much better objective entity, which can be observed.
53. Shiller (2000), p. 109 It. edn and ch. 5.
54. See Hayek (1988), p. 251.
55. See Cesarini and Gualtieri (2000), p. 46.
56. Shiller (2000), pp. 52f. It. edn.
57. For an overview on 'newsmaking' and the news values guiding it, see Wolf (1985), pt 3.
58. See Shiller (2000), pp. 110f. It. edn.
59. See Tivegna and Chiofi (2000), pp. 34 and 180f.; Kapferer (1987), ch. 16.
60. See Shiller (2000), pp. 116–19 It. edn.
61. See Sarcinelli (2000), p. 17.

PART II

The time of finance

7. Paper finance and the relationship to the world

What has changed in finance over the last decades? Do technological innovation and the launch of the 'new economy', with all their promises and threats, really mark a transition to a completely different financial world? Or are they only further developments of speculation and credit as we have known them for centuries? Perhaps this question is difficult to answer because we do not really understand what is happening. It might be useful to use time as a reference. In financial markets, the future is produced using expectations about the future, in a circularity where one loses sight of the difference between reality and illusion (section 1).

Finance seems to deal only with abstractions and flimsy entities, neglecting the concrete reality of goods, production and wealth consumption. As in other areas of society, however, with respect to the economy, one should abandon the idea that observation and reality are separate, and consider how the descriptions of the world change the world described. This breakthrough, which goes under the name of constructivism in science and performativity here, starts from observers observing the world and each other, and tries to describe the resulting reality (a reality made up of objects and observations, which observe objects and are sometimes themselves observed, observe others and the way others observe them) (section 2).

This flexible and non-univocal reality is related to the structure of contemporary society, which refers to an image of reality that corresponds to the categories and criteria of the area at stake in all fields (science and economy, as well as rights and art, education and family). This image of reality is not valid in an absolute way. The reality of science is not that of art, nor that of the law or family, and none of these is arbitrary or able to be invented at will. Reality always sets very precise constraints, but these are not dictated by an independent world. From another point of view, these constraints may be different, and they may change over time (section 3).

The madness and obscurity of financial markets seem to refer to another kind of rationality, one based on the mutual observation of observers (which is not only gregarious behaviour, but also the foundation of reality), on the reflexivity of time, a rationality that is produced by our expectations and projects, and on the orientation to risk (section 4).

1.   REVOLUTION OR CONTINUITY?

In this part of the book, we shall discuss the so-called derivatives, which are very special financial instruments with a set of characteristics that make them extremely interesting for the purposes of our analysis. For some time now, derivatives have had a broad, but dubious, visibility. These highly technical, innovative and rather opaque tools have become famous in the media as the object of many discussions, articles and various reflections. By now, references to futures, options, swaps and other such similar things can be taken for granted, even outside the strictly economic field. The assessments of their role and their consequences are also very forceful and emphatic. When the Italian Minister Giulio Tremonti defined them as the plague of our century in the summer of 2008, it was asked if the perspective was too negative, not if the phenomenon was really that relevant. Despite this over-exposure, or, perhaps, because of it, it is less and less clear what derivatives are and how they operate.

As sociologists know very well, when this lack of clarity develops, it is hardly by chance. It is rarely an error. Despite the diminished transparency and the inaccuracies in the debate, if a phenomenon receives this reputation, there is usually a reason, even if it is not always the one that draws the attention of the public. The leading hypothesis of this work is that derivatives, because of their 'secondary' nature (they are called derivatives because they 'derive' from something else), highlight and exacerbate all the trends we have presented concerning financial markets, money and the management of time in the economy. Derivatives, one could say, are the extreme implementation of economic rationality. In fact, they are so extreme that they mark the point where the perspective is reversed and one is forced to reconsider familiar theoretical assumptions and face a new stage of development (which, however, once accepted and understood, is not so new any more, given that the premises have been operating for so long). Our hypothesis is that the new financial instruments appear so obscure and incomprehensible because we continue to look at them with categories that are inadequate, even for 'primary' financial markets. Forced to realize this, we must try to develop a different approach.

Perhaps Tom Wolfe was right when he prophesized that we are facing the end of capitalism[1] (an impression shared by many others during the events of the summer and winter of 2008, which would have been unthinkable before). The bankruptcy of famous and reputed banks, the collapse of insurance companies, public rescues and the direct intervention of the state in the economy all served to reinforce this position. However, every end is also a beginning, one that does not come out of nowhere, and, according to one's point of view, one can decide whether to stress break or continuity, the end or the evolution of the capitalist economy. The new dynamics of financial markets can also be seen as an epochal break, marking a transition to a radically different economic organization or a new form of money, or seen as the evolution of tools that have already existed for centuries, if not millennia, that are simply used in more and more reckless ways.

What matters is that a higher level of reflexivity and abstraction comes into play, which at a given point becomes autonomous and follows its own development. Although one could speculate before the 1970s, speculation now refers only to speculation and, so to speak, 'feeds' on itself. Although markets have always had their dynamics, which are led by the mutual observation of observers, this observation has now become the real object of transactions. Economic dynamics have always been for the production of the future; however, the future now depends on the expectations for the future, not on the present data and even less on the past. The phenomena to be explained are concerned with this new form of self-reference of financial markets, which does not imply isolation. The problem is that these abstract and opaque movements have a heavy impact on all areas of society. The so-called 'real' economy is not independent of the financial economy, even if, in the light of the new instruments and the new financial dynamics, it is less and less clear how these interdependencies work or can be controlled.

It is taken for granted that speculation played a role in the dizzying ascent of the price of oil in 2008, especially in derivative markets. However, at the same time, we know that the demand for oil from emerging countries (particularly China and India) has also increased – that is, the situation of the 'real' economy has changed, and suffers severely from the increase in prices. Do financial markets react to the situation of the real economy or vice versa? Do 'real' expectations orient the movements of 'paper money' or is it the trends of finance that shape concrete expectations? Do we refer to the world or to finance, or to how finance observes the world and the future that awaits us? What is 'real' and what is 'paper', if the economy no longer works with barter and with the immediate satisfaction of needs? What have derivatives to do with it? Why do we tend to blame them for this new form of closure and the self-reference of financial markets?

2. CONSTRUCTIVISM IN ECONOMICS

All these questions remain difficult to answer, so long as we continue to consider the economy and the world as two separate areas, where there are objects and real needs on the one side and payments and credits on the other, separated by the 'veil of money' that marks access to an area where different criteria and relevances hold. This is the attitude we adopt when we separate world and finance, real wealth and paper wealth. The criticism of money as a neutral screen (the 'veil'), which does not belong to the world, is at least as old as Keynes.[2] So, too, is the criticism of the 'autarchic' attitude of economic theory, which is open to the contribution of other disciplines such as psychology, anthropology and sociology. So far, however, this openness does not seem to have led to a genuine transformation of the basic assumptions of economic reflection. A simple broadening of the theory (as in Akerlof's 'psycho-socio-anthropo-economics'[3]) is one thing. However, the breakthrough that leads to the idea that money and its dynamics (including economics) are not simply an image of the world but real objects of the world, as goods among others that contribute to the constitution of the world that money itself monetizes and translates into capital, is quite another. According to this approach, money is the 'duplication' of all goods and commodities in monetary sums and, at the same time, is itself a good that can be exchanged and evaluated, and is influenced by the dynamics of prices and their corresponding movements (that is, money is both outside, and inside, its object).

This breakthrough is far from new. It corresponds to similar changes of perspective in many other areas, such as the change in perspective that characterized the philosophical reflection of the twentieth century, beginning with the way in which language is considered. Language is no longer considered an external description of the world, but as something that belongs to the world that it describes. It has consequences and affects things. Language is itself a thing, and even makes things. As a result, it has become necessary to develop a theory that takes this into account and draws out its consequences. The theory of language in the twentieth century, with all its developments, has followed this line of development. Economic reflection is due to make a similar breakthrough, radicalizing the ideas it has maintained for some time; ideas that have not yet been consistently followed through.

Only recently have some approaches been developed that start explicitly by rejecting the separation between the 'economic world' and the social world, and trying to study the variety of connections between them. Callon's (1998) very influential study refers to Granovetter's (1985) social network analysis and proposes the 'embeddedness' of markets in the overall society.[4] Abolafia (1998) observes markets as generators of specific cultures, places of interactions and repeated transactions that develop a series of guidelines and criteria that guide their further development. A tradition of research has been developed that is driven by the idea of 'performativity'[5] – that is, by the assumption that the cultural and theoretical presuppositions of economic operators affect the way markets work, changing the economy as a whole. Ideas and cultures are forces that operate in the very field these same ideas and cultures aim to describe and understand. MacKenzie showed how the models developed by economics affect the very economic reality to which they refer, which changes by conforming (performativity) or deviating (counter-performativity) from the image proposed by the theory. The theory is observed as an object among others in the field of the economy, and contributes to changing economic reality as a whole.

Our proposal is placed in this framework, even though it stresses the reference to the theory of society to a greater extent, and this with a significant shift of accents. The studies on performativity aim to show how economics (communication about the economy) changes its object (economic dynamics). This is certainly very useful. The Black–Scholes formula, for example, refers to a model of financial markets which, although it did not correspond to the reality of finance at the time when it was first introduced (at the beginning of the 1970s), has become increasingly accurate as the formula has been used to guide operations. Reality adapted to the theory.[6] We would like to show that it is not only observations, but the very operations of the economy (transactions, speculation, trade in derivatives and other assets), that change the economy, that build up elements of the world that operators observe and take into account, and to which they orient their choices and decisions. It is not only the 'external' communications of economists and the cultures of operators that change the reality of the economy, but also the very operations of the economy itself, which has to do with a world comprising expectations and operations. Even without referring to a theory, operators face a reality made up of objects and observations, goods and money, data and bets on productivity, values and prices (where prices themselves change the value). The reality of the economy is produced by the economy itself.

Our description of economic dynamics, as presented in previous chapters, with its emphasis on the informative value of prices, the self-referential dynamics of markets, the creation of needs by the economy that must in turn satisfy them, the production and duplication of scarcity, tried to show just this fact, and can now be used as a premise for what ensues. The novelty of derivatives and the corresponding financial markets lies first of all in their making this turning point inevitable. It has never been as evident as it is now that, without this step, one cannot understand what is going on and fails both in describing these dynamics and also in attempting to provide practical tools. The widespread discourses about the 'opaqueness' of the new financial instruments, which are so complex that they are misunderstood not only by the uninitiated, but also by the operators, are indicative of the lack of an appropriate and workable explanation of what is happening. Operators are in the paradoxical situation of knowing what to do and how to do it (relying even on algorithms and very refined techniques to guide their behaviour and their decisions), and simultaneously not knowing what is happening or what it is that they are really doing. It is evident that financial markets – apart from the recurring crises, errors and bubbles – do not proceed arbitrarily. However, it is equally evident that nobody really knows where they are going or what mechanisms guide them.

Nobody claims to be able to predict or control the dynamics of markets. However, by broadening the perspective from the idea of the economy as an isolated sector to that of a view of society as a whole (with the economy as a part, which presupposes society and helps to bring about its realization), one can see parallels and connections, constraints and influences, allowing at the very least an understanding of how economic dynamics can be completely contingent and non-arbitrary at the same time, how they can be self-referential and oriented to the world – that is, how it is possible to give up the assumption of an independent outside world (the fundamentals of the economy, needs as an anthropological entity, even the gold standard exchange) without giving up the presence of constraints and the reality of the economy as a whole (including futures, options and other exotic and scarcely tangible objects).

The development we intend to propose for the economy reproduces what has been called the constructivist turn in other areas. It corresponds to a basic transformation of the structures of contemporary society. It is not by chance that MacKenzie refers to language studies (the theory of language acts with the famous formula 'How to do things with words'[7]) and epistemology (Barry Barnes's work[8]) to frame the breakthrough he invites economic theory to fulfil. Constructivism has been discussed, for the most part, in the case of science. The term often refers to the controversial problem of the relationship between theories and scientific descriptions and their reference to the world. This is the modern (or postmodern) legacy of the old debate between realism and nominalism. Constructivism[9] can be seen as the outcome of the epistemological debate of the last century, which goes beyond falsificationism, the end of the 'grand narratives' and the hypotheses about the social construction of science to say that science does not aim to know an independent reality, and that it cannot be the criterion of truth measuring the adequacy of its propositions; science can know only the reality built by its very operations. This is sufficient to constrain its operations and distinguish between real and false propositions in a unique and reliable way.

Since Heisenberg, we have known that science is confronted with a world that cannot be seized and always depends on the tools and view of the observer. Scientific observers inevitably face their own world, the world as it appears through their conceptual (theories) and practical tools (methods), not an independent world. This does not mean, however, that they face an arbitrary world, where 'anything goes', or that there are no objective criteria by which to distinguish between truth and falsity. On the contrary, reality (whatever it is) actively contributes to distinguishing between acceptable propositions and propositions that must be rejected, even if the result is not knowledge about an independent world. It is not necessary to know an outside world in order to refer to a reality that discriminates between scientific operations. This reality, however, will only be *one* reality among others, that of the observer concerned, and not *the* reality as such. There can be many realities, while there should be only one world. Reality, then, is only the hetero-reference of science, not an independent world. The way that science sees the outside world is on the basis of its instruments and categories, on the basis of the way it projects something different from itself and then faces it. This something different is never the world as such, existing apart from any observer. Each system has its own hetero-reference, which changes and evolves with the evolution of the operations of the system. This is its way of facing another – *its* other, not *the* other as such (which is always inaccessible).

The problem with the theory of science is its ability to describe the way that science deals with its hetero-reference, constructs it own reality and then learns about it, and describes how these operations affect our relationship with the environment, be it through technology, ecology, or any of the other various applications of knowledge in different fields. That the reality of science is not an independent given makes it no less real, as the consequences of research into our work and daily life abundantly show. The fact that science knows only its own reality by no means makes it a 'paper science' that is different from hypothetically real knowledge. It is simply the only way we can know, and the criterion is rather the rigour with which the operations are carried out.

Constructivism aimed to change the approach of the theory and, in particular, to move from what is called first-order observation to so-called second-order observation[10] – an apparently minor change that entails a cascade of consequences. The initial distinction is quite simple. The first-order observer observes data and objects in the world, while the second-order observer observes observers, who themselves observe data and objects in their world. Through the observed observers, the second-order observer observes a multiplicity of different worlds, those of all other observers. This obviously has consequences for their ontology, now fragmented into a multiplicity of reference realities. The point is that the second-order observer is inevitably a first-order observer facing their world and their objects, who can be observed by a further observer (who can be the observer themself, if they move to the second order). The second-order observer, who observes observers, cannot avoid also observing themself as an observer among others, and possibly distinguishing first- and second-order observation (by themself and others), nor can they avoid observing that they also observe others, others who are also observing them and their observations, in a mirroring of perspectives that soon becomes staggering. Second-order observation inevitably includes a reflexive component (that is, the theory always also observes itself when it observes its objects) and a component of abstraction. The reality of second-order observation is the reality of constructivism, referring each datum to the observer at stake and every reality to an intertwining of observation perspectives that affect and influence each other (this same thing happens in financial markets, and produces a similar bewilderment).

3.   THE SOCIETY OF SECOND-ORDER OBSERVATION

According to the systemic theory of society,[11] it is no coincidence that today's science works in this way. Constructivism corresponds to the structure of contemporary society. It is articulated in many distinct fields, each oriented to its own function, priorities and criteria. The perspective of science is hence quite different from those of politics, law, education, religion, art and economy. The post-modern aspect of this condition lies in the fact that none of these perspectives can claim priority and dictate rules to the other fields. Policy cannot tell science which propositions are true, in the same way as religion cannot tell art how to operate, and law cannot indicate to the economy how to gain profits. There is no univocal hierarchy with one function at the top, as there was in the past for religion or politics. There is not even a 'grand narrative' that can unify the various perspectives of different functional fields. Coordination can only be achieved at the level of second-order observation, given that each observer can observe the observation of others and the differences between them, and this without the possibility or need for a common reference world.

With this in mind, some variants of constructivism become obligations, not only for science, but for all other areas of contemporary society. Indeed, in all fields a similar orientation can be seen, which builds up references that hold, even if they are contingent, and work, even if they are not independent. Each sector of society must learn to assume certain references as valid that are not absolute, and do not apply to other areas or at other times, but that, nevertheless, suffice to orient their operations in ways that are neither random nor arbitrary. The system (and not the world) binds itself. This is why the constraint works with reference to the specific situation and to the problems of the area at stake. The issues of politics are not those of law or science, art or education, and, therefore, they require specific solutions. The exclusion of arbitrariness depends on the internal operations of the system, not on the presence of an independent reference. This is the root of the constructivist turn, which, while difficult to accept, is already implemented in the concrete practice of the operations of contemporary society.

Let's look at a few examples in addition to science. Particularly evident is the case of the legal system, which moved some time ago from an orientation to natural law ('right' by nature and valid in the same way at all times and in all circumstances), to positive law ('set' by a decision and valid because of it). Modern law now applies and must be followed in accordance with a decision that could have been different and will probably change in the future, not in accordance with something external and absolute. It is a contingent law, but cannot, nevertheless, be broken. So long as it holds, it must be followed, even if we know that it can be changed in other circumstances. The validity of the law depends on the operations of the system, but this does not undermine it. On the contrary, today it would be difficult to accept a law that claimed absolute and universal validity. The difficulties of the Western world in comparison to fundamentalism are an example of this fact. Its legitimacy would be weak, and rely far more on the use of force (which would be needed in order to exclude the possible arising of different perspectives of observation) than on the plastic and fungible reference to the intangible strength of public opinion (to the observation of observers). In the same way, it would be difficult to accept scientific research statements that claim to express the absolute truth. The truth of science is acceptable because it is presented as hypothetical and provisional.

Similarly, art abandoned imitation as the basis of its appropriateness and its criteria (imitation of the outside world or imitation of ideal models). Art no longer imitates eternal models, but instead produces its forms, which must be convincing, on the basis of the interplay of distinctions that they themselves bring into work and make perceptible. Observing a work of art (figurative arts, as well as a song, a poem, a dance), the spectator does not observe the world, either as it is or as it should be, but the perspective of the artist and their construction of their own world, which persuades (if it persuades) on the basis of internal criteria and self-adequacy. In other words, they realize a second-order observation.

Numerous other examples exist. Education, for instance, no longer aims at teaching content, but at teaching to learn, with all the consequent problems this entails. Here again, we see a movement to second-order observation, observing the pupil with their perspective and specific autonomous construction of a reference world. This poses issues much more complex than the simple transmission of competences about a world assumed to be given, equal for all and in all circumstances. We can also turn to families, which are now based on the observation by each member of the idiosyncratic and unrepeatable observation of each other member, where love implies the availability to agree to take as a reference this contingent and unmotivated perspective. According to the modern semantics of love, one does not love a person because they are beautiful or rich or intelligent or good (that is, for external reasons), but because they are as they are, with their irrationalities and peculiarities (that is, for reasons internal to the love relationship, which binds itself). This, as we know, is fragile and difficult to stabilize.

Our focus, however, is the economy. It is in its dynamics that we wish to verify if these same guidelines hold (and how) – in other words, a kind of constructivism that leads to a switch to second-order observation in order to explain the criteria and orientation of the operations. In the case of the economy, in order to explain what is actually happening, must we describe how operations bind themselves and build up non-arbitrary references that drive further operations? Do we need a 'positive economy', as we have a positive law?[12] If so, then, as for the other areas considered, it is no longer useful to go on using external references like the status of production, the availability of goods or other economic 'fundamentals' for the economy. Rather, we should be able to describe how economic dynamics work without them.

In this view, the economy is not devoted to the satisfaction of needs (from the primary needs to the indefinite multiplicity of induced needs), but to the management and circulation of specific forms of time binding, where everyone is oriented to their future perspective and to the perspective of others. It is at this level, at the level of second-order observation, that needs generate, addressed to the indeterminacy of the future and, as such, always inexhaustible. One always has needs, because one does not know what needs will arise in the future. In order to satisfy these needs, one will need money, money that, for this same reason, is chronically scarce (despite how much one has of it). The world (object of first-order observation) has little to do with it, because it is only present and, hence, inevitably inadequate with respect to future needs, and because the observation of the availability of goods is not useful. The world does not tell us what is perceived as scarce (because others also want to appropriate it), or which time horizon is activated (which future one refers to). We must observe observers, and observe them in time.

Monetization, with its translation and homogenization of any relevance into a sum of money, means an uncoupling from the simple reference to the world and needs, and an implicit reference to observers. Only in this perspective can money (by itself devoid of every utility and of its own value) become the object of need and, thereby, scarce. One needs money and not goods. This makes sense only through the reference to others, who accept it and give access to goods. The goods themselves can then remain indeterminate (even more so if the indeterminacy of time is projected over time, as in the case of credit, which sells money against money – that is, time availability projected over time; the future management of the future). Financial markets, which operate at this level, mark the accomplished abstraction of economic dynamics, and work on the basis of the endogenous creation and management of uncertainty, with its own specific forms of rationality.

The constructivist turn, when applied to the economy, involves the abandonment of any reference to a given external world, even in the form of the discourses about the difference between investment (which should operate in the real economy) and speculation (which should be a mere financial transaction), where the second should refer sooner or later to the first. Otherwise we have to deal with a pathological development, with a crazy economy, with gambling and a total lack of control. Derivative markets show us a financial world that is not crazy and is not made of paper, but cannot be understood so long as one keeps an external reference. Indeed, as all acknowledge, we do not understand anything. Because of this, the inference is made a little hastily that, because we cannot understand, it must therefore be wrong.

4. THE RATIONALITY OF FINANCIAL IRRATIONALITY

We shall try to describe the rationality of financial irrationality – that is, to describe all the countless breaks in the consolidated model of economic rationality that are constantly produced in the markets of the 'new economy'.[13] This reconstruction will be guided by three basic assumptions, which will transpose the general approach of constructivism into our field of research.

First, the mutual observation of observers (in this case financial operators) must not be understood as a pathology, one that, even though we must take it into account, contradicts the 'physiological' functioning of the markets because of different causes such as affective or cognitive limitations of individuals, 'noise' produced by the intervention of media or policy, limits to the circulation of information, opaqueness or other 'imperfections' of markets. The observation of observers by other observers is usually presented as the source of 'anomalies' in the market (which implies that there is a 'normal' condition) and of the reprehensible 'gregarious' behaviour of individuals who, instead of accurately assessing the available information, are misled by the behaviour of others and activate positive feedback loops and other forms of imitative correlations, thereby greatly increasing the riskiness of markets.

According to our approach, second-order observation is a structural condition of modern society and the basis of the only form of reality still viable. Observers do very well in observing each other because the world is not a primary given (not even for the economy), but comes into play when one observes what and how other observers observe. The reality of the modern economy is the reality of second-order observation. The world exists through the observation of others, who are themselves oriented to other observers. It is at this level that factors such as the return to fundamentals, the rush to raw materials in times of crisis and similar trends come into play (not because one refers to an independent reality, but because one observes the trends of the market – that is, observes the observation of others in the balance between self-reference and heteroreference of the markets). One observes what others observe. One observes the observation of the outside world, not the outside world as such. In this sense, gregarious behaviour is absolutely physiological and, indeed, inevitable. This does not mean that we do not make mistakes, as the recurrent crises, failures, and the outbreak of the speculative bubbles dramatically show, but that the error is not the abandonment of the world but the way of assessing and managing the internal constraints of the economy. In science, it is also simply not true that all statements are equivalent, but it is not their adequacy in relation to the world that discriminates between acceptable (true) scientific communications and wrong (false) research directions. The eye of the researcher must turn to the ways in which the financial economy binds itself and its operations, not to a correspondence with an alleged given world.

Second, in financial markets, one deals primarily with time relations – that is, one handles time. The primary role of time for economic communication in derivative markets becomes evident and absolutely essential. Old antagonisms, like the one between production and finance, definitively leave space for new variables like volatility, which becomes the main factor that moves the bargaining, and actually applies to temporal relations. The time of financial markets is a very abstract and reflexive time, and modern society is not yet accustomed to it. These markets are oriented to the future (think of *futures*), and not simply because they try to anticipate future states in the present, in the sense of foreseeing or guessing what they will be. Derivative instruments are used to manage the difference between the present future and the future presents in the present, between what one can expect to happen tomorrow, today, and what will actually be achieved tomorrow, as a result of what one does today in order to prepare for it. Derivatives allow one to make decisions today that affect the way the future will be, while preserving the freedom to decide one way or the other when this future will be present. They leave the indeterminacy of the future open, and, at the same time, produce it with their decisions. They produce indeterminacy while reducing it.

This extremely unlikely situation is the most abstract development of the complex management of time in the modern monetized economy. If it is true, as Shackle maintains, that money has always been time, then derivatives sell time in the form of the management of uncertainty. They sell time in order to decide about time using time, through the difference between presents that affect each other.

Third, the rationality of derivatives is the rationality of risk, which contradicts the current logic of rational calculation.[14] In risky situations (and, in financial markets, there are only risky situations, which are sought and actively produced), it is not rational to follow criteria of rationality. Instead, one should use them in order to deviate from them and generate profit opportunities. The rationality of risk interweaves social uncertainty (the fact that no one knows what others do) and temporal uncertainty (the fact that we do not know what the future holds) in order to condition them mutually and generate opportunities. If the behaviour of others or the trend of time were known, there would be no opportunity for speculation and profit, which are actively produced by the mutual conditioning of equally uncertain operators. The point lies in using constraints in order to generate opportunities.

In financial markets, one sees that risk is not a damage or nuisance, but can become a resource – indeed, the main resource for managing money under conditions of high uncertainty. The movements of markets show how the paradoxes of the risk society (the attempts to avoid risks are themselves risky, and risk is the only security) do not necessarily result in a stalemate, but can be actively used as opportunities to bind time and generate opportunities. In financial markets, one can earn, even when the economy goes bad or in situations of crisis, by selling uncertainty or following its orientations (in the form of volatility). Profits in derivative markets are often independent of markets, and relate to risk and its trends. The study of derivatives has the great advantage of showing how this risk rationality is already operating and how it works in the movements of very structured markets, which cannot be reduced to the rules of a 'first-order' rationality.

Recent events show that this does not exclude crises or problems of various kinds. These problems, however, do not relate to malfunctions of derivatives, which work too well and produce such complex situations that they become opaque and difficult to regulate. Instead, the problem is that we are not equipped to deal with the consequences of such an efficient working of tools that we do not yet fully understand. The fact that derivatives, which are detached by two steps from the data of the world, work well does not imply that the world goes well or that their consequences are positive.

NOTES

1. Cited by Massimo Giannini in *La Repubblica Affari & Finanza*, 30 June 2008, p. 1.
2. We have already seen it in Chapter 4.
3. For example in Akerlof (1984), 'Introduction'.
4. Assuming, however, an anthropological approach hardly compatible with systems theory, which takes communication as its primary reference. Callon (1998) proposes to develop a sociology of markets whose 'embeddedness' depends on the 'real man', placed in a 'bundle' of links and connections (p. 51), overcoming thereby the abstractness of *homo oeconomicus*. Systems theory starts, on the contrary, precisely from the abstractness of economic dynamics in order to explain its role in society: it is always a matter of communication.
5. See in particular MacKenzie and Millo (2003); MacKenzie (2005a, 2006, 2007).
6. This is the argument of MacKenzie and Millo (2003), to which we shall return later.
7. See Austin (1962).
8. See Barnes and Edge (1982); Barnes (1983).
9. I refer here to Niklas Luhmann's version, as found in Luhmann (1990a), pp. 508f. or in Luhmann (1988b). Under the label of radical constructivism more simplified theories also circulate, lacking the coupling with the general theory of society that is the strength of the approach of systems theory.
10. For the distinction of first-order and second-order observation see von Foerster (1981).
11. Here I am referring again to Niklas Luhmann, for example to Luhmann (1997), pp. 743f.
12. Milton Friedman spoke as early as the 1950s of 'positive economics', which rejects any realistic assumption and is not intended to provide adequate descriptions of an external object, but is adequate if it 'works'; i.e. if it has effects on the economic dynamics. See Friedman (1953). As positive law, positive economy is part of its object, and works if it can create constraints that orient its operations.
13. See also Esposito (2005).
14. See above, Chapter 5, section 4.

8.   Derivatives

Derivative contracts, which were the focus of financial innovation over the past decades, are strange and very abstract tools that do not refer to goods or assets directly, but to changes in the value of goods and assets (those they 'derive' from) (section 1). They do not refer to the present but to a future date for which they have already decided some of the conditions. One will buy or sell (or have the possibility to buy or sell) something at a given price, even if still unaware of what the situation or prices will be at that later date. Derivatives are needed because we are unaware of these things, in so far as they refer to what people expect or fear from the future, and deal with the resulting uncertainty, an uncertainty that is bought and sold with great freedom with respect to goods and becomes the real object of exchange.

In derivative markets, one buys and sells risk, and one can make substantial profits (section 2). Risk is indeed a risky object, and far more so than the goods that 'normal' trading deals with. It produces a 'leverage' that multiplies profits and damages, because it allows one to 'free' oneself from a reference to the world. When risking on risk, one only has to deal with uncertainty and its trends, and not with the goods themselves. In this way, one can even earn a great deal when the market goes bad or lose when the market is good.

Risk has always been traded in markets. What is new is the development of markets that deal only with risk, which have learned to standardize risk enough to be able to exchange it and give it a price (section 3). This is far from simple; in order to determine the correct price for a contract that refers to the future, it seems necessary that one know the future. A market for risk could only be constituted upon the realization that what is bought and sold is not a future given, but today's risk. One pays in order to eliminate uncertainty or to achieve opportunities, and these are all present conditions. Derivative markets refer to the present way of seeing the future, not to the unknowable future that will come about later. The uncertainty about the future is a present given that can be priced.

This kind of traffic makes sense only when markets become unstable, as happened in the 1970s after the abandonment of Bretton Woods agreement, because they no longer refer to an external reality, but to their own reality that is created by financial transactions and the way they are observed (section 4). The guarantee of their functioning should be the internal and paradoxical mechanism of arbitrage, which creates an order by eliminating imbalances. If there are differences in price somewhere in the markets, then someone will take advantage of those differences in order to obtain profits, and they will then disappear. Arbitrage works best when it does not exist.

Derivatives can be used for arbitrage, which should be a riskless activity that refers only to the present state of the market. One can also refer to the past or to the future, with hedging or with speculation (section 5). One hedges in order to eliminate the risks that one is aware of, and speculates in order to exploit the opportunities of the future, hence creating risks. All financial transactions are risky, because the future, when it comes about, is always different from what one expected. When one tries to protect oneself, and thus perhaps feels safe, one makes the future even more unpredictable.

1. SELLING POSSIBILITIES

Derivatives are financial contracts that have the (very interesting) peculiarity of depending on something else. Their price is calculated (derives) from the value of something else that is defined as the 'underlying', and this can be anything: financial instruments such as stocks, indices, currencies, rates, and also natural facts like the amount of snow falling in a resort, the wheat harvest, or the price of pigs. One could say that derivatives are tools located at the second order of observation: they vary on the basis of variations, not in reference to the world. It is not surprising that they deal primarily with contingency and its trends[1] – that is, with variations of data that could be otherwise and whose variability becomes the real object of negotiation.[2] All the features of derivatives can be traced back to this distance from the world, to which they refer through reference to something else. In this sense, they have a high degree of independence. Their trends can be positive when the economy, and the underlying, goes bad, or vice versa, because they are not directly connected to the world, but to the way one observes the world and negotiates it.

Here, the reference to time, which is also articulated in two steps of abstraction, comes into play. Derivatives are 'term' contracts, whose execution is deferred in time. They are made on a certain date, but refer to a future date, when the goods will be delivered or one of the parties will decide whether or not to do a certain thing (to buy or sell the asset). Derivatives handle the management of the future in the present. They do not directly refer to the future, but to the way the future will appear in the future – a deferment and a doubling that constitute the basis of their abstraction and of all the flexibility and complexity they introduce into financial markets.

The main forms of term contracts are futures and options; from these, a huge variety of combinations develops (swaps, warrants, and the cloud of 'exotic' contracts). The difference between futures and options is the type of contingency that they leave open.

Futures (like forwards, which are similar in many respects) are agreements between two parties to buy or sell something at a future time and at a given price, a price already fixed in the present and usually different from the current market price of the asset or activity at stake (spot price), as well as the future market price. The advantage is the present binding of the future transaction price. This protects against variations. If the price rises, then the one who bought the future contract makes a profit, and in any case does not have to worry about the movements. It allows for speculation – one can sell the right to buy to others.

Options differ from futures in that the bearer acquires the right but not the duty to the object of the contract. One can decide at a later time if one wants to buy (or sell) – that is, if one prefers to exercise the option or abstain from it. The decision depends on convenience. If one bought an option to buy (call option), then one will exercise it only if the price fixed in the contract (strike price) is lower than the market price at the expiration time.[3] The opposite is the case of an option to sell (put option), which will be exercised only if the strike price is higher. In this case, one says that the option is 'in the money' – that is, involves a gain if exercised, while it is 'at the money' if there is no difference between the prices, if one doesn't earn anything, and 'out of the money' if, by exercising it, one loses money. With the option, one sells contingency, the opening of the future. For the bearer, the future remains open even if time has gone by and the future has become present, because the bearer is not bound to the state of things. He/she can still decide one way or another.

What is bound is the present, because, unlike the future, the option has a cost. To hold onto the opportunity to change one's mind, one must pay a premium, which is much lower than the total value of the transaction. The price of options depends on the quantity and quality of the contingency that they make available. It is higher if many possibilities remain open. Their value is made up of the difference between the strike price and the current price of the underlying on the one side, and of a 'time value' that corresponds to uncertainty (or hope, as one usually reads in the description of options) on the other. As their expiry approaches, their value decreases, because there are fewer possibilities, and hence less contingency. This explains why options 'out of the money' have a value, even if they are not convenient at present. The value corresponds to the hope that the fixed price will come about, and is higher when there is more time and the trends are less predictable. In the vicinity of the expiry, an option that is out of the money is worth nothing.

Derivatives can afford this freedom from the world because they do not refer to the world. What is bought and sold is not the goods at stake (not even indirectly or delayed), but only a commitment by the counterparty (an attitude of the observer). One buys and sells only a promise, and it is on this that the whole traffic of transactions is focused.[4] Most derivative contracts close without the exchange of anything more than the mutual observation of observers and their expectations. In most cases, the underlying is not delivered, because the contract is sold, allowing one to earn from the difference between prices, or is not exercised because of inconvenience. One might never even think of exercising it, because it has been undertaken only as coverage for an opposite contract – that is, one buys a call and a put for the same underlying, in order to be protected regardless of how the prices move. In many cases (more and more frequently), the underlying cannot even be delivered, because it is something intangible like a stock index.

It is interesting that the traffic of derivatives can only work – that is, really serve to observe the observations of others and produce the future – if the agreements governing the delivery of the underlying (even if it will not be delivered) are fixed in every detail. The quality and quantity of the goods, mode and place of delivery, for example, must be precisely specified. It is necessary in order to maintain the link between futures price and spot price, between observation and the world. It is necessary in order to bind second-order observation, thereby eliminating any arbitrariness. Even if it is not an observation of the world, it must be a non-arbitrary observation of the observation of the world (a hetero-reference) that respects its bindings and its references. It is not simply an invention or a product of imagination.

The history of the legitimacy of term contracts shows the doubts and functioning of this market of observation. It shows the difficulties in accepting the non-arbitrariness of transactions (which do not refer to goods or performances in the world, but to the attitude of the observers), which are nevertheless not uncontrolled or completely hazardous. It is the old question of the distinction between promise and bet, of the separation between speculation and mere gambling. An issue that has always created legal problems in term contracts is whether or not the sale is effective without the transfer of possession.[5] Until the nineteenth century, contracts were not considered valid in England if the seller did not own the goods (even prospectively). The mere promise was not considered a commercial value, but only a bet, which was unreliable and negatively evaluated. For a long time, the criterion remained the 'intent test', which concerned the actual intention of the parties to exchange the goods. The mere observation of observers and of their expectations did not appear sufficient, which obviously created great difficulties in the case of contracts where the delivery of the underlying was not only unnecessary, but impossible. In the 1980s, a more liberal legislation was introduced, given that future contracts had already become essential for financial circulation as a whole. In fact, a condition has been recognized in which the intertwining of transactions, with their mutual constraints and the links between different presents, is sufficient to effectively exclude any arbitrariness and to create a unique reference of reality.

2. THE TRADE OF RISK

The true cornerstone of derivative contracts is leverage. By committing a small sum (or even nothing), an investor handles much larger sums and is able to obtain the corresponding profits (or suffer the corresponding losses). For example, one who buys futures acquires the future right to deal with the assets and receive the same gain as the owner, without having invested the sum required to possess them. If the value of an asset moves from 10 (the price fixed in the future contract) to 12, the owner of the future contract can sell it and gain 2 as the owner (and can possibly invest the remaining capital in other derivatives, thereby earning more money). If things go wrong, however, they must cover the full amount of the asset, with risks that can become unlimited.[6] In the case of options, the risk is smaller, because those buying them risk only losing the value of the option (which is worth nothing if it is not convenient to exercise it), and not the full amount of the asset. If, however, they invested all their money in options, then they can lose their entire capital and, hence, much more than they would have lost if they had bought the asset.

Leverage depends on the fact that, when trading with derivatives, one does not buy goods, but transactions. One does not invest in assets, but only in the movements of assets, which depend far more on their upwards or downwards trends. One who deals in ships or oil buys the objects at stake in accordance with their value. One who buys derivatives on ships or oil does not buy any object, but only the expectation that their value will increase or decrease (and earns proportionately more should the values move, but owns nothing should the values stay still). They have bought no goods, only expectations about the goods. These become valuable under conditions of uncertainty, when we do not know what to expect, while they are of little worth if we know with reasonable certainty how things will go. If the expectation is right, then one receives the corresponding gain; one loses if it is wrong. Leverage, in essence, depends on the fact that one buys/sells observations – that is, one acts at the level of second order. Only in the event of a crisis does one have to go back to first order in order to see how things are.

Derivatives, in fact, are needed to manage uncertainty, and have spread when financial markets have gradually become more uncertain and unpredictable. As Grossman argues,[7] derivative markets exist for some commodities, not for others. Why? The answer is that some markets are riskier, information is more uncertain, and we need tools to distribute the risks over the operators in accordance with their propensity to risk. Uncertainty, shared by everyone, is transformed into a resource to be exchanged and is used to obtain profits, because derivatives allow one to buy or sell the risks associated with the possession of an asset without having to buy the asset itself. What circulates in derivative markets is information (not about the goods, but about the expectations and intentions of other operators). The problem to which these tools respond is that 'market participants lack *current* information about the future trading plans of other participants',[8] and the movements of derivatives make this information available. They inform us about what the operators expect for the future in the present, and not about how things are. Futures and options are needed in order to take a position on future movements and to make this position visible.

However, they are only expectations. Their circulation actually increases uncertainty, which can be transferred to others when one buys certainty, or transferred to those who are more interested in assuming it. This is what happens in derivative markets, which have developed significantly in recent decades because uncertainty has spread in all markets. In this sense, derivatives are 'commodified risk'. They allow one to buy or sell exposure to the fluctuation of the values of assets, without having to transfer the ownership of the assets.[9] The expenditure concerns only exposure to risk, not the property of the underlying. It concerns only the perspective of the observers, not the state of the world. This is what leverage hinges on and what allows for the multiplication of the performance of the money invested. It is also what the complex strategies implemented in derivative markets are based on. They are aimed at compensating for, and combining, different risk profiles in order to obtain a profit, regardless of how things go. The operator should be able, in the face of any movement of the markets, to achieve earnings. Unlike one who operates in goods or actions, one who deals in derivatives (that is, in contingency) has a much broader range of possibilities and can take advantage of price movements. For example, they can buy both put options and call options on the same underlying, but with different strike prices, or buy and sell call options at different prices, or even combine options with the same strike price in order to speculate on the speed of markets and on the passing of time. In any case, they operate with open possibilities, with the expectations of operators, and have very little to do with the state of the world.

3. THE PRICE OF UNCERTAINTY

The spread of derivatives gave rise to the 'new finance' of the last decades, which has profoundly transformed the functioning and importance of finance in the economy as a whole. But are derivatives really new? In what respects are they new? The issue is controversial. If derivatives are understood in the very general form of 'sales of promises', where a contract is assigned before the date of performance, futures can be traced to ancient Mesopotamia, where a future performance was fixed in the present in order to protect against changes in the prices of the goods.[10] Options have ancient origins as well, as they can be traced back to Thales of Miletus, who, expecting an exceptional olive harvest, paid the owners of the mills in advance for the right to use them and negotiated the fee in advance. As in all option contracts, if his prediction were wrong he would only have lost the sum advanced.[11] The number of examples that could be offered is large, given that they can be found in Rome and throughout the Middle Ages. Even the sale of indulgences can be considered a somewhat atypical form of derivative, providing for the future delivery of the negotiated goods.[12] That there are so many possible examples should not be surprising, since concern about the future has always been a problem; there have always been attempts to protect against possible damages.

However, the point here is different. It is not so much the occasional occurrence of single agreements concerning future performances, but the existence of special markets, where one negotiates the protection itself, and not the transfer of specific assets (which is delayed and protected in various ways). In derivative markets, one does not deal with goods, but with the willingness to make transactions – that is, with the risk (whatever the asset concerned, whose characteristics are mentioned only to bind the contract and do not come into play in determining the value or price). In order to develop these 'second-order markets', it must be possible to sufficiently standardize the primary contract (the underlying) and to acquire an abstract contract, which is uncoupled from the physical quality of the goods exchanged (wheat, olives, livestock) and the persons of the parties (a contract that can then be sold and can circulate among different people).[13] Although the trade in futures has existed for some time, a genuine market for futures developed in Europe and the USA only in the second half of the nineteenth century.[14]

However, futures are not enough to start derivatives finance. The real sale of contingency is achieved with options, which are much more difficult. In the case of options, which have a cost, there is the additional problem of measuring and determining the specific price of the derivative contract – that is, price risk (a risk that concerns future events). This determination must be unique, yet standardized, in order to be the object of transactions. The problem is an important one, considering that one has to assess the cost of the risk of binding itself in the present (while the future remains completely open and one does not know what it may hold), and not only to negotiate the future price of the transaction in the present. Even though trading in options has a long tradition, it is not surprising that the first options market was established in Chicago as late as 1973, at a time when the available financial techniques were undergoing a dramatic evolution. It is not by chance that it was in the 1970s that the new finance was born, and was linked to innovations so radical that they have been compared to the introduction of paper money.[15] Although derivatives have been known for millennia, everything changed a few decades ago.

How did everything change? First, derivatives have become available that take abstract entities as their object and can be settled only by cash, like options on stock indexes. They refer to standardized objects and allow for expectations to be standardized. Above all, a way has been devised to give risk an apparently objective price, by means of the famous Black–Scholes formula to price options.[16] All previous attempts, up to that of Nobel prize-winning Paul Samuelson, had been blocked by the idea that, to give a value to the option, it was necessary to know the value of the underlying at the expiry (that is, the idea that in order to know the value of the future right to buy or sell something one needed to know the future value of that thing), because this decides whether the option will be in or out of the money. In other words, it was necessary to know the future (in particular a future present), which is notoriously impossible. And, indeed, a solution was not found. The fundamental turn at the basis of the innovation introduced by the formula is that the authors[17] realized that it was not necessary to know the future, because the present value of the option does not depend on what will happen (the future present), but on what operators presently know about the future, that is, on the present future. It does not depend on the world (the future), but on how observers observe the world today. One has to know only how risky the asset appears today, because this is what operators are willing to pay for – a value expressed by the volatility of the asset, which can be calculated.[18] The future remains open, but the risk is a present problem, and it is risk to which one must refer.

A seemingly objective method for pricing options then became available, and a market could develop that trades these specific objects, that trades contingency and risk. These cost more when markets appear turbulent and animated (with greater volatility), and less in quiet times. This is the novelty of financial derivatives. They are financial instruments that refer directly to finance (to stock indexes, exchange rates and the like), and are completely uncoupled from production. They are related only to money, to the economic management of time.[19] They deal only with the present observation of the future and the resulting contingencies. They combine and articulate these with one another, offering derivatives of derivatives, like options on futures, options on options, and other more and more imaginative forms. The point is not to know the future, but to sell and circulate projections of the future, which are intertwined and combined with one another, in order to produce what will actually become the future present. The point is not to predict the future, but to observe observers. This is the great novelty of today's financial markets, which was not possible or necessary in the past. They are the markets of the risk society.

4. INSTABILITY AS A PROBLEM AND AS AN OPPORTUNITY

Derivative markets have expanded dramatically in recent decades, and this process has accelerated more recently. The sums of money handled in these markets are impressive, significantly higher than the world economic production and the value of the stock market. The figures generate a big effect, but have a relative significance, not only because many of the contracts are never performed, but also because many opposing derivative contracts are often stipulated on the same underlying in order to protect against various kinds of risk. Hence the contracts cancel each other out. Nevertheless, they contribute to the total estimate of derivative trade, which is grossly inflated. The official figures measure only a part of the phenomenon because, aside from the contracts that are negotiated in the stock exchange, there is also the opaque and poorly controlled nebula of contracts that are negotiated 'over the counter' (OTC), where the parties treat the standardization, and escape the constraints, of official markets, which require a series of rules and controls, with clearing houses, protection against market risks and daily adjustments balancing profits and losses. In free markets, the conditions of derivatives can be adjusted to the needs of the customers, creating ever more imaginative and idiosyncratic contracts, which neither correspond to the forms and controls provided by the stock exchange nor appear in the official estimates of the volume of markets.

The takeoff of derivative markets is often linked to the famous abandonment of the Bretton Woods agreement in August 1971. President Nixon decided to put an end to the global trade and finance management system that was founded in 1944, thus establishing the exchange rates between the major currencies in relation to the dollar, while the dollar itself was connected with gold at a price of $35 per ounce (the last remains of a 'real' constraint on the movements of finance, which maintained the idea that the movements of coins and assets referred to an independent value, precious metal). What was surrendered in 1971 was the symbolic presence of an external reference, acknowledging the duty and burden of the markets to steer and control themselves.

Markets must now learn to do this on their own, and as a result they face new risks and unknown opportunities. The liberalization of the markets led to the fluctuation of exchange rates, to instability and large oscillations in financial prices, ultimately giving rise to new speculative opportunities (for example, arbitrage possibility[20]), which greatly increase the magnitude of international capital flows. They also give rise to uncertainty and risk of a qualitatively different nature.[21] The new financial market is much more volatile, unpredictable, and subject to 'contagion' phenomena that expand rapidly and out of proportion to the initial problem. It is a market that is now directly addressed to second-order observation. These uncertain and self-referential markets, which create the problem, also provide the solution, in the form of new financial tools addressed explicitly to the management of risk (that is, of observation). The growth of derivative markets is connected with the liberalization of financial markets, which made them both possible and necessary. Most of today's derivative products did not exist before 1970. According to MacKenzie, they are not an evolution of previous forms, but new entities, which have been consciously invented in order to cope with circumstances that did not exist before.[22]

It has been said that derivatives are the bridge between the real economy and money,[23] between the real economy and the financial economy. Once the link has been established, it is difficult to keep the two areas separated. These mix and intertwine in a situation where it is increasingly evident that finance is absolutely real, even if in a different way. The 'imaginary' character of derivatives is often perceived as a disturbance, and one therefore talks of paper wealth.[24] This happens because derivatives are highly abstract monetary forms. Even when they refer to concrete entities such as agricultural crops or raw materials, their value lies in the claim about future states of the world. Often, the underlying is also abstract, consisting of rights to future payments, values of indexes, and similar entities. The reality references are created by derivatives themselves, and are oriented to such data as the LIBOR (London Interbank Offered Rate – the rate of interest at which banks can borrow money from other banks in the interbank market – a completely abstract entity, which is absolutely clear and reliable in financial trading). Even if everything is virtual, MacKenzie maintains, it is a 'material production of virtuality',[25] a virtuality that generates a reality that can serve as a reference. This reality is located at the level of the observation of observers. One does not observe the prevailing opinion, but what the prevailing opinion considers to be the prevailing opinion.

The key mechanism for the functioning of these self-referential virtual markets is not prices, and certainly not values, but the coordination of price differences provided by arbitrage. It does not assume any intrinsic value of the assets. It only observes and exploits the price differences – that is, entities that are internal to the dynamics of the markets.[26] If the same asset has different prices in different markets, arbitrageurs buy it at the lower price and resell it at the higher price, making profits, and, in the mid-term, they balance the markets. The assumption of arbitrage makes it possible to think that markets are ordered, even without an external reference, because any imbalances are deleted by the simple dynamic of markets, which exploits the differences in prices in order to generate profits, thereby eliminating them. The cornerstone of the functioning of capital markets and of risk management markets, arbitrage, in its standard description, does not require capital (which can be obtained with short-sales) and does not entail risks.

This sounds paradoxical, and, like almost all key mechanisms, arbitrage actually has a paradoxical foundation, because it works best when it is absent.[27] Markets are optimally coordinated when no arbitrage opportunities are available – as supposedly happens in derivative markets, which are highly interconnected and supported by complex technologies that reduce them to a single global market. This market should negatively prove the assumption of arbitrage, which works because it is not there. In fact, recent experiences and, in particular, the much-discussed failure of the LTCM Fund, show that this is not the case and that even arbitrage is not a riskless activity. Like the idea of an objective value of options calculated by the Black–Scholes formula, the assumption of ordered markets regulated by arbitrage relies on a simplified image of financial markets and, in particular, on a model of time that refers only to the horizon of the current present, not to the presents that will become real in the future. What observers expect is one thing; what happens (and happens as a result of the expectations of observers) is another. The reality of financial markets is not an ordered one, but a reality that is structured in relation to an always-open future (a future that is always heralding risks).

5.   ARBITRAGE, HEDGING AND SPECULATION

Derivatives have to do with time, and can be seen using the standard distinction between the three different uses of these tools: for purposes of *hedging* (as reduction of already existing risks), *speculation* (looking for risks) and *arbitrage* (riskless activity) – where hedging is directed to the past, speculation is aimed at the future direction of the market, and arbitrage operates on presently connected markets.[28] According to the current definition, only speculation should imply risks. Only the future should be risky.

Derivatives are used for purposes of *arbitrage* when they are used to obtain a profit by entering simultaneous transactions in multiple markets – for example, when the price of a stock or another asset is different in different markets. Arbitrage strategies often involve the short-selling of assets without owning them. Assets are sold without owning them, borrowing them from another operator through a broker, and buying them at a later time to give them back to the lender. The operation is profitable if the buying can be done at a lower price because, in the course of time, the value decreases or because (as in the case of arbitrage) the asset is cheaper in another market. The profit should be certain, and it does not even require the availability of capital for the trader. It does not require the prediction of the future either, because the calculation refers to present data. As we have seen, however, arbitrage is based on an ambiguity, in so far as its existence relies on the inefficiency of markets, which should be excluded by the model taken as a guideline. In well-functioning markets, arbitrage should not theoretically be possible.

The main goal of derivatives, and the reason why they have been introduced into markets, is *hedging*, which is achieved when contracts are used to reduce the risks an operator is exposed to – for example, pre-existing risks such as the decrease of the wheat price at the future time of harvesting, while the expected profits have already been invested, or (dealing with the euro) the increase in the dollar price in three months, when one will have to buy something from a US vendor and must schedule the cost today. In buying a future, then, one can fix the price to be paid or to be received (if one sells) in the future today, and does not have to worry about it. With an option, one gets the same assurance without sacrificing the possibility of taking advantage of favourable price movements. However, one has to pay an initial price for this possibility.

Upon closer inspection, however, the assurance offered by derivatives looks a little doubtful. One is actually protected from adverse movements, but cannot be at all certain that the overall result of the transaction will be better. One risks losing a possible gain, or having needlessly paid the price of the option. It is only in reference to the risk perceived in the present that we can feel safe and, in this sense, it is true that hedging is turned to the past. One acquires certainty only with respect to existing risks, while the future course of events remains fully open, with all its contingencies and unpredictabilities. All insurance coverage may involve additional risks because of moral hazard or the observation by other operators. In any case, hedging does not eliminate the risk. It only distributes it across different time horizons, implying further risks when the assurances are themselves handled for speculative purposes.

Hedge funds, which have been so ill famed in recent times as a source of the turbulence in financial markets, were, as the name suggests, initially introduced for the purpose of hedging – that is, as a protection against risks.[29] Their founder, Alfred Wislow Jones, devised a combined strategy of short-selling and leverage in 1949. Through leverage, one can increase liquidity, and use it to buy assets with a good potential for growth, and, at the same time, short-sell assets with an opposite trend, thereby earning if the market falls. The overall strategy should protect from fluctuations and still allow for good earnings. In fact, the presence of such operators in the market, who spasmodically tend to exploit opportunities in the short term, increases the volatility and instability of the markets and makes them increasingly difficult to forecast. Markets become more abstract because these operators, in order to hedge, use strategies that protect them independently of the movements of the markets, that is, they use 'market-neutral' strategies, whose success does not depend on the trends of the markets, which suffer the consequences and become more unstable. As in all other cases, those who protect themselves against risks can be the cause of major risks for others. By themselves, hedge funds cannot be defined as risky, but their activity increases the risks of the overall financial system.

Derivatives can also be used for *speculation*, using financial leverage to over-proportionally exploit market trends. With a very limited initial expense, one can obtain the same earnings as the operators who work in the market of the underlying, whose movements are correspondingly amplified. Speculation addresses market trends – that is, the present future, what we expect to happen tomorrow in the present, and, thereby, change the conditions that will have to be faced tomorrow. It produces a future that is different from the one expected. The market becomes much more restless, unstable and responsive, since the perceived trends, when they are the object of speculation, strengthen without control, dragging behind them non-speculative investment. Risk then increases, not only because traders expose themselves to losses that can quickly become gigantic, but also because the uncertainty and unpredictability of markets for all other operators increase, affecting production and consumption. The future then comes about as it comes about – with speculators still trying to exploit its opening, while retaining the possibility of making a different decision at a later time.

NOTES

1. I refer (here and hereafter) to the concept of contingency of modal theory, where contingent indicates what is neither necessary nor impossible. One encounters contingency when there are several alternative possibilities: something is, but could also not be, or be otherwise.
2. They are also called contingent claims.
3. Or in the previous period, according to the kind of option.
4. See Swan (2000), who proposes to define derivatives in general as 'sale of a promise' (p. 17).
5. See ibid., pp. 205f.
6. Second-order observation remains bound to the corresponding first-order observation.
7. See Grossman (1977), p. 62 and (1989).
8. Grossman (1989), p. 135.
9. Bryan and Rafferty (2007), p. 136. See also Arnoldi (2004), pp. 23ff.
10. See Swan (2000), p. 279.
11. See Millman (1995), p. 26 It. edn.
12. This is the opinion of Swan (2000), p. 290.
13. See MacKenzie (2006), p. 14.
14. According to Shiller (2003), in Frankfurt in 1867, in Chicago in 1871, in London in 1877, and then in many other places.
15. See Millman (1995), p. 26 It. edn. The suggestive history of the opening of an options market in Chicago, with all related uncertainties and resistances, is narrated in MacKenzie (2006).
16. See Black and Scholes (1981).
17. As, previously, the Italian Vincenzo Bronzin, but in a context that did not permit him to promote that innovation – indeed not even to grasp it: see Hafner and Zimmerman (2009).
18. We shall come back to the corresponding procedures and to volatility estimates: see below, Chapter 10.
19. See LiPuma and Lee (2005), p. 411.
20. One talks of arbitrage when one takes advantage of the differences between the prices of securities in different markets. We shall return to the meaning and the consequences of arbitrage.
21. See Pryke and Allen (2000), pp. 265ff.; Eatwell and Taylor (2000), pp. 102f.
22. See MacKenzie (2007), p. 359.
23. Bryan and Rafferty (2007), p. 145.
24. One example among many: Giorgio Barban Avaretti on *Il Sole 24 Ore*, 30 December 2007.
25. MacKenzie (2007), p. 372.

26. See Mandelbrot and Hudson (2004), p. 243 It.edn; MacKenzie (2005a), p. 562 and (2006), p. 268.
27. See Miyazaki (2007), p. 397.
28. See Miyazaki (2007), p. 400; the standard distinction can be found for example in Hull (1991), pp. 6ff.
29. See Manuli and Manuli (1999).

9. The production of the future

If financial markets have become markets of the observation of observers and time, and derivatives are tools for buying and selling risk, how does finance change with the spread of derivatives?

Derivatives make money work differently. They allow one to buy and sell assets without owning them. They are a new form of money independent of the property of the exchanged objects (section 1). Property reassures about the future because it warrants that one will enjoy a good, even if others might want that good. Money extends this assurance to different goods in the sense that to have money means to have future property. Derivatives let this safety about the future, which they sell and exchange, circulate, without linking it to the property of the goods (or any other property). They deal with safety and uncertainty.

If one deals with future uncertainty, however, one actually deals with the future, and does so with very complex and formalized techniques that allow for a picture of the future and its possibilities to be negotiated in the present. However, when these forecasts are correct, the future comes about differently because it reacts to these very forecasts. The real future is different from the expected future and holds surprises, even, and especially, for those who have tried to prepare themselves for the various possibilities (section 2).

What is the advantage of such trades? Derivatives increase the liquidity of markets – that is, the available future. The number of possibilities to be conceived and dealt with grows, as do opportunities and risks. It is not at all certain if and how these possibilities will come to be realized, but the present must take them into consideration and face a much more complex world, where possibilities produce or restrict other possibilities. In derivative markets, one handles risk – that is, distributes it. One protects against some damage, thereby producing both opportunities and other possible damages, for both oneself and for others. The propensity to risk increases because others speculate on it, or because the future is bound. Risk management produces a more complex future, as well as unmanaged risk (section 3).

The problem with risk, and why it cannot be disposed of, is that we prepare ourselves for what we expect, not for the unforeseeable events that occur with financial crises, for example (section 4). The 'rationality' of risk would require an ability to calculate and face what one does not know in advance, without knowledge of when or how it will appear. In the field of reinsurance, techniques have been developed to deal with unknown future threats not perceived as risk, not by attempting to predict the future or its possibilities (as statistics does), but by preparing for a future that is different from what is predictable.

1. A NEW FORM OF MONEY

How are we to interpret the impact of derivatives on financial markets? Are we to interpret them in terms of continuity or in terms of breaks? Do we start from what is known in order to understand their novelty? Instead, some propose that we consider them a new form of money, specific to financial capitalism and its movements, highly abstract and connected with the availability of computers.[1] However, why should they be a new kind of money? How do these tools superimpose on the function and the operating mode of money that have given rise to the modern self-referential and future-oriented economy?

As we have seen,[2] money, as a form of time binding, is able to coordinate different times (in particular, the present and the future) because of its peculiar ability for homogenization. Monetization makes the property of very different goods (furniture, jewellery, food, as well as land and labour) equivalent by converting them into a quantity (a sum of money) that can be compared and exchanged with any other sum of money. From the point of view of the capital they represent, all goods are equivalent and, hence, homogeneous. Money can bind the future because it makes every property equivalent to any other. Thus it allows the availability (or the transfer) of present goods equivalent to the indeterminate goods it makes accessible in the future. We attributed the primary function of money to this performance, to its ability to act as the medium of deferment. The classic functions of means of exchange and store of value remain consequences of this performance. If derivatives are a particular kind of money, do they also do something similar? How?

Bryan and Rafferty maintain that derivatives are a new form of money because they have a specific ability to bind the future by relying on a peculiar form of homogenization (blending),[3] a second-level homogenization that presupposes the abstraction of the modern economy and the transformation of goods into capital. Derivatives are able to equate different forms of capital (and not different forms of goods), which can be converted.[4] In the previous economy, one distinguished between different kinds of capital: production capital, commercial capital (linking offer and demand) and credit capital, generated by the circulation of capital itself. In the traffic of derivatives, all forms of capital become equivalent, because they can be converted one into the other in order to generate the liquidity that circulates in the market.

What is the mechanism that allows derivatives to gain this degree of freedom? In the traffic of derivatives, the dynamics of investment is independent from property. One can invest in a title, thereby influencing its movements and achieving profits or losses without needing to own it. As in short-selling, where one sells something one does not have, with derivatives, it is enough to be able to manage certain transactions, speculating on trends and expectations. When dealing with futures, one invests in the future movements of an asset that one does not possess (and will often never possess, given that the future will be sold before the expiry). Options give the freedom of never needing to possess anything. This independence of money from property is a fundamental novelty and represents a decisive change in the operations of finance and the economy as a whole.

The reference to property is, of course, central to economic dynamics, and constitutes the link with the 'real world'. Monetization gave rise to the modern economy, with its autonomous dynamics guided by its own criteria when money realized a 'second codification' of property, making the corresponding time binding much more flexible and fungible.[5] The first form of protection against the uncertainty of the future was supplied by property, which gave the holder the possibility of enjoying goods even if others aspired to them. When goods are scarce and of interest to many, the owner has the recognized faculty of providing them as they see fit, even if they do so poorly (wasting or using them inadequately). If something belongs to me, I am free to spoil it or make it go bad, even if others need it. Society (that is, others) guarantees me in this condition (an amazingly unlikely combination).

Monetization makes this mechanism much more efficient. It starts the autonomous dynamics that define the economy and make it largely independent of the specific characteristics of goods. Property remains the prerequisite, with the (unlikely) forms of social support it relies on. However, it is translated into an abstract measure (the price) that circulates independently and is not constrained by the specificity of the context. If my property has been paid 1000, I can spend these 1000 to obtain any other good with unspecified characteristics without caring about the fact that the original transaction had to do with apples, houses or livestock. Money always presupposes property, but makes it abstract and independent of the specificity of the object (I can change it into any goods), of the social relation with the parties (I can pay anyone), and of the time of the transaction (it can be anytime).

Derivatives seem to untie the relation of money with property, allowing one to buy and sell securities that one does not possess. In financial markets, only money circulates, without any coupling with property. Is it still money? How? One can say that it is a new form of money, which presupposes the abstraction achieved by monetization, but takes it a step further. It abstracts from the specificity of the capital, making every form of capital convertible into any other, and finally equivalent to money itself. Untied from property, the circulation of investments (the 'new' money) becomes pure liquidity, which proceeds freely, transforming money into money – that is, buying and selling money in order to buy and sell (only) further money. As the 'first' monetization achieved independence from the characteristics of the goods (again, a sum of money is the same if one has sold horses or wheat), so too the 'second' monetization achieve independence from the characteristics of the capital. In derivative markets, one can earn, even if the underlying is doing badly, in the same way as one can lose, even if the stock is increasing. One does not depend on the investment. One does not own it, not even partially, as in the case of stocks. Instead, one depends on the observation of investments in the market – that is, on the speed and intensity of capital movements, whatever they refer to.

The most evident function of derivatives (also recognized by their opponents) is to create liquidity, greatly increasing the mass of circulating money. Every kind of capital can be used as underlying in order to generate additional traffic of currency, to enter new investments, to retreat and invest again. The markets become more mobile, flexible and dynamic. This money, in exorbitant amounts, circulating at very high speeds and seemingly unlimited, is, however, different from the money we have known for centuries, which is the basis of modern monetization. It is different because it can increase indeterminately. It does not need to remain coupled to the property of goods and assets. The money expressed by derivatives is also different because of its second-level 'blending' function. It not only homogenizes the various forms of capital, but also eliminates the very distinction between capital and money. Ultimately, everything becomes liquid. Money itself takes on the features of capital (for example, it can generate further money[6]).

As Myron Scholes pointed out in his Nobel prize acceptance speech (1997), speaking about the progressive confusion of the distinction between debt and asset, every capital can be immediately translated into money, even when it is negative capital (that is, a debt). Even a debt can become the basis for creating wealth, as is shown through the use of the pyramid of debts by banks. Banks lend money. Traditionally, this money was thought to be that deposited by customers. Today, however, the guarantees at the basis of the circulation of capital are increasingly the debts of those contracting loans or mortgages, which flow in other banks and transform into cash. In practices such as securitization,[7] one cedes activities or goods through the emission and placement of bonds. These can be real estate, contracts or other, but the transferred goods are more and more often credits (the debts of customers), transferred to others on payment of cash. The manoeuvre has little to do with the concrete goods (properties) at the base of the pyramid (such as houses or cars, which are often the object of other loans), but relies on a hazardous and reckless use of time. The goods are always the same, but different payments (those of the borrowers, those of the first bank and then those of all other financial operators) overlap each other – that is, there are several deferments, several spaces of time overlap each other. The manoeuvre, as the crisis or the outbreak of speculative bubbles has repeatedly shown, does not work when these times pile up. Everyone wants to cash in at the same time and the game of deferments implodes on itself.

As traditional money is based on the homogenization of goods to bind the future, so derivatives, realizing the dizzying performance of the creation of the future, achieve a second level of homogenization to bind time in a new way. They can thus be considered a new form of money. In this case, however, the presupposition is a new step of abstraction that allows for a formerly inconceivable freedom of movement – a 'dematerialization' that leads to the financial replication of any investment, without needing the money to make it. At this level, it no longer makes much sense to keep the distinction between real economy and paper economy, since everything is homogenized in an indistinct flow of abstract money. In this kind of economy, where investment has become autonomous from property, it should not surprise us that the constructivist turn prevails almost as a necessity.

2. THE PRESENT FUTURE AND THE FUTURE PRESENT

Derivatives are a highly self-referential form of money in the sense that they do not refer to anything external, but only to money and its circulation. In financial markets, money stays for further money. Its value is created, not in reference to the world, but in reference to the future. According to Rotman, derivatives are double objects, which are bought and sold only in order to generate further buyings or sales – that is, to allow money to buy and sell itself.[8] If our approach is correct, however, then money is time, and indeed the circle of derivatives, either vicious or virtuous, makes sense only if time comes into play, unfolding the tautology in an orientation towards the future. In Rotman's terms, a derivative is a form of money (Xenomoney) that creates its reference by itself, 'a sign that creates itself out of the future'.[9] The value is generated in the present calculation of future performances, which in turn become part of the present.

In operational terms, the extreme abstractness of derivatives, whose value is now uncoupled, not only from the features of the goods but also from their property, allows money to turn directly to its primary function, the management of time (in particular, the future uncertainty that interweaves present decisions in a new way – up to the point where what is bought and sold is uncertainty and related risks, the future itself). But how can one sell (or buy) the future? Here we turn again to the distinction between the two forms of future: the present future (tomorrow as it appears from the perspective of today) and the future present (the one that will come about tomorrow). All transactions in derivatives have to do with the management of this difference and with the relationship between the two perspectives – with the fact that future-oriented expectations and decisions affect what will become present in the future. The future is not the present future or the future present, but the difference between the two. It exists because the course of time generates a present that is the outcome of past expectations and decisions, but is different from them. If the future is made up of the combination and interchange between present future and future present, then the market of derivatives can be seen as a great apparatus for the production of the future. This becomes the reference for the empty sign of money, and is produced as a result of financial transactions.

How does this happen? Financial decisions are rarely driven only by intuition, but tend to rely on very complex mathematical systems or computer programs that are based on past stock market data (time series) and formulas, and claim to identify a set of rules to be used as a guide for the prediction of future events. It is not simply a replication of the past in the future. No one actually expects historical trends to continue over time. The point is to start from the past to imagine how the future will deviate from it. One starts from the past in order to imagine a different future. As we shall see in the next chapter, the famous formulas to price options use variables such as volatility to give these kinds of indications. These mechanisms, however complex and refined, produce an image of the future that should orient current decisions in the present, an image that constantly changes since negotiations always refer to the current present, which is different in every moment. The value of futures contracts, for example, is updated at the end of each day of trading, coupled to the movements of the market (marking the market). The present is rewritten every evening, zeroing the contracts and rewriting them at a new price.

The markets of term contracts refer to a future date, the 'term', and make it the object of current negotiation. The future, which is by definition only possible, becomes something concretely existing. In this regard, Arnoldi talks of the virtual existence of the future in the present,[10] which leads to an interaction of the present with the future and can generate such a precise thing as a price. Derivatives have an object only if their calculations include the contingency of future events and refer to it, thereby turning it into a present given. Throughout this process, they only have to deal with the present future, which is not the future, and price movements always produce surprises that would not arise if there had been no speculation about the future in financial markets. The future projections to which operators are oriented are correct and incorrect at the same time. If done well, they anticipate the way the future would have come about if there had been no attempt to foresee it. In this sense, they sabotage themselves. The future arises precisely out of this interaction between expectations and operations.

In this sense, it is correct to say that the future of derivative markets is produced by financial operations that are oriented to the future but, as often criticized,[11] in a much more complex way than current models assume. The point is not that the future projection is wrong, although it obviously can be,[12] but rather that it is right or even too right.[13] That is precisely why it does not work. The future depends on the present, but in a strange way. Mandelbrot speaks of 'dependency' to indicate the possibility that the levels or the variations of prices, at a given time, influence the levels of prices at a later time with a 'push' effect.[14] This produces a 'turbulence' and translates into the financial world the ineliminable vagueness of the future, ineliminable because it is produced by the present operations that try to bind it. The future present is unpredictable because it is produced by the very present that tries to predict it.

The series of financial prices seem to have a 'memory', which means that what is happening today affects what will happen tomorrow, and variations tend to strengthen each other. This sort of continuity, however, is a 'second-level' continuity concerning variability itself. If there is a variation, it is more likely that another variation, either upwards or downwards, will follow. The only continuity is produced at the second order of observation and helps to predict the orientation of the observers, not the movement of the markets. The future remains totally open, even if our way of predicting and devising is less so.

3. MANAGEMENT OF RISK AND NOT MANAGED RISK

In the markets, however, some people earn money. In the game of inde-terminacies and expectations, some results are achieved. This does not happen randomly. Which logic is followed in order to have an orientation in this abstract and self-referential world? Is it possible to find a form of rationality at this level? Those who earn do not succeed because they cor-rectly foresaw the future and guessed the prices, given that there is nothing to foresee, aside from the refutation of one's own forecast. The correctness of the operation must concern something else.

Let's go back to the takeoff of derivative markets in the 1970s, usually connected with the abandonment of the Bretton Woods agreement and the resulting increase in indeterminacy and risk in the markets. Derivatives were created in order to manage the multiplication of risks in liberalized markets, where risk takes on a different connotation. In production-oriented markets, as in all previous economies still referring to production as the reality index, risk was an extrinsic problem and a condition linked to unmanageable external factors that must be kept under control and possibly eliminated. However, in the abstract financial markets oriented to the circulation of money, risk becomes a resource and an opportunity, something endogenous, specifically produced by markets and their move-ments. The issue is no longer to eliminate risk, but to produce and repro-duce it, manage it and make it the object of exchange. Risk is no longer a problem, but a source of wealth. In derivative markets, one does not negotiate goods, but the risks associated with investments and the uncer-tainties linked with price fluctuations. 'Modern finance is a building based on the sale of risk.'[15]

This kind of risk is different from the specific risks that loomed over pre-vious markets and every form of economic enterprise – that is, credit risk, transaction risk, exchange risk and so on, each related to a specific context and the concrete conditions of the transaction. Derivative markets deal with risk as such, an 'abstract risk'[16] that subsumes all the various forms of risk and has its own circulation. This 'riskiness' is expressed by volatil-ity and its trends. Risk becomes the object of transaction, it is bought and sold, without having to buy or sell the goods or the assets, whose prices rise and fall. Goods, but also currencies, stocks and other financial enti-ties, are not negotiated. They constitute the underlying which is essential for measuring and quantifying risk and its movements, but is not directly involved in the negotiations. It is not bought and does not constitute the value for which one pays. The traffic of derivatives is completely uncoupled from the property of the underlying. You can gain or lose from the movements of an asset without possessing the asset itself, even if the asset follows an opposite trend – that is, it loses or gains. What is negotiated is pure risk exposure, and the value of derivatives depends on factors that measure the risk of the investment. These facts are the time left before expiry, and volatility (uncertainty).

In this traffic, risk becomes a resource because it is and remains ineliminable, and it is greatly increased by the operations of financial markets. Despite all hedging intentions (and also because of them), with derivatives, financial markets have become much more risky. This should not be surprising. It corresponds to the fact that the present management of the future produces a future present that is more and more complex and unpredictable. The very willingness to take risks generally tends to strengthen itself. In a market where operators observe each other, with respect to their risk exposure, speculation orients to speculation and tends to emulate the search for opportunities. If some operators risk, then it is more likely that others will tend to do the same. So, too, they tend to retreat in times of market restriction, without reducing risks.[17] There is also a distinction between specific or individual risk and systemic risk. Hedging operations can serve to reduce or control a specific risk for a given operator, but tend to generate additional risks for the financial system.[18] For example, portfolio insurance schemes aim to ensure the bearer a certain return, independent of market movements. They tend to accentuate trends because, when the market falls, the managers sell stocks or futures on stock indexes, thereby accentuating the decrease. The same happens when the market rises. Although the original intention was to hedge, the result is an increase in the volatility and, therefore, in the riskiness of the market, with an overall destabilizing effect.

It makes no sense to turn to derivatives for safety. If this were possible, there would be no derivatives. Derivatives aim at risk sharing, with appropriate markets managing it in more and more sophisticated ways.[19] However, risk management is risky anyway. Hedging operations circulate in the markets, generating further speculation that is more distant from the original prudent intention. The very possibility of hedging produces the phenomenon of moral hazard. Knowing oneself to be protected from damage, one is willing to dare more. Operators consider only one aspect of risk, the specific risk they can identify and want to manage. They do not take into account the systemic risk, considering it an 'externality' beyond their control. But systemic risk exists, is important, and multiplies. The result is a situation where the sum of the risks managed by investors is much less than the overall risk for the system,[20] which is not managed at all. The management of risk produces unmanaged risk. The distribution of risks, rather than reducing them, increases them, since the measures available to deal with individual risk are inadequate to deal with systemic risk. Risk becomes a 'self-mediating agent'[21] that follows its own (systemic) dynamics, regardless of the individual risk calculations from which it starts.

4. PREDICTING THE UNPREDICTABLE

Although operations in the markets are still guided by mathematical models and probabilistic procedures, there is now a widespread conviction that these models are inadequate in providing reliable guidance, and can even contribute to an increase in the opacity of markets. Apart from the procedures used, the methods tend to be pro-cyclical, in the sense that they predict future movements, or at least their orientation, based on past experience.[22] Even the most refined models, using statistics and chaos mathematics, start from some idea of measurability and controllability. Even when it is acknowledged that prices are not predictable, one still tries to describe their swings. The problem is that, under conditions of quick and turbulent innovations like those that characterize finance, the greatest risks often come from completely new events. The models should then somehow succeed in predicting the unpredictable.[23] The high reflexivity of markets, obsessively intent on observing themselves and their own movements, condemns every continuity model to sabotage itself.

Risk (and relative markets) seems to follow a model of rationality that is very different from the current one. It seems to follow a rationality where a decision is right when, from the current point of view, it is wrong, and vice versa. One should be able to observe the present and the future at the same time, and then look for difference rather than for identity, just as the future present derives from the present future because it deviates from it and not because it conforms to it. A situation that is so full of paradoxes presents only insoluble puzzles. However, once again, practice shows that things happen, and not randomly. The most effective instruments were not developed in financial theory, but have been found by insurers involved in problems of reinsurance, which is practically the equivalent of the distribution of risks on financial markets. One takes on the risk of someone else against an advantage. In this case, the issue is the possibility of transferring the risks associated with the insurance against a catastrophic event to financial markets, at the cost of some form of payment (securitization of catastrophe risk). The problem lies in the unpredictability of risk and the impossibility of quantifying it, which must somehow be calculated.[24] The resulting practices are very opaque, and appear to be 'a special kind of alchemy'[25] from the point of view of the current logic, because they use very limited statistical techniques, and have to do with unlikely, and usually unprecedented, events. It is a question of 'thinking the unthinkable and quantifying the unquantifiable'.[26]

Nevertheless, a market of innovative tools for the management of reinsurance risks has been developed, and it seems that investors are interested in it. 'Risk networks' arise where uncertainty is valued as a resource, a set of techniques that enable the management of catastrophic risks to leave their contingency completely open. One does not know what they will be or when and how they will arise, but is still prepared to face them. This is possible because financial markets that are specialized in the management of risk, which in this area comes to the foreground and openly appears as the object of bargaining, come into play. What is interesting is that the solutions found are not based on some form of calculation of catastrophic risks (that would be paradoxical), but on the concept that nobody needs to know 'what is going on'.[27] The financial instruments seem to be appropriate for taking this into account.

The point is the management of time. The temporal problem of insurance, which is an 'after-the fact industry', since it sells to customers something that has not yet happened, is normally not perceived as a risk.[28] The profit of the insurer relies on the consideration that the resulting uncertainty could be an opportunity. This current presence of an unknowable future is the object of the insurance. The techniques developed in recent years, particularly in reference to events such as terrorist attacks, do without statistical procedures (disposed of as 'archival–statistical knowledge') since these procedures are always based on the processing of past data, which are irrelevant when facing unprecedented events. The techniques are based on the concept of 'enactment', relying on no archive of past events and using the past only in order to obtain different information. More concretely, we could say that one starts from an inventory of risk elements, from information about the vulnerability of these elements, and from a threat model (all present data) in order to build a future frame that is different from everything known (different from the present future). One starts from the past in order to project a future that is different from what appears predictable. Past events are used to project an uncertain future event that is 'diverse' from the available data[29] (discontinuity), not to determine averages or distributions – that is, not in the sense of continuity. The resulting model is used as preparation for surprises, the development of a competence as paradoxical as the object to which it refers. Mathematical models and computer databases are used, but in a radically different way. They are used, not in order to predict what will happen, but to prepare for something unpredictable.

How this approach can be translated into a technique to be used in financial markets is not yet clear. However, it would be a way to put into practice the 'risk rationality' required by a temporal orientation that is different and much more complex than the cause–effect rationality associated with a linear time model.

NOTES

1. See Rotman (1987); Pryke and Allen (2000); Bryan and Rafferty (2007); LiPuma and Lee (2005).
2. See Chapter 4.
3. Bryan and Rafferty (2007), pp. 140f.
4. See LiPuma and Lee (2005), p. 411.
5. See Luhmann (1988a), pp. 197ff.
6. This is the thesis of Bryan and Rafferty (2007), p. 153.
7. We shall see this more specifically in Chapter 11.
8. Rotman (1987), pp. 150ff. Ger. edn.
9. Ibid., p. 153 Ger. edn.
10. See Arnoldi (2004), p. 24.
11. See only, out of various approaches, MacKenzie (2006) and Mandelbrot and Hudson (2004).
12. This does not necessarily mean that the speculation is not successful.
13. See the case of the LTCM fund discussed in MacKenzie (2005b).
14. See Mandelbrot and Hudson (2004), pp. 97 and 122 It. edn.
15. Ibid., p. 69 It. edn. See also Arnoldi (2004); LiPuma and Lee (2005); Pryke and Allen (2000).
16. LiPuma and Lee 2005, p. 413.
17. The case of the failure of the LTCM fund has been reconstructed in MacKenzie 2006 (ch. 8) along these lines: even if the fund itself did not undergo excessive risk, did not exaggerate in leverage or in formalization, the result was penalized by the imitation of others who wished to repeat its successes, dramatically altering the situation of the market.
18. The language of financial operators indicates, often with α, individual risk, which depends on the ability of the operator and remains undetermined, and with β, systemic risk or market risk. We shall come back to this point in Chapter 11.
19. See Demanges and Laroque (2006), p. 9.
20. See Eatwell and Taylor (2000), p. 46.
21. LiPuma and Lee (2005), p. 419.
22. We shall come back to pro-cyclicality in Chapter 13.
23. An attempt in this direction was proposed by Benoit Mandelbrot, making use of fractal mathematics, and has been the object of considerable attention in the financial world (perhaps more at the theoretical level than in actual practice): see Mandelbrot and Hudson (2004).
24. See Bougen (2003); Collier (2008); Ericson and Doyle (2004); Grossi and Kunreuther (2005).
25. Bougen (2003), p. 258.
26. Ibid.
27. Ibid., p. 271.
28. See Ericson and Doyle (2004), p. 142.
29. See Collier (2008), p. 233.

10. Trading uncertainty

Like current financial markets in general, the market of derivatives produces the future and produces risk. Conversely, however, what actually
happens is often different from what operators (and most theories) think
will happen. Risk management is based on an assumption, one implicit
in the techniques prevalent in the 1970s and involved in the generation of
their calculations, that unpredictable risk behaves in a predictable way.
Our inability to know the trends of the world generates risk. However, we
can know the trends of risk. Even if our expectations are often wrong, we
can at least expect to be able to obtain a certain kind of security from risk
calculations (section 1).

Markets are unpredictable because we cannot know if they will move
upwards or downwards, if an asset will display good or bad behaviour.
Volatility measures these changes and increases when turbulence (of the
market or of an asset) rises. The financial techniques for risk management
assume an ability to control this unpredictability. This assumption is made
because, even though one cannot know in which direction the market will
go, one expects to be able to know how volatility will move. In calculating
implied volatility, one should be able to predict whether the movements
will be broad or narrow, fast or slow (even without predicting if they will
go up or down). Against these movements, one seeks protection through
various strategies that compensate for them, allowing one to operate with
risk without risk (section 2).

This has seemed to work for several decades. For example, the success
of the Black–Scholes formula to price options is rooted in this idea. The
formula, however, only worked so well because, for a certain time, volatility adjusted to the estimates of the formula, not because it predicted the
actual movements of volatility. Implied volatility does not calculate how
things will go, but how operators expect things to go (and, at that time,
operators formed their expectations starting from the results of the Black–
Scholes formula). This is why an unrealistic formula (and one presented
as such) could seem to be the correct guide for market trends (section 3).

The assumption of financial engineering, also on the basis of the Black–
Scholes formula, is that risk (that is, the unpredictability of markets)
shows an order according to which many risks can be neutralized by

compensating for them, by and with one another, in preparation for anything that might happen. A residual risk (called β) remains, one that cannot be eliminated but is instead evaluated by the market, which finds that assets that are more risky cost less and assets that are less risky cost more. A prudent (and technologically equipped) operator can then manage the risk of their investments, without ever being surprised by the surprising movements of the markets. The idea that implied volatility objectively measures risk starts from the same premises (section 4).

The security offered by these calculations, however, only concerns the risks that operators can expect, those that can be inferred from past movements. It does not concern those risks that are unpredictable. Markets, however, occasionally behave in a radically different way, in a way that contradicts previous operations. For example, in certain situations, markets seem to expect unforeseen events and, as a result, they seem to consider it less of a risk to engage in risk than to behave cautiously (and risk is indeed cheaper). This goes against all risk management models, and even seems to increase risk. If one knows that operators use models for the prediction of risk, then one predicts the unpredicted. Operators no longer expect markets to behave as the models indicate, and markets actually do not behave in that way. The estimates projected by the Black–Scholes formula no longer work. Volatility becomes volatile, reacting to the idea of a regular volatility. Risk is shown to be unpredictable precisely because it does not follow a random walk, but 'remembers' past experiences and reacts to them, even if one does not know how. Were volatility turbulent, it is likely that it would change again, but this can increase or decrease as well. If risk has its own rationality, it is certainly not that of a predictable order (section 5).

1. THE CALCULATION OF RISK IN A RISK-NEUTRAL WORLD

The markets of derivatives (and the entire 'new finance' they drive) are actually markets of risk. If this is not taken into account, they may seem mysterious and incomprehensible, as though driven by an uncontrolled irrationality. This is because their movements cannot be accounted for (or, at most, only indirectly accounted for) by the actual traffic of goods and services. Although the movements of finance affect the production and trade of goods and may refer to the movements of goods and services, the logic of finance is different from theirs. What is sold when selling the movements of money is risk, the operationalization of the management of time that defines the economy. When economic transactions become self-referential, as is the case in financial markets, the function of time binding becomes the sale of future uncertainty – that is, the management of the difference between the future horizon of the present and the future present. This is nothing other than the traffic of risk.

If this is the case, then we must understand both which mechanisms regulate these trades and their underlying logic. We must understand the mechanisms according to which someone gains and someone loses, because such gains and losses are not random. By now, we can identify the tools of this movement. They are transactions of derivatives, which allow for the buying and selling of pure risk, the exposure of the movements of goods that do not need to be actually possessed. All the expense is devoted to risk exposure and not to the underlying asset. After all, if things do not go as expected, one does not actually own anything, not even a depreciated good. But how can one buy and sell risk? How is it measured? How much does it cost? How can one calculate its changes? At what price are futures and options traded? The answers to these questions come to describe the whole issue of derivatives of the last few decades.

The problem lies in the pricing of uncertainty, in estimating the 'vagaries' of the future, knowing that they are interesting precisely because they cannot be foreseen. In this case, the advantage of derivatives is that they operationalize the problem. They must do this in order to give the uncertainty a precise value and to track its movements. The uncertainty of the future is expressed by the fact that the future price of an asset does not coincide with the expected value of the future spot price. In other words, the future price in three months is not the same as the expected price of the asset three months later.[1] The present estimate of the future is different from the future estimate. The estimate of risk marks the difference between these two prices.

If risk must be bought and sold, however, the price must have objectivity, albeit a provisional one, and the measure used to determine the amount to pay must stand as a fact, one that properly, or at least adequately, represents the object at stake.[2] Only in this way does hedging, for example, make sense. The coverage with derivatives must reflect the movements of the underlying market. This is why, according to many observers, modern finance was born in 1973,[3] when a way was devised to give risk a price that seemed to be objective and independent of the idiosyncratic estimates of each individual. This date corresponds to the spread of the Black–Scholes[4] formula to price options in financial markets.

The scheme is ingenious, and presupposes a precise conceptualization (and neutralization) of risk. The basic uncertainty, as we know, is grounded in the fact that, however we try to predict and prepare for it, the future will come about in an unpredictable way, sabotaging any policy of neutralization of risk, and, as a result, risk remains. This is why it is so difficult to price options. One thinks that, in order to fix the price, one ought to know (or at least estimate) what price the underlying asset would have at maturity. One should know the future present. On this level, there is obviously no possible objectivity. Black–Scholes's solution avoids the problem by changing the time perspective and moving to that of the present future. It remains the future, and therefore includes the knowledge that one cannot know what will happen, but has a kind of objectivity, one that is based on what one can presently know of the asset at stake. This knowledge pertains not only to its present and past values, but also to its volatility, to its variability in time, and to its tendency to react to circumstances. This variability can be calculated, generating a value that stands for the level of risk. Taking into account volatility, time (the longer the time, the higher the uncertainty and risk), and the present value of an asset (which includes an estimate of its riskiness), one can give the option a price that allegedly corresponds to an objective estimate, a price that all operators can agree upon and that they can take as a basis for their calculations.

The weakness lies in a detail, in the fact that the whole calculation presupposes a 'risk-neutral' world (a financial world where future risk, although unpredictable, behaves similarly to past risk). The weakness lies in the belief that, while we do not know what will happen, we know in which dimensions it will happen. While the calculations allow for occurrences of the unpredicted and the unexpected, they fail to admit that these, by definition, cannot be predicted or expected. While one can be protected against these errors, and complex techniques of hedging have been developed, one remains exposed to completely different threats. The future present remains open.

2. THE MYSTERIES OF VOLATILITY

The variable that corresponds to risk in the markets of derivatives is referred to as *volatility*. This expresses the intensity of the variation of the price of the underlying asset, the speed of the market. Volatility is a value that corresponds to the amount of the variation, not to its direction. It does not tell us if an asset is good or bad, only the degree to which it fluctuates. If one knows that an asset has low volatility, for example, one can expect that its value will not decrease sharply, nor will its price increase significantly. If volatility increases, the risk to which operators are exposed also increases, given that unpredictability increases. The problem is that future volatility remains unknown, and, therefore, unaccounted for. While one can know its past, operators are interested in future risks, which cannot be known. The information we can gain from the past indicates only what observers expect in the future, not what the future will be. These predictions, based on this information, affect real movements, although nobody knows how.

Those who buy or sell options deal with volatility,[5] with an estimate of operators' risk. In other words, they deal with second-order observation and its variations. The trend of volatility is often more important than the price of the underlying asset. Those who trade with options are successful if they are able to guess how operators expect prices to change (by guessing the management of risk), not by guessing how prices themselves will change. If, for example, one buys a call expecting an increase, a situation can arise where, while the market rises, the volatility decreases, causing the option to lose value (risk seems to decrease). When selling only volatility, earnings can occur even when the market does not full or rise. In general, if volatility increases, the value of options rises (risk increases). If it decreases, they become cheaper.

This form of market can be understood in terms of taking place at two steps of abstraction from the actual data of the world. It therefore requires a constructivist approach in order to be properly accounted for. The movement of derivatives reflects only the observation of observers. This observation occurs both reciprocally and in time (an observer observes himself in the future). It cannot be explained by referring solely to the price of the assets. The underlying asset comes into play only as a reference for measuring volatility and its variations, for observing how the other operators observe and what they expect based on such observations. As is always the case with observations of observers, the concept of volatility depends on the perspective adopted, and cannot be fixed univocally. It always depends on both the observer and on time. We can distinguish between the following three kinds of volatility that correspond to the observations gained from three distinct perspectives.

First, *historical volatility* is relative to the past and is measured by the deviation of the values of an asset from the average. This form of volatility is a direct measurement of the price movements of the underlying asset in a given time. It is high if the asset was turbulent, low if it remained quiet. Like all data based on the past, it remains a kind of reference that appeals to certainty, but says little about the future trends of the asset at stake in a restless market. There is nothing that prevents a stable asset from beginning to oscillate suddenly. Historical volatility can, however, affect the other kinds of volatility.

Second, *advanced volatility* expresses the subjective expectations of a single operator and, therefore, how one expects the asset to behave. Like all subjective perspectives, it is always uncertain and opaque. One cannot know with certainty what people think, or if they are right.

Third, *implied volatility* is strange and self-referential. It has become the key concept for the traffic of derivative markets as a whole. It does not depend on the price variations of the underlying asset (as historical volatility does), but on the prices of the derivative itself. It does not measure how turbulent the movements of the underlying asset are, but what the changes in the expectations of the operators about these movements are. Different derivative contracts on the same underlying asset (for instance a stock) will normally have different implied volatility, depending on the duration of the contract (an option expiring in six months will have a different implied volatility than an option expiring in one month for the same underlying asset). Implied volatility is not a datum because it refers to the future. It expresses an estimate based on the perception of the operators on market movements (not the movements themselves, which are of course unpredictable, but on reasonable expectations based on past movements and on the available information).

One often hears that implied volatility indicates the 'sentiment' of the market and of the investors at a given time. This makes sense only if we consider the fact that this 'sentiment' can be very different not only from what will actually come to be true (as measured by a future historical volatility), but also from what the individual subjects believe and expect – that is, from their actual 'sentiment'. The distinction between advanced volatility and implied volatility indicates that the latter does not claim to reflect what the operators really think, but what one generally thinks they think. In other words, it indicates the prevailing opinion on the prevailing opinion. In this sense, everyone thinks what they want (and then use this perspective to make profits, or at least to try and do so), while the world goes as it goes, ultimately confirming or rejecting this opinion. Implied volatility can be understood to measure this perception of the prevailing opinion, the projection of the future from the considered present (which, in itself, remains a simplified entity, one that neglects all contingencies that may intervene in the course of time and all deviations in the perspectives of individual operators). It is primarily an entity that assumes a certain continuity between the past and future, which, while not at the level of the world, is at least at the level of risk perception. The measure makes sense only if one assumes that risk perception follows a constant trend and expects that an asset that was turbulent (or quiet) in the past will continue to follow this trend. In actuality, it may rise or fall (this cannot be known), but one claims to possess the foresight to know if it will move more or less broadly and/or quickly.

Implied volatility, then, is not 'real' volatility. It does not reflect the risks of the market, but only those risks that the market expects. It is, however, a calculable measure, which has its own objectivity to which one can refer. Implied volatility is actually the reference for the models of risk assessment, for the models to price options (starting from the famous Black–Scholes formula that seemed to give objectivity to the indeterminacy of the future and of expectations). The great advantage of the Black–Scholes formula is that it found a way to estimate implied volatility (which, while as circular as the notion itself, may in fact depend on such circularity in order to work in the first place). Implied volatility can be calculated by reversing the Black–Scholes model (which gives options a price). Once the price of an option is known, one inserts it into the formula, retrieving a value for volatility that can be used in future calculations. One thereby builds the future by projecting the known data forward from the past, thereby exposing oneself to future reactions to these projections.

If one accepts the procedure of risk assessment proposed by the Black–Scholes formula (as was the case from the mid-1970s until at least the second half of the 1980s[6]), one can assume that others will also use it to build their strategies. Although there is an apparently objective basis upon which one can deal with risk, this basis actually has very little objectivity. Since risk is an increasingly urgent problem, the notion that it can be dealt with in a non-arbitrary and non-subjective way has led to the multiplication of risks that everyone can observe in the market of derivatives (which is, in essence, a macroscopic version of moral hazard expressing the reflexivity of economic action at all levels).

Today, the market of derivatives is both extremely technical and formalized, with the calculation of implied volatility serving as a cornerstone and, in some instances, almost as a substitute for reality. Not only are complex strategies of hedging and speculation realized through such means, but also those of 'volatility trading', with options and swaps on volatility, reflective strategies based on the expectations of the evolution of volatility, ultimately serving to yield concrete gains and losses. Starting from the calculation of volatility, other measures can be inferred that allow for considerations on the sensitivity of options with regard to other factors that affect their prices. An example of such measures are the famous 'greeks' (so called because they are conventionally indicated with letters from the Greek alphabet), where the variation in the price of the option is relative to the variation in the price of the underlying asset (δ – delta), the decrease in value of the option as the deadline approaches (θ – theta), the relationship between the price of the option and the interest rate (ρ – rho), the variation in the value of the option relative to the variation of the volatility of the underlying asset (vega), the variation in the option when the underlying asset has an infinitesimal change, or its elasticity (ω – omega). A reflective wireframe of calculations of calculations is thus produced that allows for more and more detailed guidelines in the vague and uncertain management of risk, guidelines that become more reliable the more they are used to direct operations.

3.   THE RIGHTNESS OF A WRONG FORMULA

The component of performativity of financial markets, rightly underlined and analysed by many authors,[7] now comes to light. MacKenzie, in particular, has reconstructed the history of the success of the Black–Scholes formula from this perspective – that is (in our terms), from the reality perspective of second-order observation. Today, after the experience of the inaccuracies and problems of the proposed solution, it is easy to say that the formula 'is simply wrong'.[8] It is far more interesting, however, to ask how it could have been 'right' for so many years, effectively guiding the forecasts and behaviour of operators. Even if the Black–Scholes formula is wrong (by now an established fact), it is not wrong in a simple way. To study its ups and downs can be very informative about the working of derivative markets.

Because it seemed to eliminate the component of gambling, the availability of the formula notoriously led to an enormous expansion of the market of options and of financial transactions in general. One thought that by applying it, one could perfectly hedge each transaction, and then eliminate all risks, that it was possible to operate in a risk-neutral market. Gambling turned into financial engineering. But was the market really risk-neutral, or was it the operators who viewed it as neutral?

The Black–Scholes formula and the quantified calculations on derivatives can only be reliable if a number of assumptions about the functioning of markets hold (as its authors explicitly declared). It is interesting that everyone knows that these assumptions are unrealistic, and *a fortiori* were unrealistic in 1973, when the formula was proposed. The formula assumes, for example, that there are no transaction costs, that all profits are subject to the same tax rate, that there are no arbitrage opportunities (because they are immediately deleted when they come about), that all participants can borrow money at the same interest rate at all dates of expiry, that the assets are perfectly divisible and the stocks do not pay dividends.[9] These assumptions are necessary in order to suppose that the behaviour of the financial system reproduces the behaviour of a physical system, as it is described by the model of Brownian motion used by Einstein to deal with random movements of particles in fluids. The mathematics under the Black–Scholes formula[10] is a stochastic calculation that reproposes, for the case of financial markets, the formulas of the physics of particles for Brownian motion. There too the problem was to predict something unpredictable, because it was random and subject to the endless contingencies of time, but could be handled using stochastic techniques that assumed a 'normal' distribution (the famous Gaussian curve). Using the theory of probability, the unpredictability of the physical world was 'normalized' in a format that allowed for forecast and calculation.

If the assumptions of the Black–Scholes formula were realistic, the same treatment could be used for predicting the movements of financial markets, recognizing their random nature and the basic statistical order.[11] The problem is that, when applied to the behaviour of operators who observe each other and plan their future, the model involves a series of extremely doubtful assumptions, which have been criticized by many authors. The above assumptions regarding the functioning of markets are necessary to describe the behaviour of each single operator as the movement of a single particle in a fluid – that is, without 'stickiness' or applicability to other operators and over time. Particles do not observe the future and do not observe each other.

But these assumptions could hold only (1) if people were rational in the sense of the classical rationality model, but we have seen (and behavioural economics continually confirms) that traders in the market follow another kind of rationality, one that is much more complex and reflexive; (2) if all operators were equal, like the molecules of an ideal gas, but investors are different from one other, have different goals, perspectives and attitudes toward risk, and influence each other on the basis of this difference; (3) if price variation were continuous, but we know it follows a discontinuous pattern, with leaps and sudden changes; and, especially, (4) if the movements of markets did not have their own memory, and each was independent of the others and of the history of market movements (that is, if they were Markov processes), but a significant dependence has been observed, so that the levels of prices and their changes at a given time affect the levels at a later time, in ways that cannot be represented by a Gaussian curve. Volatility, the key index of market movements, does not behave in a statistically controlled manner (that is, with a predictable unpredictability), but is itself volatile (without thereby being accidental).

Current models of economic behaviour tend to register all these deviations as 'anomalies'. When the anomaly tends to become normal, however, one might ask if it would not be better to consider the irregularities as a basic feature of the phenomenon, rather than as imperfections or defects. Mandelbrot proposes extending the concept of hazard on the basis of formalization, overcoming the constraints of the bell-shaped (Gaussian) curve that is still the basis of the statistical models used in finance and, in particular, of the Black–Scholes formula. In his opinion, there are formulas (like Cauchy's formula) that allow for more irregular and unpredictable forms of randomness, thus more adequately reflecting the evolution of markets, which do not behave in the ordered way predicted by normal distribution. Extreme values and fluctuations are much larger and frequent, expressing a law of power, where variations affect and reinforce each other.[12]

Our point here is one that concerns the 'mystery' of the correctness of an incorrect formula. How could an unrealistic model like that of Black–Scholes become the reality reference for the financial market as a whole? Instead of being considered a simplified support useful for decision-making, the Black–Scholes model seems to have assumed the role of a faithful description of reality, a sort of 'fetish' that allows one to choose the correct behaviour.[13] How can this development be explained? What does it teach us about the functioning of financial markets?

When the Black–Scholes model was proposed at the beginning of the 1970s, it was not plausible, and its authors have repeatedly reported their difficulties in finding a publisher for their article. Not only did the application of the complex mathematical procedure appear laborious and difficult, but also the assumptions of the model were clearly unrealistic – and indeed the fit of the forecasts was quite poor. In the financial markets of the early 1970s, it was not true that there were no transaction costs (there were instead high commissions), the price of actions did not follow a continuous trend, information was not immediately available to all operators, there were still legal constraints and significant levels of distrust concerning short-selling, and it was not possible for all operators to borrow money at the risk-free interest rate. Some of these conditions have changed as a result of technological development, which has greatly increased the transparency and speed of the markets, as well as the spread of information. In addition, one of the major advantages of the Black–Scholes formula is its compatibility with the use of computers. One needs only to insert the necessary data (all available except the ineffable volatility, which can be calculated with a standardized procedure) and the machine produces the required information.

Once the Black–Scholes formula was published, and operators began to realize the advantages to be gained from it, markets changed in order to adjust to the formula and to the increasingly widespread use of it, and finally produced a 'Black–Scholes-world',[14] which confirmed the predictions of the theory. This world, however, would not exist if the theory did not exist and find itself established as a guide to the behaviour of operators. The model gradually became popular among financial operators because it seemed to solve their problems of uncertainty and arbitrariness, both practically and convincingly. It seemed to provide a standardized procedure with which to design investments, a procedure common to everyone that could be jointly observed by operators, making the market much more transparent. In particular, the Black–Scholes model was intensely used in the practice of arbitrage (of options, futures indexes and other highly reflective assets with high leverage). This, as we have seen, is the cornerstone of the idea of an ordered functioning of markets because it should eliminate any imbalances without assuming the rationality of investors, simply enabling the autonomous dynamics of markets. Price differences are exploited in order to gain a profit, and thereby eliminated.[15]

This kind of procedure, if intensively used (and, during the 1970s, the Black–Scholes formula became the guide for the behaviour of the majority of operators), has the effect of moving prices towards an always higher conformity with the estimates of the model. The financial world tends to increase liquidity, to spread information, to remove legal constraints and transaction costs, to normalize short-selling, and to behave generally as the initially unrealistic options pricing model requires. The calculations guided by the Black–Scholes model offered more and more accurate forecasts for the behaviour of the markets, so that, in 1987, the fit between estimates and options prices was so good that it could be said that it was 'the most successful theory not only in finance, but in all economics'.[16] Thus the establishment of the model and the complete integration of finance and economy were sanctioned. MacKenzie's argument is that the theory adequately describes reality, not because it is realistic in an absolute sense, but because reality itself changes as a result of the theory – that is, because of performativity, which explains how a 'wrong' theory could work so well and appear so plausible for so many years.

4. THE ORDER OF RISK AND THE DISORDER OF THE MARKETS

As Hull remarks,[17] it is difficult to verify empirically the models for pricing options and other derivatives, such as the Black–Scholes model, because their validity depends on the features of the model and on a number of assumptions about the efficiency of markets. If the forecasts are not satisfied, perhaps the forecasts were wrong. However, it might also be that the market did not behave efficiently. On the other hand, if the forecasts are satisfied, it does not necessarily imply that markets are efficient. The issue is to know whether or not the market itself is efficient.

The Black–Scholes approach, together with a consolidated tradition of market studies, explicitly assumes that financial markets are (or at least can be) efficient markets. We have discussed the efficient market hypothesis (EMH) and the underlying theoretical assumptions.[18] All the additional assumptions required for the application of the Black–Scholes formula are actually linked with this basic theory. Only under these conditions does it make sense to assume that financial operators behave as particles immersed in a fluid, subjected to random collision, leading (at the level of large numbers) to a macroscopic order that redeems the microscopic disorder. The particles follow no plan and move randomly, but their overall movements can be foreseen and systematized. The hypothesis underlying the models for pricing options (that is, the models actually used in financial markets to face the future) presents the same pattern. Even if financial movements remain random and operators are irrational, their trends show regularities, which are measured by volatility, which one can rely on in the design of one's investments. Markets as a whole, then, are rational – or, at least, efficient – and one can devise rational strategies for moving within them.

The first transposition of the EMH to financial markets spread in the 1960s in the form of the capital asset pricing model (CAPM). It was a balance model for financial assets that allowed one to settle the correct price for each asset, and then build an 'efficient portfolio' (or even an optimized portfolio) – that is, a collection of assets that should lead to the maximum possible profit independently of market movements. It is a technical and formalized version of the old traditional idea of the 'right price' as a reference for markets, with the difference being that this correctness is no longer measured by alleged extrinsic qualities of goods, but by the level of risk associated with the transaction. In this sense, it is 'right' that the price of a financial asset is higher if the one who buys it risks more. The rest follows accordingly and is relevant only in so far as it affects risk assessment.

The key variable of the whole calculation is called β (which we have already encountered as the index for the level of systemic risk or market risk). The basic idea is that one can objectively measure an ineliminable risk of the market that cannot be avoided, even with prudent and reasonable behaviour. This risk is called systemic risk; the right price of an asset depends on it. There are no riskless investments, but there are more or less risky investments. The right price of each title supposedly includes a component of risk assessment. Therefore a riskier asset costs less (to encourage investors to buy it despite the uncertainties to which they expose themselves), while a less risky asset is more expensive (a kind of cost for security is added). In an efficient market, all prices are right. If a right price calculation is available, all markets become efficient because, if the price were lower or higher than the correct one, there would be a race to buy or sell the asset, until equilibrium was reached (arbitrage).

The construction holds only if one can objectively calculate the riskiness of each asset. It is here that we must deal with the coefficient β, which indicates the level of systemic risk of each investment. The market, as a whole, will always have β equal to 1, but individual financial activities can have β lower or higher than 1, depending on how risky the investment is (in a relative sense) – that is, depending on the fact that it entails higher or lower risk than that which is inevitable for the market (systemic risk). β, however, does not depend on the fact that a given event can be harmful to an operator (for instance, fears of an increase in the price of oil). It is an objective measure of risk, one that is valid for everyone and is independent of the contingencies and the idiosyncratic situation of the investment. Financially, these specific risks can be eliminated by buying other activities that follow an opposite trend. For example, one can protect oneself with activities increasing their value if the value of oil decreases, so that gains and losses compensate for each other. All risks that can be compensated for by diversifying one's position in the market (that is, articulating it on several investments not related to each other or compensating each other) are deemed eliminable. These risks do not intervene in the determination of β, which measures only the level of unpredictability of the market, namely the higher or lower variance in the movements of the asset (or of the market as a whole). β becomes the measure of the unpredictability of the market.

Each operator can build a portfolio of assets that exactly matches their propensity to risk, paying more for safe assets and less for risky ones, gaining or losing only in accordance with the risk assumed. This is the efficient portfolio promised by CAPM, which neutralizes all risks that can be eliminated with a careful analysis of the market. The model, which was very successful[19] and is still used by many operators, was strongly criticized because it assumes a substantial continuity in the behaviour of the market, excluding rare and extreme events, and especially excluding any correlation between the behaviour of different operators and between the present behaviour and future market trends (all factors that are central to our analysis).[20] What interests us here is the continuity of this approach with the current models for pricing options – that is, with the prevailing references in the traffic of derivatives, which lead to a maximum abstraction of the orientation to risk and its trading. The Black–Scholes model, guiding the overall setting of derivative markets through performativity, starts from the same assumptions of CAPM (and inevitably suffers the same weaknesses).

In both cases, the central element is the claim to determine risk (of the market as a whole and of each single investment) objectively, a risk expressed in one case by β, and in the other case by implied volatility.

Like β, the measure of implied volatility is derived from the previous movements of the market, assuming (without declaring so) a form of 'second-order order', assuming that, even if risk is inevitable because the future is unpredictable, one can at least rely on the fact that riskiness can be predicted. One can know how much risk one undergoes with a certain investment (even if one doesn't know how things will go). Risk is risky, but it is assumed that riskiness is not. With regard to the movements of an asset, this means that one assumes the ability to predict how turbulent its behaviour will be, without knowing whether its value will rise or fall. One believes one can make this assumption because the future volatility mirrors the implicit volatility reliably enough to price options addressed to future variations. The price of options is the price of risk. One pays for the level of uncertainty that one protects oneself against through the option.

Derivative markets project the model of order formalized by CAPM into the future, the idea of an efficient market, a market that is not guided by arbitrariness even if it is based on random movements, because this randomness has an order that can be detected and used as a reference in investment decisions. The CAPM concerns the financial market (where risk is a component of investment choices), and the Black–Scholes model applies the same assumptions to derivative markets (where risk is the object: one deals with riskiness and its trends). The approach, however, is the same and, hence, there can be various mixtures. An operator who wants to avoid risks can choose to diversify their investments (according to the models of portfolio theory) or can realize hedging operations, compensating for the risks with opposing oriented derivatives. In both cases, the ability to detect a second-order order (an order of risk, the last legacy of the idea of efficient markets) should lead to the possibility of a second-order safety (a safety compatible with risk). Even if the world is full of risks, one thinks that an investment strategy protects against riskiness. One should not discover afterwards that one is exposed to a higher level of risk than one chose to be.

In our view, the weakness of the model, the confusion of present future and future present, is always the same. Implied volatility, taken as the measure of risk, does not deal with actual future contingencies, or even with riskiness (nothing guarantees that a turbulent asset will go on being turbulent in the future), but concerns the expectations of observers on riskiness, what everyone expects others to expect – that is, the implied volatility, the level of restlessness of a financial activity as one can imagine it on the basis of its past restlessness (the present future). This is the measure that guides options pricing models. It is only at this level that one can find an order (a supposed efficiency), but this measure can appear objective only because the expectations of the observers are confused with the actual development of the world (which is often not efficient at all). The safety provided by the calculation of riskiness concerns only what one expects others to expect. Here the model is completely reliable, as the performativity effects accompanying its diffusion show. If everyone uses the Black–Scholes model, everyone expects a given volatility trend, and volatility tends to follow that trend. But there is no guarantee that common expectations are correct, if and when the circle of performativity is broken – that is, in all cases where, for various reasons, what operators actually expect departs from what is deemed reasonable to expect. In this sense, advanced volatility departs from implied volatility. This typically happens in cases of panic related to stock market crashes, in coincidence with unforeseeable events, and, in general, in all cases where the confidence in the basic order of markets is shaken, albeit in the abstract and intangible order at the level of risk. Operators begin to expect unforeseeable events and, hence, an irregular and disorderly development of riskiness itself. For this kind of situation, the available models are by no means equipped.

5.   THE VOLATILITY SMILE

The central point, and the problem with the whole construction, is whether it is realistic to expect risk to behave in a predictable way – that is, whether it is realistic to expect risk to follow an ordered trend that can be inferred from its past trends. As long as this is the case, the Black–Scholes model is appropriate – and this is the case as long as the model is considered appropriate. As we have seen, this was the situation until the mid-1980s, as long as there was a high correlation between theoretical predictions and the behaviour of the markets. Since 1987, however, things have begun to change, and one now sees that portfolio insurance cannot protect against all uncertainties. A different quality of risk is discovered, a 'market internal risk',[21] which does not behave according to the model and expresses the so-called (and much-debated) volatility 'smile' or 'skew' in its formalization.

What does this mean? The calculations of volatility predict a given trend of risk, which must remain substantially stable.[22] The Black–Scholes model assumes a volatility with a regular evolution, one that allows for the calculation of implicit volatility, which will be used in the forecasts for the different financial activities. Volatility should increase when time distance increases, but should be the same for all strikes (that is, for the different expected prices) at a certain expiry. On the contrary, however, one sees that options that are distant from the level of the index (out of the money) – that is, more risky and presumably more unlikely – tend to have higher implied volatility than options that are closer to that level (at the money) – that is, less risky. The riskiest options are proportionately more expensive than less risky ones. This clearly contradicts the assumptions of the model: riskiness is under control and one pays for safety, not for risk. It seems that the prices reflect a situation in which risk appears less risky – that is, in which unforeseen movements are expected; a situation in which it is considered likely that unlikely events will happen, so that those who risk more risk less with regard to disappointment.

It is not by chance that this configuration appeared after the crisis of 1987, when, on 19 and 20 October the markets were submerged by a wave of sales, with a fall of more than 20 per cent – an event whose probability, according to the calculations used by financial theory, was less than 1 in 1050. According to the calculations, it was a practically impossible event, one that nevertheless occurred[23] and produced a kind of shock, highlighting the vulnerability of markets and the fact that the best hedging techniques cannot guarantee against exposure to risks. The fit between theory and markets was lost (and can no longer be recovered). One began to observe that the variability of markets does not follow a normal statistical distribution (as the movement of particles in a fluid, the Brownian motion that served as a model for options pricing techniques), but shows the complex trends of chaotic systems, with the possibility of much wider and much more frequent fluctuations. One saw that markets can show 'wild variations'. The volatility that detects the level of irregularities of markets does not behave in a balanced and predictable way, but itself tends to be volatile and erratic. Deviant movements are not neutralized by an order inherent in the market, but can instead feed on themselves and increase enormously, and occur much more often than the insignificant frequencies one predicted. The risk calculation systems used in financial markets do not take the inherent risk of markets reacting to themselves into account and, therefore, underestimate them, thereby serving to become an additional factor of (intrinsic) risk.

From 1987 onwards, the Black–Scholes model began to be questioned, limiting its scope and entering a series of 'adjustments' that attempted to account for the exceptions and contradictions that were accumulating, as always happens in defence of a dominant paradigm. One generally tends to try to save the model, because of its well-known practical convenience, presenting it as a 'useful approximation' to the forecast of market trends that is to be eventually integrated with additional considerations. But the criticism is much more radical than this, maintaining that the basic approach of the model does not work and is even harmful. One uses 'the wrong number [the measure of implied volatility] in the wrong formula [Black–Scholes] to get the right price'[24] – the price that is then used as a reference in markets, producing a series of distortions.

Markets have absorbed this experience and have appropriated the expectation for catastrophic events. In the face of the forecasts of the models, they now exhibit phenomena of 'counter-performativity', such as those that the 'volatility smile' detects. When sudden price changes occur, people tend to think that the hedging models do not work. They therefore abandon these models, further strengthening the originary movements. In the face of a fall in prices, one immediately tends to sell, even if the hedging calculations indicate that one should wait in order to achieve the designed hedging. This cascade of sales, in turn, produces new sales, leading to a further fall in prices. Markets react to themselves, and this distorts the calculation of risk (if it was set without considering this reflexivity).

In this setting, the very success and spread of portfolio insurance systems becomes an additional risk factor, especially given that they were designed and implemented with the support of computers. One even talks of 'model risk' in order to indicate the particular kind of instability that results from the technological support of transactions. This obviously requires models that are compatible with computer implementation (such as the Black–Scholes model), but makes them indispensable because, without their processing capacity, it would not be possible to achieve the complex calculations required. The 'technosystem' that guides the transactions, however, is often based on strict rules. For example, it can compel one to sell titles automatically when a predetermined risk threshold is reached, without considering the context or the mutual observation of observers.

In general, the problem with the models of risk formalization is that they assume that risk behaves randomly, with a random walk that should para-doxically make it predictable. Risk, however, remains uncertain because it does not move randomly. Instead, it presents a series of correlations and stickiness that makes it partly predictable (albeit only locally and in reference to contingent situations), and a reflexivity that produces sharp discontinuities and abrupt changes.[25] Risk movements remain risky. It is therefore particularly risky to think that they can be controlled. Typical correlations are imitation phenomena where the level of risk depends on risk perception, as is shown in the much-discussed cases of 'gregarious behaviour', where operators mutually observe and orient to each other, eventually leading to congestion in the same strategy and sabotaging its outcome, or cases of positive feedback where buyings and sellings provide information that gives rise to further buyings and sellings, influencing the level of prices. The prices of assets, then, are not determined only by the level of risk and by the expected profits, but by price movements themselves.

Risk moves in a non-random way because of forms of dependence, where the past influences the future, and this not in the sense of continuity.

What happened yesterday affects what will happen tomorrow, but not necessarily because things will be the same. In fact, as in episodes of counter-performativity, it can happen that one behaves in the opposite way because of past experience. The past teaches, but we do not know what it teaches. The trends of volatility show this. A wide variation makes a further variation more likely (thereby increasing the frequency of extreme events), but we do not know in which direction. A growth in volatility can be followed by a further growth, but volatility can also decrease abruptly.[26] The presence of (second-order) regularities increases uncertainty rather than reducing it, and the memory of the past seems to introduce a further unpredictability, because it makes the structure of expectations even more complex and interconnected.

All these alleged risk anomalies are based on reflexive configurations, excluded by current models. We need a theory that takes account of risk riskiness, and of itself in its effects on its field of application.[27] Nobody knows, however, if and how such a theory can be translated into models. The 'volatility smile' would not be an anomaly to be corrected, but evidence of how markets learn from experience and from past risk, as well as how one can try to deal with these. They deviate from past expectations as a result of these expectations. One cannot protect against risk, because this very protection generates new risks (for oneself and others), but one can try to apply a form of rationality that includes the volatility smile and its consequences for markets. According to this rationality, paper markets are not unreal, and their operations are (often) not irrational at all. We should, however, find out what kind of reality and what kind of rationality are at stake.

NOTES

1. There are technical words to describe this circumstance. The situation where the futures price is below expected future spot price is called 'normal backwardation'; the one where it is higher is called 'contango'.
2. See MacKenzie (2007), pp. 368f.
3. For instance MacKenzie (2006), ch. 5; Mandelbrot and Hudson (2004), p. 161 It.edn; Millman (1995), p. 47 It. edn.
4. Or Black–Scholes–Merton, as MacKenzie calls it, in order to acknowledge the role of Robert C. Merton. Actually, however, in the debate on the pricing of derivatives, one speaks mostly of the Black–Scholes formula, and we will conform here to the prevailing habit. See Black and Scholes (1981).
5. The operators themselves say this: see Caranti (2003), p. 107.
6. Cf. MacKenzie (2006), ch. 5, pp. 119ff., for a convincing description of the career of the Black–Scholes formula and of its performative aspects.
7. See above, Chapter 7, note 5.
8. Thus Mandelbrot and Hudson (2004), p. 259 It. edn.

9. See, for example, Hull (1997), pp. 49 and 239.
10. As under the model proposed by Maurice Bachelier 70 years earlier: see Bachelier (1900). On the history and context of options pricing models see Hafner and Zimmermann (2009).
11. On the construction of the reality of the calculus of probabilities, see Esposito (2007).
12. See Mandelbrot and Hudson (2004), pp. 11ff. It. edn.
13. See Maurer (2002), p. 24.
14. MacKenzie (2006), p. 166.
15. See above, Chapter 8.
16. Ross (1987), p. 332.
17. Significantly, in a book devoted to the explanation and concrete description of the use of derivatives, and not to epistemological or theoretical matters: see Hull (1997), p. 507.
18. See above, Chapter 5.
19. One of its proponents, Harry Markowitz, received the Nobel Prize for economics in 1990.
20. The failure of the fund LTCM, which relied essentially on arbitrages starting from the assumptions of the CAPM, is often regarded as a major evidence of the inadequacy of the model.
21. See MacKenzie (2006), pp. 183ff.
22. We do not focus here on the paradoxical aspects of the alleged 'risk stability'.
23. See Mandelbrot and Hudson (2004), pp. 6ff. It. edn; MacKenzie (2006), pp. 184ff.
24. See. Rebonato (1999).
25. Mandelbrot and Hudson (2004), ch. XI, speak of two forms of wild variation: discontinuity (which depends on the features of the event) and pseudo-cycles (which depend on the order of occurrence of the events).
26. The technical espression is 'autoregressive conditional heteroscedasticity'.
27. Systems theory speaks here of 'autology': see Luhmann (1997), pp. 16ff.

PART III

The time of the crisis

11.   The crisis – presuppositions

In this third part, we shall deal with the financial crisis of 2008. We shall do so with regard to the following three questions. Was the crisis avoidable? How did it develop? What can we do now?

If, as we have seen, theories and techniques about financial markets are based on faulty or, at least, overly simplified assumptions, and risk management produces uncontrolled risks, was a crisis bound to arrive sooner or later? If one were to have asked for a forecast, one's question would have been meaningless, given the impossibility of an answer because the future is always open. However, at an *ex-post* reconstruction, one can see the correlations between a certain (past) vision of the future and the (today present) future which actually came about.

The uncontrolled increase in risks began with a new trade in safety, the buying and selling of guarantees for the future. This was connected with the impression of being able to govern the risks of tomorrow in the present (section 1). How did the future escape this control? What mistakes were made?

One of the reasons for the crisis was the change in the conception and management of risk (section 2). The development of techniques for risk assessment for those granting loans, which allowed them to calculate the possibilities of delays and defaults, to foresee these and compensate for them with one another, and to promise the creditor that they would achieve a profit regardless of how things went, is an example of this. Profit relies on the management of risk as such, no longer needing to distinguish between 'good risks' and 'bad risks'. A wise manager should earn in every case. Risk, which was formerly a threat to be avoided, is instead an opportunity for exploitation.

The techniques for risk assessment were applied in a pyramid of increasingly opaque credits, based on a simplified image of the future (section 3). The starting point was loans with which to buy houses, which were granted without guarantees, relying on an increase in the prices of real estate. Residual risks were neutralized by compensating for them with other credits and distributing them among many creditors in a chain of securitizations (ABS – asset-backed securities – and CDO – collateralized debt obligations). At the highest level, the transaction concerned only abstract risk, with no connections to the initial investment. Derivatives allow one to gain from risk even when one is not exposed to them. One can insure against damages that do not affect oneself. This enables one to collect the repayment without having suffered the losses. However, one takes risks in the management of risk, often without realizing it.

The reality reference of markets has shifted to the future: it is based on the future that the risk or rationality of an investment is measured. Because the future is not present, one must refer to the way in which markets foresee it. One must refer to a series of techniques and devices that make the future appear to be an objective fact (section 4). To find out what an investment is worth, one refers to the judgements of rating agencies, which rely on calculations to estimate risk (the same calculations that led the regulation of financial markets over the last years). Although it is often said, it is not in fact a simple matter of deregulation, but a strict and rigorous regulation, the regulation of the future world that is expected by markets.

In order to evaluate assets, one moved from the past price to a 'fair value', which referred to the future (mark-to-market), a future that had dissolved into a nebula of projections based on unobservable data, where reality comes to be confused with the model or even with myth (section 5).

When they work, these techniques allow one to use the future in the present, thereby increasing the available possibilities (measured by liquidity). However, in so doing, one binds the future (present) tighter and tighter, and, should things not go as expected, one finds no further possibilities, but discovers that the future is no longer available (section 6).

1.   THE SALE OF THE FUTURE AND ITS PROBLEMS

There have always been people who have criticized the prevailing economic models for being based on faulty premises and, by extension, have criticized their practical application as dangerous, even irresponsible. This criticism became more prevalent with the great crisis of financial markets in 2008. The disturbing impression was one of gigantic movements of money without any orientation, driven by erratic and irrational movements, and without any real knowledge or understanding on the part of either the politicians or the economists of what was happening or how they should intervene. Such a criticism was clearly too harsh. In the management of the crisis, many analyses and concrete measures were produced, while the sequence of events that led to the collapse (starting from the management of the US sub-prime loans) was identified with clarity and remained undisputed.[1] Nevertheless, there were no clear answers to the following fundamental questions. What had really happened? What was one buying and selling when handling paper money? How and why did virtual finance flows affect the ability of citizens to satisfy their needs – the available goods and services? To what extent can these flows be meaningfully multiplied, while keeping in touch with the 'real economy'? What is really the reality of the real economy?

It has been said that the crisis marked a historic turning point both in the economy and in Western society. It marked the end of an era of irresponsible expansion of credit, and the inability to understand the evolution or meaning of speculative bubbles.[2] Why was it irresponsible to sell guarantees and assurances in a market that called for these assurances and used them in order to produce further availabilities of money, to circulate it and increase itself? What misuse ensued during this irrational euphoria, when everyone followed the behaviour of others, forgetting the world and its constraints? What are these constraints, given that we have known for some time that prices do not, and cannot, reflect any external objective value, but instead correspond to values that are produced by markets themselves – that is, by the economic dynamics they should regulate? At what point does the mechanism become irrational?

In the following pages, we shall try to describe the financial crisis. We shall start with the dimension of time, from the perspective that has guided this entire work. If it is true that time, in its essence, is money, and that financial markets are a mechanism for the present management of the uncertainty of the future, can the crisis of 2008 be accounted for by the use and economic construction of time? Why was it wrong to sell one's own future and the future of others in the present? How did it happen that the future was not in agreement with the projections of operators?

2. LOVE OF RISK

Everything can be traced back to the 1970s, when a change in the concept of risk began to develop, leading up until the crisis at the beginning of the following century.[3] In the 1970s, a probabilistic approach to risk began to spread (starting with the USA). This approach reified risk as an entity that could be defined objectively. It was linked to the use of models of 'credit scoring' that promised to calculate accurately the probability of insolvency (default) in the granting of credits, to enable safe and motivated decisions. These models had already been available for a few decades, but had been formalized to forms of 'risk pricing' that radically transformed the image and management of future uncertainty.

The technologies used, supported by probabilistic procedures, should have allowed those who were granting loans to obtain profits, not only when the creditor promptly paid their debts, but also when they paid them late, even when they did not pay them at all. Risk is identified, calculated, evaluated and negotiated in the markets as an entity in itself, in the process of the 'commoditisation of everything',[4] which takes advantage of the uncertainty of the future and turns it into a resource. This refined and technical process no longer considers risk something to be avoided (in accordance with the traditional understanding), but as the neutral object of the calculus, where negative possibilities (default risk) join positive ones in a general evaluation of profitability. There is no longer 'good risk' and 'bad risk'. However, there are different possibilities that are opposed to and intertwined with each other, in a complex game of compensations that should always allow for a gain. The problem is not the insolvencies, which can become virtuous if carefully managed, but the inability to calculate future opportunities properly. The problem is not the future, but insufficient preparation for it. For those who are able to properly deal with it, the problem should not exist.

In a kind of zero-sum game, one based on a combination of conditionings and counter-conditionings, absolutely rational and guaranteed by guarantees and countermeasures, the image of a future comes about that, although unknown, cannot produce bad surprises. Because all events have already been considered and managed by a prudential calculation, one can use this calculation in the present in order to prepare for the events that will make current behaviour virtuous. The future, which has not arrived, can offer no resistance to the constraints that are imposed on it. These constraints are used in order to generate liquidity, to generate present availability. This availability is not groundless, but assumes that the future will follow the expected course (with a certain flexibility, measured by probabilistic techniques). One does not fix how things will necessarily go, but considers a range of possibilities (that the debtor is timely, that they pay late, how late, or even that they do not pay at all). If the variability of the future falls within the expected range, then there is no problem. There is no lack in the consistency of 'paper money', which matches actual availabilities (those availabilities and games of correlations between presents and futures that have always been the backbone of a monetized economy). In such cases, there are no losses. Because a certain variability is allowed, the course of the future is not restricted to a single possibility (that the debtor pays on time). One has the impression of being able to leave it open, of not having to consider the possibility that the future will not behave as it should. One can be free to enjoy the assurance of those who do not have to fear that things will go badly.

It is not a matter of recklessness, but of highly formalized techniques that have gradually changed the ideas of prudence and foolhardiness. It consists in a formalized and computerized revision of the old distinction between gambling and speculation, with the legitimization of the speculator as being wise, a person who performs a service for the collectivity. The gambler is the one who artificially creates risks (which would not otherwise exist), while the speculator assumes and manages the inevitable risks, especially in business, and does so in a professional way that allows him/her to deal effectively with such risks.[5] The speculator, far from being a dangerous individual, would be a responsible person, relieving other operators of the inevitable business risks and managing them both competently and cautiously. The speculator would be an expert on risk, who attains greater results for everyone. A century later, this idea has transformed into a kind of 'love of risk' that has come to replace risk aversion,[6] leading us to conceive of risk as something positive and productive. Were the future not uncertain, there would be nothing to earn. There would also be less wealth for everyone. If properly prepared for and managed, risk cannot produce any negative surprises, given that the cautious and prudent business person is not one who looks for safety (which does not produce possibilities), but one who calculates and manages contingencies. These are not disorders, but 'market opportunities for the wise';[7] market opportunities for the one who takes risks, despite knowing what they are doing. The trader has become a sort of mythical figure.

The main problem with the concept of risk circulation is not recklessness or irrationality (the famous irrational euphoria), or even an excess of gambling that leads one to see only the positive side of the investment (which can bring benefits) and to overlook the negative side (which implies only small and unlikely losses for risk managers).[8] The main problem is an excess of rationality, which is reliant upon a simplified idea of the future and its network of uncertainties. In cases of crisis, the future 'doesn't agree'. It not only behaves unexpectedly, but also unpredictably, sabotaging the whole construction. It is, however, a rather subtle matter, and it remains for us to examine how this happens in detail.

3. REPACKAGED AND REDISTRIBUTED RISKS

How do techniques for risk management and risk marketing work? It began with models of 'credit scoring', which allowed institutions granting loans (banks or others) to categorize debtors in accordance with their default probability – that is, their reliability in promptly paying the installments of the loan. This is not done (as one might have thought in the past) in order to select only acceptable debtors and to reject others (that is, to exclude the insolvencies). On the contrary, as the policy for granting credit cards (in particular the ill-famed revolving cards) shows, a creditor who does not pay on time is often more convenient, and is therefore actively sought by companies. One who does not pay is not rejected. The purpose of credit scoring is not to exclude candidates. No one says that the risk of insolvency should be avoided at all costs. On the basis of formalized models and probability calculations, debtors are divided into groups in order to associate the loans with graduated interest rates. If the creditor seems reliable, then the rate is low. If the risk is high, then the interest rates increase. The one who grants the loan should then have a guarantee for securing profits even if there are delays. When the latecomer finally pays, the higher rates allow for greater earnings. The creditor, on the other hand, has money available in the present with which to seize chances and take advantage of opportunities.

This kind of reasoning has helped to produce sub-prime mortgages, granted to debtors whose reliability is below the acceptable standards, and even without any guarantee (such as the so-called 'ninja' loans: 'no income, no job, no asset'). In the USA, the guarantee was derived directly from the future. Even if the debtors did not have the money to pay off the instalments, the increase in real-estate prices would have led to an increase in the value of the house to which the mortgage referred, and upon which the bank could make up its credit or grant a new mortgage in order to acquire the money to pay for the first debt. In some cases, the bet on the future was more hazardous still, as in 'adjustable rate mortgages' (ARM), where one pays a reduced rate in the first years, and an increased rate thereafter (relying on the growing value of the house, which should make it possible to withstand higher rates).

There are also those who do not pay at all. However, it seems possible to insure against these eventualities. First, higher rates should cover a number of insolvencies. Second, there is the possibility of insuring oneself. Since the mid-1980s, the practice of securitization has spread, leading to the 'originate and distribute' model that became infamous during the crisis of sub-prime mortgages. The agencies that grant credits (banks, and other institutions that do not necessarily own big capital and often depend on short-term credits and need liquidity), 'package' their credits in bonds that are sold in the market at a price that reflects the level of risk. They are sold at a discounted price with respect to the nominal one, in order to account for the possibility that not all payments are successful. The buyer buys the claims of the seller, and hence the right to collect them, paying a little less than what they should be worth, because they can only be collected in the future and because it is always possible that something may go wrong (there is a certain amount of risk). Risk is calculated with sophisticated stochastic techniques. This procedure gave rise to 'asset-backed securities' (ABS), the infamous 'toxic' assets that have spread financial risks and the corresponding fear in markets. The original calculation, however, was far from irrational and seemed to reflect sound risk management strategies.

In the case of real-estate loans, the procedure remains plausible, and corresponds (as all loans do) to a practice that allows for the transformation of wealth that cannot be spent (illiquid) into available monies, such as when one asks for a loan offering the goods one owns as a guarantee (in the case of mortgages, the guarantee is the house). This seems to suit both parties, and satisfies their needs at the most convenient time and under optimal conditions. Here we find an interesting clause: the wealth at stake does not yet exist. The basis of the transaction is future wealth (this gives rise to all kinds of complications, given that the future is far more uncertain and flexible).[9] In ABS, the lending institution asks another institution for a loan, warranting this with the expected flow of instalments from the first loan (for example, a mortgage). If the calculation is reliable, then the manoeuvre corresponds to making time fluid (the basis of all the operations of the monetary economy). The transaction offers liquidity against risk. It gives one party (the creditor) the opportunity to use the future in the present, while the other party uses its present (its liquidity) in favour of an expected future (when it will collect the credits).

All the operators involved knew from the beginning what they were doing. They assumed, in accordance with the model of the prudent speculator who professionally manages risks, that those who buy and sell bonds would be able to assess the magnitude of the risk they undertook and insert it into an overall strategy.[10] The problems started at a later stage, when structured finance and derivatives came into play. Once risk (future contingency) had been objectified and become the object of transactions (running risks), nothing hindered the movement of those risks forward or the selling of this second risk, or any subsequent risks. This takes place when ABS, along with other assets, are themselves 'packaged' in other bonds, called 'collateralized debt obligations' (CDOs), which are much more abstract.

Like ABS, CDOs collect assets and include them in structured schemes (the so-called structured finance), which should allow for their mutual compensation. Assets are organized in tranches, with a rating assigned by the competent agencies (the famous 'votes' from AAA to BB), expressing the riskiness of the investment, and they are then associated with different interest rates. Greater riskiness corresponds to a higher rate. These products are then traded on the market, in a traffic that no longer concerns goods or risk, but an abstract riskiness that has nothing to do with the original investment, or even with the kind of future to which one binds oneself. What is bought and sold is binding, circulates in the markets and produces additional bindings. Those who buy a CDO buy a risk with a corresponding reward; they do not buy the asset or the underlying goods. All that they know is the rating that has been assigned, the assessment of investment risk. The fact that there was a house and a (more or less reliable) promise for payment of the instalments of a loan is completely opaque at this level. What is bought is the abstract riskiness of the investment for the one who decided to grant the loan. One does not buy a present good or a future availability, but the availability of a future availability, the possibility to decide one way or the other in the future, the possibility to choose one's own future. One buys and sells the openness of the future.

This riskiness is associated with, compensated for, and balanced against the riskiness of different investments. It is then possibly sold again in more and more abstract markets. CDOs multiply themselves. They are repackaged in CDOs of CDOs, which can be resold in third-order CDOs, with increasingly daring risk reflexivity, gradually losing any contact with the present or the original bindings. Risk seems to depend on the riskiness of risk management (on the ability to offset risks with risks, to anticipate them, and to react to them), and no longer on the world. The future seems to depend only on an ability to combine bindings and bindings of bindings (how a decision expands or shrinks the options of other decisions), on the ability to manage the present future. The future presents are completely ignored.

The process accelerates further when derivatives come into play. These, due to their vocation, always have to do with the marketing of risk. In this case, the tool adopted is CDS (credit default swaps), a tool that was also common during the financial crisis. Swaps, in general, are agreements between two companies to exchange future cash flows, under conditions where both parties benefit. Swaps on interest rates, for example, refer to practices where a party commits itself to pay, for a certain period of time, a predetermined fixed rate on a given capital to the counterparty. The counterparty assumes the commitment to pay a variable rate on the same capital for the same period. The agreement becomes interesting for companies that would profit from a financing with fixed rates. However, they are for various reasons forced to use variable rates, while other companies are in the opposite situation. Swaps can actually turn fixed rate loans into variable rate loans, and vice versa. The same mechanism is used for the exchange of any kind of payment (on currencies or other), and in all cases where contractors obtain mutual benefits. CDS are a special kind of swap that applies to credit risk, and require a buyer and a seller. The buyer pays a periodic amount of money to the seller in exchange for protection against a credit (like the credits of ABS or CDOs); the seller commits themselves to pay the buyer back if the creditor defaults.

In this formulation, which is the original one, CDS is a tool for protection, much like insurance. The buyer pays the equivalent of an insurance premium and is insured against the risk of an adverse event (the failure of the creditor). But CDS has a very peculiar feature, one that makes these swaps unique. Unlike insurances, they do not require that the buyers actually own the assets for which they want protection, or even that they really suffer a loss. It is as if one were insured against the fire of a home one does not own, or against the risk of accidents to someone else's car. If the damage occurs, then one collects the repayment without undergoing the damage. The highest speculative potential of these instruments is clear, and they spread in an explosive way in the markets of structured finance. They are explicitly oriented to risk (to the risk that CDS isolate and commercialize, without the 'burden' of the property of the fluctuating assets).

If one expects a title to cause problems, then buying a CDS enables one to 'bet' on its movement, allowing one to collect a refund in the event that difficulties actually arise. This speculation is equivalent to short-selling an asset that is expected to depreciate, but with much higher margins because of the flexibility of the contracts. In highly volatile markets, the availability of such contracts has the effect of further increasing trends, pushing declining markets even lower, with consequences that are difficult to calculate (given the disproportion between the cost of the investment and the magnitude of the effects). Warren Buffett compared CDS to time bombs that threaten both those who deal with them and the financial system as a whole. He went so far as to define them as 'financial weapons of mass destruction', with indeterminate but potentially catastrophic damages.[11] The availability of these tools in abstract financial markets (as a consequence of the use of derivatives, securitizations and all the apparatus of structured finance) had the effect of exacerbating the autarkic construction of the future that we shall have to face when it becomes present.

4. THE REGULATION OF THE MARKETS TO THEMSELVES

For a certain period, the highly rational mechanisms of structured finance dominated markets, turning them into risk markets linked to derivatives, and hence different from previous finance. Financial markets have always been turned to the future, but only in recent decades have they explicitly carried out the 'commercialization of uncertain futures',[12] with specific advantages and specific risks. These markets extended, eventually reaching a nearly incomprehensible circulation of capital (the traffic of derivatives in 2008 was ten times the worth of the amount of the world GDP). How is it that such a takeoff could have come about?

At the origin, there is certainly an increase in the circularity of financial markets and their mechanisms. The reference value of investment, which should guide market prices, is not the productivity of businesses, the reliability of debtors or some other external criterion, but the assessments provided by rating agencies. The figures, expressed as combinations of As and Bs, should offer the information that is necessary for markets in a concise way. But AAA, AB ratings (etc.) speak only to the creditworthiness of the examined entity, not to the goodness of the investment. They are only concerned with risk assessment, not with the state of the world. This is indeed the only object that circulates in financial markets. It is with respect to risk that ratings give operators equivalent transparency, standardizing very different, often complex and obscure investments and allowing for their comparison on the basis of a simple system of letters.

Risk assessment is nothing more than reading the future, where the present is used only in order to give forecasts a basis. The present choices of operators refer to the future, at least in so far as the future is foreshadowed by the evaluations of rating agencies. Similarly, the votes of rating agencies are not an objective reading of the future, but based on calculations produced by the financial system in order to orient itself based on contingent criteria. The calculations of Standard & Poor's, Moody's, Fitch and so on rely on risk estimation algorithms similar to those used by the operators themselves (for example, those used to give ABS or options a price), with the same assumptions regarding a dependence on the past and the construction of the future. Guided by the apparent objectivity provided by ratings, operators reflect on their own criteria, which are transformed into quantified data, and derive a transparency that is largely based on the fact that they observe themselves and their reference world (in a manner that is also observed by others[13]). However, this is always the present future, not what will be present in the future.

The same circularity can be seen at the level of regulation. Financial markets seem increasingly to rely on self-regulation, which works only if it produces limitations – that is, if it can exclude possibilities and generate constraints. In the case of positive law, which is respected (when it works) precisely because it refers to itself, the production of contingent norms applies in virtue of a decision (not referring to external criteria). The self-regulation of markets, on the other hand, seems to be based more on the lack of reliable criteria than on the availability of its own criteria, and does not seem to be able to oppose market trends once they are in motion.[14]

Meanwhile, the evolution of financial technology seems to be gradually obliterating the distinction between banks (with their complex hierarchical organization, constraints and checks) and other, far less controlled financial institutions that produce assets and let them circulate in markets.[15] The majority of derivatives are not traded in the stock market, but in over-the-counter (OTC) markets, which are far freer, more imaginative, and less regulated. They are free from the restrictions of standard contracts, centralized controls, clearing houses and other protections from market risks. These markets offer contracts that are tailored to the needs of customers, and are ready to adapt to the movements of markets. However, they are also much more obscure and difficult to control. Every exchange is carried out without knowledge of others, without clearing houses, and without the possibility of knowing the movements or the level of exposure of other operators.

Faced with this situation, the authorities seem to have realized that the idea of central control has become unrealistic. They have moved in a direction that some have called deregulation, while others consider it a more flexible and complex (perhaps even more rigid) form of regulation. The basic principle is different. It is not that there are no rules, but the rules are increasingly contingent, refer less to fixed criteria and parameters, relying instead on the perspective of the operators. For the USA, the turning point is often located in the Gramm–Leach–Bliley Act of 1999, which introduced liberalization of the banking system, overruling the distinction between commercial banks and investment banks. The so-called Basel II agreements were decisive for the G10 countries, establishing the minimum capital requirements for banks in relation to the risks taken.[16] Each bank is required to set aside a certain amount of capital to ensure its solvency, representing 8 per cent of the 'activities adjusted according with risk credit' (that is, of the potential capital the bank should collect on the basis of the granted credits, evaluated according to criteria and taking into account the possibility that some debtors do not pay). Banks, in substance, must have in cash at least 8 per cent of the money they abstractly own.

How much this 8 per cent is depends on how risk is calculated – that is, on the estimate of insolvency risk for the companies to which the banks have granted credits. Previously (in accordance with Basel I agreements), the 'riskiness' of companies was evaluated according to historical criteria, by referring to the age of the company, its property and its previous activities. The objection was that these criteria were of little significance in the dynamic and future-oriented markets of the time, and had to be replaced with other forward-oriented criteria, which would allow one to assess whether, how much, and for how long a company would generate an income. When the present is mainly concerned with building the future, history cannot teach us what to expect. It has been recognized that financial markets that use innovative and structured tools require a more sophisticated and flexible risk analysis, one turned to the future rather than to the past.

The decision was then made to rely on risk management programmes in order to assess the riskiness of credits. The ratings could be external if attributed by acknowledged international agencies (the usual Standard & Poor's, Moody's etc.), or internal if based on calculations made by the banks directly. The decision was made to rely on the future (as the present sees it), in order to determine which present is needed. On the basis of these calculations, the amount of capital reserves could be established, the constraint to be imposed on the present in order to enable it to prepare for the future. If the criteria are internal to the banks, then, in practice, each of them is entrusted with the production of its own future, forfeiting any common constraints. This relies on the assumption that banks themselves do not go blind, but project and carefully prepare their movements and constraints. It is not true that there are no rules. According to many observers, a precise application of Basel II criteria would indeed lead to a substantial increase in capital requirements, but in a more flexible way. It would be linked directly to the future horizon of the operators who are building it. Banks, therefore, cannot act recklessly without worrying about possible damages. They are required to behave prudently, in accordance with constraints that are strictly imposed and regulated by international agreements (referring, however, to what they themselves have evaluated as the risk they take). What is not clear is whether this increases or reduces the openness of the future as a whole.

5.   MARK-TO-WHAT?

The problem is the ability to evaluate wealth, to give a reliable price to the assets that are circulating in markets, in order to understand how much freedom (how much contingency) one has in the present and in the planning of the future. This is a far from easy problem, which during the crisis became a mystery, guided by the anguished question, 'What's this stuff worth?'[17]

There are obviously accounting procedures, but these have become circular with the spread of structured finance and new speculative tools. Previously, one referred to *historical cost*, to the price paid when an asset was purchased. This was an admirably simple, univocal and common measure, one that unfortunately became increasingly inappropriate as a result of the dynamic nature of markets and their orientation to the future. If the purpose is to evaluate how much wealth one has, the past value is an unreliable reference. The value of the asset could have changed, as is usually the case. The present does not continue, and it does not represent the past. What is required is an estimate of the 'true value', and there was a search for procedures that could indicate this. A criterion for *fair value* was established, and it became a cornerstone of international accounting,[18] no longer referring to the past, but to the market. This immediately adjusted values to the present situation. If the market rises or falls, the value of the asset adapts to the variation. Budgets record the new available wealth, which can be taken into account in investment strategies.

The problem is that what really warrants evaluation is not the present but the future, given that investment strategies are increasingly based on the present use of future availability. This is why the present that is recorded by the market, as the past reflected by historical cost, can be such an unreliable guide. In phases of strong upward or downward variations of assets (in bubbles or crises), the market price is not fair at all. In fact, it is not even realistic or true. It does not express the real potential of the asset, and it often does not even indicate future wealth. Its advantage is its apparent objectivity. It should, at the very least, serve as a common reference that does not depend on the perspectives and inclinations of operators (or even on their honesty). In increasingly abstract and hypothetical markets, this condition is also little respected, as indicated by the practical use of fair value.

When it must be translated into practice, one resorts to 'mark-to-market', which is a methodology for ascribing a value to a financial tool on the basis of the current market price. This method was initially developed for futures that had to monitor the reliability of the estimates continuously. The problem is that, in many cases, one cannot refer to the market for the evaluation of the assets, because not all economic activities are listed in the stock market, or because a corresponding market does not exist (for example, for complex financial tools). The apparent objectivity of fair value (which is not so fair by itself) is overshadowed by subjective elements, which become increasingly invasive as the evaluation becomes more abstract. A 'hierarchy' of levels of fair value has been adopted, which corresponds to an increase in the subjectivity of evaluation (which, in times of crisis, is immediately associated with a growing risk of the investment). Level 1 is that of liquid or quoted assets, where one simply has to look at the market price. Level 2 is that where one 'pretends' that there is a market and calculates a value based on the market prices of similar assets or on pricings like those provided by the Black–Scholes formula and implied volatility. These are still based on data that are 'observable', with a known methodology. Level 3 comes into play when not even these observable data are available, and 'unobservables' are used instead – that is, one uses one's own evaluation models. One invents a virtual market through some kind of procedure and uses it as a reference to fix prices. In cases such as these, one talks of 'mark-to-model', of the reference to a fictional objectivity that increases the discretionality of the evaluation with criteria that can become increasingly idiosyncratic and imaginative and can even degenerate into what Warren Buffett condemned as 'mark-to-myth'.[19]

What is the problem? What makes the 'myth of the mark-to-market'[20] dangerous? The price, however calculated, does not express an objective value, but a crossing of observations of observations about supposed needs and future contingency. It is an internal construction of the economy. This also applies to prices that are 'really' fixed by the market, and even historical prices. We always move within a fictitious reality that is constructed by the economy in order to gain an orientation that is not based on independent objective data. What is the problem with the growth of subjectivity, which goes from mark-to-market to mark-to-myth, given that we saw that the market price is not 'true' at all (in any sense of the term)?

From historical price to fair price and, then, to an orientation to models, what changes is the temporal frame. Historic cost corresponds to a long time period, which binds the future to the past and maintains a certain stability with respect to the ever-changing events of the different presents. Mark-to-market, on the other hand, refers to the present and to the 'here and now', constantly reviewing the past on the basis of current data. It corresponds to the model of the quoted company, which is looking at the increase in the value of stocks. In mark-to-model, it is the future that shapes the present. The problem is always the construction of the future, and the bindings that the different ways in which to regard or evaluate the present impose on what will be possible later on. The more the future is 'used' in the construction of the present, the more the success of the strategy depends on the fact that the future corresponds to what we imagined (or to the range of possibilities taken into account). Things can go well, and then we earn much and the strategy is advantageous. However, things can also go wrong, and then we do not even have the freedom that is available to those who have turned to stability (to historical cost) – that is, to the simple openness of an unknown future.

6.   THE PRESENT USE OF THE FUTURE

With the different forms that we have been considering (credit scoring, risk management, structured finance, securitization, ratings, fair value, to changes in the regulation), the financial system seems to be turning to autonomous criteria, referring to its own future projection rather than to external evaluations or historical data. Why? What benefits come from this kind of orientation?

The key word is *liquidity*. The different tools share the ability to make liquid out of any capital, that is, to use any thing in the present, which then becomes widely available.[21] This helped many families buy houses and goods that they would not have been able to afford otherwise, and helped companies to carry out projects that would have otherwise been impossible. One example of this is Google, which produced real wealth on the basis of claims that were initially based only on confidence in the future. Liquidity enables one to build a future, one that would not have been realized otherwise, in the present. Houses are actually bought, entrepreneurial projects are implemented. These have real consequences, producing further wealth, if things go well. As long as things work, we can all live in a better world, with more money, more available goods, and more optimism before prospects that seem to open as a result of courageous choices and a dynamic attitude. High liquidity is often associated with the optimism of markets.

We must, however, see where this liquidity comes from. We have already dealt with leverage,[22] which inflated the credit bubble of the last decades. All the money that was circulating in markets relied on the possibility of having liquid money available on the basis of an increasingly smaller capital. While ordinary obligations require a margin of 10 per cent synthetic bonds that are created with credit default swaps can be commercialized with a margin of 1.5 per cent; in securitizations the ratio of debt to net capital can reach 30 to 1 or even 40 to 1. With the same capital, by having more money circulating and allowing one to buy more things and make more investments, one can produce far more liquidity. The expansion of credit has become a kind of ideology, in a competitive situation where it is necessary to keep the minimum possible capital reserves in order to make a profit. Permanent debt has become a physiological condition. The 'love of risk' led to an inverted concept of prudence, where the prudent investor is the one producing maximum liquidity (that is, wealth) with the available capital, and the accumulation of reserves is not always the safest strategy. In order to be prudent, one should get into as much debt as possible.

As long as this worked (and it worked for several years), there were no problems and the economy went well. One invested more in both the financial and the real economy, allowing for greater production and earnings. It was not just paper wealth, but also (at least in part) a concrete availability of goods and opportunities (with the weakness that these goods were bought in the present at the expense of future availability). Everything can go well, but it can also happen that this is not confirmed when the future becomes present, and the problems can multiply out of control. This is why, as Marc Faber remarks,[23] the packages of sub-prime mortgages are so dangerous. Had they not been multiplied in the vortex of securitizations, the drop in house prices would have remained a limited problem, restricted to real estate and to the people involved in it. In the bets on betting that ensued, however, the future as a whole came into play. It was then that uncertainty spread.

The problem, Langley maintains,[24] is that the techniques used allowed one to earn profits in the present by 'colonizing the future', a future that then proved much more unpredictable, and showed a very different quality of unpredictability. These techniques took risk into account, handled it skilfully and controlled it with hedging and differentiation. However, they did not take account of the fact that risk management produces its own risks that cannot be controlled, a sort of 'macro-risk'[25] at a higher level, which no longer concerns the world, but hedging operations – that is, a risk that is produced through an orientation to risk itself. The more one uses these techniques, the more self-referential finance becomes, the more the future is put under pressure. Financial practices generate an aggregate risk of an endogenous kind, which escapes all techniques because it is produced by the techniques themselves. It is impossible to face it with more accurate risk calculations. It is the model for managing the future that must be questioned.

Where are the errors? On the one hand, they are in the persistent belief that one can rely on the past in order to predict the future. This reliance, if not on the facts, is at least on the variability, that is, on risk. Since these tools are new, the available data refer to a past that is too limited. The calculations of sub-prime mortgages were based on a few decades of continuous growth of real-estate prices, and built their estimate of future risks on this. The data also fail to consider that future conditions can change as a result of the very fact that one has relied on them. In the case of loans, which can be extended to many aspects of the crisis as a whole, this produces 'default correlations', where many debtors stop paying at the same time. This results because the market, pushed too high by the enormous granting of credits, suddenly collapses and endangers those who thought to support their mortgage with the increase in prices and had obtained the loan on the basis of this premise. The losses are not only greater than predicted, but also beyond predictability, because the risk management policy changed the conditions of riskiness.

Both good and evil, the financial tools for risk management are 'pro-cyclical' – an ill-famed term because it is linked to the acceleration of the crisis once it was put in motion. But pro-cyclicality also has its positive side, when it allows for an increase of wealth on the basis of available wealth. When this worked, no one had anything to say. By itself, pro-cyclicality is just a reflection of the circularity of financial techniques, which react to themselves and become stronger (positively or negatively). We can speak of a pro-cyclical effect when a procedure tends to accentuate trends, such as the facilitation of credit in phases of expansion, or blocking during contraction. In other words, it tends to improve things when they are already good, but also tends to worsen them when there are problems. A regulation is expected not to be overly pro-cyclical. It should be able to provide an external reference that opposes the spontaneous acceleration of system-internal trends. Otherwise, it is not regulation but simply an organization of what will happen anyway.

As we have seen, in recent decades, financial markets seem to have progressively given up this external reference. They seem to have replaced it with a reference to the future, which provided the guidelines and criteria for guiding decisions in the present. These criteria have been highly formalized and technicalized, making it more difficult to recognize that the future to which they refer is still a reflection of the present – how tomorrow's events appear today. To be driven by the future is becoming very similar to the idea of being driven by oneself from another point of view, hence accentuating one's trends through reference to criteria and rules. This is the meaning of pro-cyclicality.

The calculations underlying the grants of sub-prime mortgages are obviously pro-cyclical. In good times, they increase the number and amount of loans, and much more than can be justified by the present (where many debtors are unreliable). In difficult times, credit tightens and becomes almost blocked (even when capital and guarantees are available). The system of fair value and mark-to-market, moreover, is highly pro-cyclical. If a market grows, then the estimated wealth of businesses immediately adapts. If there is a crisis, then it makes estimated losses real. If rules like Basel II are added, which are highly pro-cyclical, then this positive feedback process strengthens even more. The banks that were guided by mark-to-market were forced to devalue many assets in their budget and to adapt capital requirements to their new accounting situation. They also had to sell assets, further accentuating the downward trend. Pro-cyclicality feeds on itself, particularly in conditions where the same criteria are followed at different points in the system.

Is it possible to do otherwise in a system that is guided by the market, where everyone observes other observers and derives the information guiding their behaviour from this observation? Is it possible to do otherwise in a system where information is primarily provided by price and not by values (which depend on prices and not vice versa)? Is it possible for a system that is based on second-order observation not to be pro-cyclical? The issue of regulation has always been the ability to prevent this excess of connection of everything with everything, to avoid short-circuiting the system in an immediate self-reference. Measures like the separation of investment banks and commercial banks, and the rules on capital requirements, are instituted in order to prevent this. The problem is that the spread of derivatives undermined this organization, leading external rules to orient themselves to internal criteria (think of Basel II). In increasingly free, opaque, and over-the-counter markets, a central bank is no longer able to impose constraints that would block the immediate reference of operators to one another. For example, we can think of the contagion of liquidity problems, which resulted as a consequence of the localized insolvencies of some banks, as in the case of sub-prime mortgages. Every problem spreads, and this at all levels, ultimately showing that the control of a future-driven market, if it is still possible, should turn itself to the management of the future and become far more complex and flexible.

NOTES

1. See, for example, the debate on the role and competence of economists in predicting and analysing the crisis in autumn 2008: see Luigi Guiso in *Lavoce.info*, 21 October 2008 or Federico Rampini in *La Repubblica Affari & Finanza*, 27 October 2008.
2. See, for example, Soros (2008), 'Introduction'; Shiller (2008).
3. See Marron (2007); Langley (2008).
4. De Goede (2004), p. 198.
5. See Henry C. Emery (1896), quoted in de Goede (2004).
6. Thus Giacomo Vaciago in an interview in *Il Corriere della Sera*, 30 September 2008.
7. De Goede (2004), p. 207.
8. According to the 'Panglossian world' discussed by Daniel Cohen in *Lavoce.info*, 16 June 2008.
9. This is also the case of sub-prime loans, which are covered by a mortgage, but on the basis of an estimated value that anticipates the future increase in prices. After some years the amount of the loan still to be returned was greater than the current value of the house.
10. In sub-prime loans, as it is well known, this was not or was true to a very limited extent, and gave rise to many problems. We shall discuss them later, but now our argument follows the alleged 'physiological' dynamics of the pyramid of loans – we want to show that even in this case the calculations were inadequate.
11. He said this in 2002, well before the imbalances of financial markets were evident to everyone: see *Berkshire Hathaway Annual Report 2002*.
12. De Goede (2004), p. 199.
13. The reform projects for rating systems, called for during the financial crisis and undoubtedly necessary, usually address only the presumed interest conflicts and the obscure relations among ratings agencies and their customers, and not the contradictions implicit in how to find, evaluate and price risk: see Langley (2008), p. 483.
14. We shall discuss the pro-cyclical aspects below.
15. See, for example, Strange (1986), p. 59 It. edn and (1998), p. 48 It. edn.
16. The author of the agreement is the Basel Committee on Banking Supervision, an international organization established by the Governors of the Central Banks of the ten most industrialized countries (G10) at the end of 1974.

17. Thus Vikas Bajaj in *International Herald Tribune*, 26 September 2008.
18. On the basis both of the IAS (International Accounting Standard) used in Europe and of the FAS (Financial Accounting Standard) adopted in the USA.
19. See *Berkshire Hathaway Annual Report 2002*.
20. Thus Luigi Zingales, 'I nodi del mark-to-market e le modifiche degli accordi di Basilea', *Sole 24 ore*, 15 October 2008.
21. The Bank of England's Financial Market Liquidity Index (FMLI) recorded in 2007 its maximum for 17 years, with a continuous increase since the beginning of 2002. Since the beginning of 2008 the index has sunk to very low levels.
22. See above, Chapter 8, section 2.
23. *Market Commentary*, October 2008.
24. See Langley (2008), pp. 480–81.
25. Marron (2007), p. 119.

12. The crisis – evolution

In 2008 the crisis arrived, spectacularly yet stealthily. Appalling financial movements, with very unclear consequences on real wealth and on the overall arrangement of the economy, captured the attention of everyone. Misconducts, transgressions and gaps in regulation were immediately identified as the culprits. However, it was also apparent that many of the disasters resulted from a fair and rigorous use of the techniques and procedures of financial engineering. These were the most worrying cases. How is one to react to risks that are produced by the management of risk (section 1)?

The problems that arose when it was discovered that miscalculations had been made spread unimpeded as a result of lack of confidence in the calculations. If the whole construction is based on risk management, and this management is shown to be unsafe, then there is nothing left on which to rely (section 2). The insolvency of sub-prime mortgages exemplified the serious problem by demonstrating that risk could show up in ways other than expected (and neutralized). The lost income of lenders had far greater consequences than the actual sums at stake, because it introduced the element of uncertainty into the pyramid of the insurance, management and sale of risks, which had been built with securitization and structured finance. Rather than economic, the crisis was a crisis of confidence, linked to the fear of having already gambled away the future and its possibilities.

This fear was due to the fact that the financial techniques that were used were 'techniques of de-futurization', which took into account a limited number of possibilities, conditioning and neutralizing them with one another and protecting against possible damages (section 3). However, the future does not allow itself to be de-futurized, and reacts to any attempt to limit it. It produces different possibilities precisely because it was constructed in such a way that one felt safe.

When the crisis burst, one discovered that one not only had made inaccurate predictions, but also had built a future that was different from that on which one had relied, thereby introducing constraints that limited the future's opening (section 4). The future had already been used to acquire liquidity in the (past) present, but the future always turns out different from expected and, instead of offering opportunities, it presents costs. Instead of everyone being richer, we have found out that we now have to pay for things that we would rather not possess.

If we had previously used too much of the future, it would seem that we are now reacting by not using it at all. We do not build the possibilities that we shall face tomorrow. The real problem with the crisis is the resulting renunciation of the future, which is expressed in the threat of deflation (section 5). The fall in prices, which may seem positive, is terribly worrying because it corresponds to a widespread lack of confidence. One prefers present possibilities over future potentialities, and therefore refrains from investing or projecting. One does not trust the future and, therefore, has less of it, because what is possible in each present depends on how the past built it (even if it then surprises us).

1. THE PROBLEMS OF TRANSGRESSION AND THE PROBLEMS OF THE RULES

The financial crisis of 2008 made an enormous impression on financial operators as well as on the general public. In more or less technical forms, the belief circulated that we were facing an epoch-making change, the end of an era, after which many things would be different – even if we didn't yet know what things or how they would change. Reasons for this included the fall in the value of securities and the capital of the banks, and a bewildering dynamism that changed situation of the markets completely every few hours, generating a volatility in the stock market that exceeded every historic maximum and overwhelmed every criterion and reference. Over a few weeks, the financial world changed faster than it had over the previous 40 years. For example, there were bankruptcies of large consolidated institutions (or rescues with public funds); investment banks that became commercial banks; the largest insurer in the world was saved by a central bank; the public acquisition of US agencies for the securitization of loans (the famous Fannie Mae and Freddie Mac) took place; there was a massive intervention of the state in the economy; and many other such changes transpired which would have been unthinkable only a few months earlier.

The general effect of the crisis was a sense of uncertainty. However, it was also the beginning of a rethinking of many of the consolidated aspects of the functioning of markets. Little confidence remained in the ideas of mark-to-market, the calculation of the LIBOR rate for interbank loan, the rules of Basel II, or even the forms of the limited liability company.[1] Suddenly, people seemed to see that the rules and principles they had relied on referred to a financial world different from the developing one, proceeding on completely different paths. Called into question was the theoretical paradigm that was more or less directly based on the idea of efficient markets (EMH), on the belief that markets, if free to develop autonomously, tend to equilibrium and to perfect competition[2] – with all of its consequences expressed in the technical management of risk, in the pricing of derivatives and in portfolio design (or, as we would say, in the construction of the future).

At the origin of the crisis, there was undoubtedly a series of distortions, which immediately drew the attention of the public and the media, as they sought reassurance through finding a culprit (or a category of culprits) to blame for the collapse. Much talk about greed (which has not been considered a flaw in a profit-oriented economy for a long time), the privileges of certain categories, corruption and conflicts of interest, the abnormal power of the CEOs of companies, the separation between managers and shareholders (with the system of incentives tending to give priority to the value of stocks rather than to the soundness of companies), the conflict of interests between analysts and managers of investment banks, the ambiguous role between controllers and operators of rating agencies, and so on, were also suggested as contributing to the collapse. The focus of these discussions was mainly the opacity of structured finance and derivative markets, which have been relentlessly exploited by banks in order both to expand the market of their securities to a public that is less and less informed about the entity or the quality of risk, and also to produce a 'shadow' financial system of extra-budgetary vehicles (structural investment vehicles and conduits), largely out of control.

All the above certainly existed, primarily because there were rules that allowed for them. These rules were there because the principles that were guiding the theory and practice of finance were blind and had shortcomings. We need to correct these distortions. We need to change the guidelines of the financial world in order to produce more appropriate rules. The latter need is a much more complex and potentially challenging goal. The most worrying part of the crisis does not concern cases where rules have been violated or where there was reckless behaviour, but those circumstances where one did what was allowed and carefully calculated the risks and the protective measures. The most worrying cases are those in which risks have been produced by risk management, with all its refined calculations of the levels of uncertainty and the techniques of hedging and diversification. There have certainly been cases of rash speculation and searching for profit at all costs, but the magnitude of the crisis was due to the consequences of a mass of apparently rational and prudent operations – following the new concept of prudence based on the calculation and management of risk. The real problem seems to be the imponderable risks that were produced by the orientation to models – that is, by the attempt to protect oneself against risk – and, against these, one cannot be protected. Nothing suggests that, in changing the rules to correct distortions, one will not produce the same effects in a different way.

2. WHAT HAPPENED? THE CONSEQUENCES OF PRUDENCE

Looking at the different steps of the crisis, one always sees the same mechanism constantly at work. A rational calculation produces unexpected consequences, generating an uncertainty that spreads and further increases damages. The sequence is well known. The starting point was the rise in interest rates by the middle of 2006, which raised the instalments of loans, including sub-prime mortgages and, especially, mortgages with variable rates, accompanied simultaneously by a drop in house prices. Many debtors had difficulties in paying the new rates, and could not even raise another mortgage on the house, because the value of the house did not increase (against the initial calculation of the lender). In some instances, it had instead decreased. Insolvencies began to multiply. This very unpleasant phenomenon theoretically should have been limited to the real-estate market and the USA, where easy credit without guarantees was particularly widespread. This phenomenon also concerned a restricted number of families and had tangible properties, however depreciated, as a reference – that is, the houses supporting the mortgages. The prediction about the future was wrong (which can happen), and one had to deal with the consequences. However, the consequences should not have spread to the world economy as a whole.

The credit-granting agencies had protected themselves against the risk of insolvencies – that is, they had behaved in a 'prudent' way, in accordance with risk management techniques (that strange prudence that almost inevitably leads to the multiplication of moral hazard). The expected future was used in order to produce further financial possibilities. The error in the prediction affected countless other areas, eventually jeopardizing the availability of the future itself. The loans at stake, both solvent and insolvent, had been packed into the first level of bonds and risk distribution (ABS), which had in turn been repackaged in CDOs. The traffic became very abstract, but the basic principle (risk distributed over multiple subjects dilutes and becomes irrelevant) theoretically should have held. CDOs, including derivatives, however, do not sell the risk of a given investment, but riskiness as such, which is relatively independent of any specific object and, hence, much more difficult to distribute or dilute. The effects of insolvencies in the first ring of the chain (the sub-primes) spread without control. The traffic of riskiness turned into a crisis of confidence, in so far as nobody seemed to know where the 'toxic' assets were localized or what consequences they could have. The whole securitization market became blocked, involving those who had nothing to do with sub-prime mortgages. Nobody bought anything; prices collapsed.

The problems should have remained confined to the market of CDOs or to structured finance using derivatives. Here too, however, risk management techniques multiply risk. Banks, the major buyers of CDOs, had often used financial leverage and had to face multiplied losses. To get cash, they sold everything, and the market of obligations collapsed. The crisis spread to the whole stock market, especially in the areas of banking, insurance and bank assets.

The market, however, was not exposed to risk unprepared. Innumerable CDS circulated, 'officially' in order to protect operators against market turbulence, but actually used for speculative purposes, reinforcing trends (upwards and downwards). Besides hedge funds, the main sellers of CDS were banks and insurance companies. The fear soon spread that, as a result of the crisis, they would no longer be honoured. Insurance companies had serious difficulties because of the number of compensations they had to bear. The US Treasury had to intervene in order to save AIG, the largest insurance company in the world. In the form of lack of trust, the spread of riskiness and of the risks of riskiness produced a block in the interbank market. Banks no longer lent money to other banks. If they did, they did so only at very high prices. Liquidity fell sharply; investment banks suffered. The symbolic event was the bankruptcy of Lehman Brothers in September 2008.

The lack of liquidity then threatened the 'real' economy. Businesses and families found no more money with which to finance their projects or consumption, to build the future. Society as a whole seemed to have no future available, and feared exposure to an unforeseeable and uncontrollable course of time without any tools or possibilities of initiative. Panic and concern spread.

The interesting thing about the catastrophic course of the crisis was that almost nothing happened. There was no war or natural disaster, no energy crisis, no annihilation of resources or of production possibilities. There were only insolvencies in a limited area of the US economy. In fact, these were guaranteed by tangible goods and supported by accurate calculations. In looking at the data, one could have come to the conclusion that, if some things had happened otherwise (if the real-estate prices had not fallen), the crisis could just as easily have not taken place. The debtors would have raised other mortgages; they would have had the money to pay the instalments; the bonds would have been repaid; the bets would have held; and so on. In the discussions on the measures to be taken in order to limit the crisis, with an enormous disbursement of public capital, the (theoretical) possibility was evoked that, in the end, the turmoil would have no costs. The state would acquire the assets and stop the panic. The situation in the markets would calm down. The prices would rise again and the state would then sell the cheaply purchased assets at higher prices.[3] Such a picture is not only oversimplified, but also completely theoretical. I mention it only to indicate that the crisis developed at the level of the future, not so much at the level of what was going on. It developed out of the fear that negative events would occur, from a lack of confidence in the capability of others to honour their commitments and, especially, from the impression of having already gambled away the possibility to affect future events. An indeterminate panic with no reassurance resulted, unleashing a 'domino effect' that led to the crisis.[4] If I fear that the future will bring damages of which I am unaware and that I cannot predict, then no warranty can calm me down; the damage can always come from somewhere else.

The real fear was in having already jeopardized the future, having used the possibilities of the days and years to come in the present, building a present that is different from the past that the future will need. This future, once arrived, will not be able to provide otherwise, because its possibilities have already been used, and it will therefore have to adapt to the constraints imposed by a past that had prepared for a different future. Is this true? Did we use the future in the present? Is this possible? Can we avoid doing this, given that every decision affects the possibilities that will be available in the future? What were the errors (if there were any)? Could we have done differently?

3.   TECHNIQUES OF DE-FUTURIZATION

The future exists so long as it remains open and unpredictable, so long as it presents a horizon of indeterminate possibilities. This is why we never know what will happen: we must always expect surprises. A future reduced to a single sequence of events would no longer be a proper future. Indeed, we should say that the more possibilities the future makes available (the more different futures it contains), the more future is open. From this point of view, not all futures are equivalent. The future is always a construction of the present. The more a society is able to use the present to increase rather than reduce the freedom of the future, the more future that society has.

Every act and every decision excludes some possibilities, thus constraining the future. If I invest in certain assets, then I spend money. That money is then no longer available. If I invest in certain assets, then I do not buy other assets. To some extent, I influence the market, which reacts to my behaviour and to the behaviour of other operators, modifying the assessments and the future price of the assets. However, my decision also opens up future opportunities. I can obtain profits, and hence have more money to spend. This gives me the possibility of buying or selling other assets. In the case of derivatives, profitability will grant me the possibility of designing and handling other possibilities. Every decision simultaneously excludes some possibilities while producing other possibilities. Obviously, not all decisions are equivalent. The possibilities that are excluded and produced by each decision are different, often incompatible. Not only does the decision determine one possibility over another, but it also determines the entire sequence of possibilities that will be produced in the future.

The future, then, is more open if it makes many different courses available. These different courses are not necessarily compatible with one another – that is, as many present futures as it is able to design, the future remains open as long as these do not reduce them to one or a few sequences of events.[5] The future is more open the more these future presents are different from one another. From this point of view, we can say that the techniques adopted by financial markets consumed the future. They restricted its freedom by reducing it to a few sequences of events, without predicting the possibility that the future presents become real in another way; a way that is different not only from what one expects, but also from all that can be expected in the present.

Financial techniques are oriented to risk in that they regard a number of possibilities, which they intertwine and compensate for, so as to be ready for the occurrence of each of those possibilities. They do not predict a single future. They generate a feeling of security about the future, because one thinks that one is protected against every eventuality, thereby feeling qualified to dare more without feeling reckless or rash. If one can be certain of obtaining profits, regardless of how things go, then why not use those profits to increase present availability? Everybody gains. Avoiding this would not be prudent, but selfish. However, the future is restricted to the number of possibilities now predictable, and one uses these possibilities without considering that future opportunities depend on the constraints generated today. Future opportunities are not yet possible. Therefore they cannot be predicted, not even by multiplying the sequences of possibilities that can be taken into account.

Is it possible to speak of de-futurization techniques[6] that reduce the opening of the future without giving the impression that that is what they are doing – that is, without identifying the future with a single chain of events? Although one does not claim to predict the future, one nevertheless expects to be able to protect oneself. The first de-futurization technique, statistics,[7] is presupposed by all strategies adopted in financial markets. It assumes a series of links between different presents, a kind of order in time, of a probabilistic kind (and, therefore, open), yet organized, allowing one to do calculations and develop strategies.[8] We have seen this in financial techniques, which claim to predict future volatility (or at least its range of variation) based on the implicit constraints from the past courses of events. They claim to derive future unpredictability from the past.

The future does not let itself be de-futurized, not because it is uncoupled from the past and has no structure,[9] but because it has too many structures; structures that depend on the present. Not only can it happen that one is wrong in one's prediction, but the very attempt to guess often makes things go otherwise.[10] The attempts of the present to strengthen the predictability of, and control over, the future (to de-futurize it) produce the opposite effect, making the future presents even more surprising. Volatility reacts with 'skew'. In this sense, it is true that the crisis resulted from the present use of the future, which adopted more and more complex and sophisticated (and opaque) techniques, ultimately limiting its opening and its space of possibilities. The present has less available future. The panic of markets was in reaction to this lack of future. It was in response to the impression that the de-futurization techniques had 'colonized it', constraining the future to a few courses of events whose possibility had already been used. In the future, should it take a different course, there will not be other courses available. The future is there, but not for financial operators, who lose their ability to decide and operate, to produce different possibilities and be surprised by them. During the crisis, they actually did nothing but wait and worry, failing to build the future in fear of a course that they cannot affect and for which they cannot prepare.

4.   THE RETURN OF THE FUTURE TO THE PRESENT

All the aspects of the crisis have the same structure. The future returns to the present, but in a different form than anticipated (when the present future becomes present, it turns out to be different from the future for which the past was prepared). Risk pricing, for instance, relied on a present assessment of the future, starting from the processing of past data, which provided the justification for granting loans (deducting the increase in real-estate prices to contain defaults in the present). When prices fell, one discovered that one was wrong, not only in making the decision, but also in the construction of the future. Instead of opening opportunities, the construction of the future only generated constraints. In instances such as these, one had to go on paying in accordance with a project that no longer corresponded to reality, which could not be changed (or could be changed only with further costs). Instead of a mortgage producing wealth for everyone (creditors and debtors), it came about that everyone was impoverished. No one could choose other possibilities because they had already bound themselves.

Where the real difficulty arises is at a higher level, when one discovers that, not only was the prediction wrong, but that it contributed to building a future different from that expected (or those expected, since one did not refer to a single sequence of events). One used a different future from the one constructed. This happened with securitizations, in accordance with the 'originate and distribute' model. The institutions granting loans did not have the capital, but acquired it through bonds that they generated by 'packing' credits – that is, by selling future payments in order to obtain the capital to finance the present credit. The bonds, in turn, multiplied themselves in the CDOs and in all further layers of credit. When the defaults at the lowest level of the chain began (some debtors did not pay), the future collapsed because everyone knew that it had been constructed in this way, that it had already been used. The model could have worked in a future without securitizations, where the damage of defaults would have remained limited (as risk calculations indicated), but it did not work in a future 'intoxicated' by a circularity without control and all past projections. One did not know if the present wealth had already been used in the past, if the alleged credit actually corresponded to a future wealth (in a future present), or if it was only the reflection of a past expectation (of a past future).

The traffic of CDS, corresponding to more and more complex ways of using the future and binding it, further strengthened the circularity. With this traffic, one bets on a certain development, which is then influenced by the bet itself; this must be taken into account. One knows that adverse effects will be amplified and that the future will be forced to accelerate itself. This serves only to multiply the uncertainty. The result was a confidence crisis, expressed by the block of credit. Nobody knew how to continue building the future. In fact, all refused to do so. None lent money, invested, or risked. The future, however, arrived anyway, and arrived in a way that depended both on the choices made and on the refusal to make them.

The crisis spread at an even more accelerated pace because it did not depend on the assessments of the state of the world or the economy (of the present), but on the uncertainty about the future, which is difficult to halt. The speed of the sequence of collapses surprised many observers, but corresponded to the same logic that supported the previous period of expansion. The more one used the future, the more one now refused to use it. This was based on the same kind of reasoning adopted in the calculation of risk. It was believed that one was acting rationally (with prudence) if one oriented one's decisions to a model of the future and constructed the appropriate past (if not predicting what would happen, at least predicting the riskiness and preparing to face it, with the right tools for the different options that could become realized). As long as one believed one was able to do so with the techniques of risk calculation and management, one decided and acted. When one seemed not to have the tools, one stayed still and waited. In both cases, one actually de-futurizes the future. In the first case, one used its possibilities in the present. In the second case, one did not produce the possibilities from which the future would have to select. Both when one thinks that the future has already begun, and when one thinks one has no future, one simplifies the situation. The future is produced as a result of present decisions and expectations, but is always different from them.

5. DEFLATION: GIVING UP THE FUTURE

This is what happened during the crisis. It was marked by a phenomenon that was the opposite of that which had characterized the previous period of expansion. It was marked by a general condition of *illiquidity*, where one did not succeed in transforming capital into immediate availability, which could be used and circulated in the markets. This applied to suspect 'toxic' assets, like ABS, which nobody wanted, as well as to large corporate bonds and other investments that had been deemed safe, but that could not be sold, even at reduced prices. However, this liquidity applied especially to credit. Everybody sought money, but no one could find any, in the sense that no one was willing to lend money (or only for the short term and at very high rates). Once again, the problem did not concern the present, but the future. Money was there, but no one trusted either themselves or others. Banks would not lend because they no longer believed in risk calculations and feared not being able to reproduce liquidity. They also did not trust the counterparty, whose solvency they could not assess. The mechanism of credit was blocked, and money was not circulating – that is, money could not be used in the present in order to produce further possibilities for structuring and building the future. One did not invest, did not project, and did not risk. While the present had formerly used the future in order to be able to do as many things as possible, one no longer used the present to build the future.

The use of the future relied on leverage, a signal of optimism towards the future and its ability to generate possibilities. During the crisis, the relationship between future potentialities and present availability short-circuited. The value of the active of many banks became imponderable, and was often devalued unimpeded, in some cases reaching negative net capital. Then an opposite process of deleveraging began, bringing back the ratio of actives and capital to less risky levels, and implying far less willingness to actively build the future and its potentialities.

The attitude towards time involved the fear that the crisis was engaging a process of *deflation*, which would be the more complete expression of a renunciation of the future[11] (the opposite of the euphoria of those who felt they were living in an already beginning future). While one had formerly used the future too much, one was now failing to use it enough. Deflation is not simply a condition of lower prices, which in many respects could be positive. After all, if monetary policies serve the purpose, and almost the obsession,[12] of containing inflation, this decrease in the cost of living should be welcomed. However, this is not the case. Deflation is an evil, one to be avoided as much as inflation (perhaps even more), because it leads to a general stalemate of economic activity. Why?

Price movements are only a symptom of a general attitude. The point, in both cases of inflation and in cases of deflation, is not the coverage of money with real goods. In the period of expansion before the crisis, an exorbitant quantity of money was in circulation, without any problems of excessive inflation. During the crisis, however, money did not circulate, even if it was said that the economy was robust and wealth factually existed (one only failed in 'liquidating' it). Whether there is more or less money in comparison with available wealth (a correspondence that we do not even know how to measure) is not the point. An attitude towards the future and the willingness to put it at stake in the design and in the present initiative, a willingness that generally depends on the level of confidence in others and in the future[13] is what counts. During the period of expansion (of high liquidity), a general attitude of optimism was circulating, one of confidence in the future and in the possibilities it held. Wealth was created by enjoying future availability in the present, which was also generated by this initiative. During the crisis, however, we were all poorer because we perceived ourselves as poorer. Deflation not only affects the consumption of goods (which cost less), but all capital (houses, reserves of banks and companies, investments portfolios, equipment and machinery), which decrease in value and do not seem to provide guarantees for future activities. Nobody had confidence, so nobody bought or invested, leading to the result that goods were actually worth less. Confidence, like lack of confidence, tends to feed on itself. During the crisis, because everyone expected others to do the same, it seemed rational to withdraw money. Previously, one had expected the opposite, and acted accordingly.

The problem with deflation is the implosion of the future with respect to the present. Everyone looks for liquidity – that is, gives priority to present possibilities with respect to future potentialities. Nobody invests – that is, nobody is willing to believe in the wealth to come. One has no future, in the sense that one is not willing to undertake it or act in the present in order to shape it. There is less confidence than actual wealth could generate. The future will come about anyway, but by itself, without the stimuli and accelerations that can result (positively or negatively) from the present initiative. In the future, less will happen. There will be fewer possible damages and fewer positive possibilities. If the future is not given *a priori*, but depends on the ability to build and promote it, we can say that there is less of it.

The problem with the crisis, both before and after its outbreak, was the lack of integration between time horizons. The love of risk, which has been accused of being the irresponsible engine of the bubble, is the exact correlate of the refusal of risk that followed the contraction of markets. In both cases, there was a lack of awareness of the risks of risk, of the unpredictable consequences arising from one's own behaviour. Excessive confidence produces risks of which one should be wary. Lack of confidence produces other risks for which one is not prepared. It is on this level that markets develop erratically and without direction, especially when they are driven by formalized techniques and by a seeming rationality. During the crisis, it became evident that trust was the key variable, the one that would decide the course of events and was more difficult to influence, not the stock market or the cost of money, which were only symptoms (as many commentators have remarked). The course of volatility showed this, exceeding every historic maximum. The VIX index rose to over 70, with impressive dynamics. The problem involved not only the decrease of assets, but also the enormous uncertainty that markets failed to control even after the collapse. Indexes had considerable rises, but these were followed by sudden collapses, while volatility remained very high and uncontrolled. Options were very expensive, indicating that no one knew what to expect. Trust had no direction.

According to Giuliano Amato, confidence is the bridge that connects finance to the real economy.[14] In our own terms, we could say that confidence connects the construction of the future to the present and allows us to use time for the management of possibilities. Although the future remains open, it is not true, as one might think according to a concept of time based only on chronology as an abstract succession of dates, that time has no structure to it or that 'in the long run everything can be'.[15] The present cannot determine how one will decide in the future, but past choices are the premise from which future choices will start and the condition for the possibility to choose in general. The date says nothing about the content or the meaning of events. However, what is possible in each present (even in the future presents when they become real) depends on how the past has prepared each, even if one decides differently than expected. Each present, when it comes to be, has limited possibilities, depending on what the society can support at any given time. Confidence is the index of this availability. The possible extension of time (how much future one has available in the present), therefore, depends on the mechanisms of confidence and those of lack of confidence, which determine the ability of society to accept the present use of the future – that is, how much operators are willing to trust each other's projections and projects (and these limits are not random at all).

The circulation of money, even in quiet periods when there is not much speculation, is based on the confidence that others accept the temporal construction of any currency holder, that one is willing to renounce having goods today in favour of a future availability. This is symbolized by the money that can be spent at a later time, and is guaranteed by the willingness of others to accept banknotes with no intrinsic value in exchange for tangible goods. This is precisely what is lacking in the case of inflation or deflation – in the one case, one holds onto the goods; in the other case, one holds onto the money. The value of money measures this willingness, which multiplies and becomes exceedingly complex when financial techniques enter the picture. However, the mechanism remains the same. It remains a social support for the construction of time, expressed by the available confidence. A conscious (and empirically appropriate) use of time would require an ability to calculate the extent of this confidence, and the limits of the 'meaningful extension of time'.[16] The techniques for this calculation, however, are very different from those adopted by financial markets, which proceed in the opposite direction. They try to limit the extension of the future through its present use. The management of the financial crisis has shown what works and what does not work in the production of the future, depending on how one binds or ignores its openness.

NOTES

1. Guido Rossi said in an interview with *La Repubblica*, 26 September 2008, that the limited liability company is at the end of its season.

2. We discussed this in previous chapters: see Chapter 5, section 1 and Chapter 10, section 4.

3. The commonly mentioned examples were the IRI case in Italy in the 1930s and the acquisition of banks by the Swedish state in the 1990s.

4. Reconstructed for example by Paul Vallely in *The Independent*, 12 November 2008, showing how the chain effects, starting from rumours about possible insolvencies of BNP Paribas securities in August 2007, rely on hypothetical assumptions that become immediately real when they change the image of the future of markets.

5. Here I follow Luhmann (1976).

6. An expression of Brunschvig (1949), p. 355.

7. See Esposito (2007), p. 60.

8. In Luhmann's terms: allowing to incorporate future events in the present present. See Luhmann (1976), p. 143.

9. Following a commonly rediscovered arbitrary course: for financial markets see, for example, Taleb (2001).

10. Soros says that the guidelines of operators (including his own) are always wrong: see Soros (1987), pp. 26ff. It. edn.

11. This was feared by many commentators in autumn 2008: see, for example, Francesco Daveri, 'Venti di deflazione', *lavoce.info*, 19 September 2008.

12. Note the criticisms of the policy for the cost of money to the ECB during the crisis, which kept interest rates high in order to avoid the feared risk of inflation.

13. See Luhmann (1997), pp. 382ff.

14. See Giuliano Amato, *Il Sole 24 ore*, 5 October 2008.

15. See Luhmann (1979), pp. 147ff.

16. Ibid.

13.   The crisis – regulation

The crisis developed as a financial crisis. It had very unclear links to the concrete availability of goods – that is, with the real economy. How and when does the loss of money become a loss of wealth (section 1)? The issue is far from easy. The fear of recession, affecting expectations before they had even become realized, spread quickly. The attempts to counter the crisis had to operate off of expectations, knowing that these would change as a consequence of their announced actions. The opacity of the techniques of structured finance makes the interventions on the crisis opaque.

Aid should have come from the policy but, in its relationship to the economy, we find the same circularity. The two areas depend on each other and yet cannot determine each other. Political intervention cannot produce wealth, even if it has effects on markets. Markets cannot decide about the intervention, although they can react to it as they see fit. However, markets do require public regulation in order to have a reference from which to start (section 2).

Can one still exercise control? Cybernetics uses a far more flexible conception of control, one that refers to unpredictable situations. It originated in the design of computers (section 3). Control, in this sense (one can speak of 'steering'), does not mean achieving a purpose because one cannot know what will be needed tomorrow. However, it does refer to the ability to connect what happens to one's behaviour and to decide differently on the basis of new data. One discovers what one should have done as a result of what one did. Because one did something, one remembers this and obtains an orientation. Tomorrow, one can decide otherwise, precisely because today's decision produced information. One can also learn from unexpected events and surprises, if one has learned to expect them.

Public measures for managing the financial crisis (from the Paulson plan to European initiatives) can be read in this sense (section 4). Traditional attempts got lost in the opacity and circularity of the dynamics of markets, while steering manoeuvres were apparently more effective. The state acts in order to give markets the opportunity to act. The state does not build up the future of the economy, but provides the economy with the premises it needs in order to be able to build up its own future. It offers the economy an orientation without imposing a purpose. Instead of refusing risk, the crisis could lead to markets where one can risk more in a less dangerous way, because one will be ready to face the risks that are produced by risk management.

1.   THE REAL COSTS OF THE PAPER CRISIS

Another mystery regarding the financial crisis of 2008, probably the most deeply felt, involved its effects on the 'real economy' – that is, the debated issue of the relationship between Wall Street and Main Street. Did the appalling collapses of financial markets, with the hundreds of billions 'burnt' in only a few days of trade, reflect the annulment of a corresponding wealth and, hence, a concrete decrease in the availability of goods? Is a world with less money actually poorer? How, through what mechanisms, and how quickly can the loss of wealth occur? Can this fallout be prevented or delayed? How?

The issue remains rather obscure, especially in light of past experience. In the background, there are always the worrying images of the financial crisis of 1929, and the Great Depression that followed. However, there are also recent examples of opposing situations, which show a relative independence of the economy from financial movements. In 2000, the outbreak of the net economy in the USA caused the biggest stock market crash after the war. However, in proportion, the effect on the real economy was utterly reduced. There was a limited loss in GDP, which was estimated at 0.17 per cent. The same happened with the terrible crack of the stock markets in October of 1987, which did not lead to a recession. The role of speculation on the price of raw materials, in particular on the huge movements in the price of oil during 2008, remained very unclear. The price of oil passed from approximately US$60 per barrel at the beginning of 2008, to a peak of US$147 in July, when it was feared (and expected) to reach a level of US$200. However, it then decreased in the autumn to under US$50. This kind of movement in price inevitably affects production costs, the expenditure of households, and the development of the (real) economy. How much do these depend on real factors and to what extent are they pushed (and manipulated) by financial speculation?

Real factors exist. These are recognized by everyone. The development of the economies of India and China led to hundreds of millions of new consumers and raised demand, albeit certainly not to such an extent as to justify the doubling or tripling of prices in only a few months. The financial manoeuvres in the NYMEX (New York oil market) reached an impressive magnitude, with futures contracts referring to a billion barrels per day, while the production of crude oil was only 85 million barrels per day. It was difficult to think that the bets of financial operators, both downwards and upwards, were not affecting price movements. However, it was much less clear how, or how effective, these affectations were. If it is true, as Luigi Spaventa maintains, that betting on a horse does not foster its victory,[1] then it is also true that financial bets affect expectations, which are much more sensitive to the observations of the expectations of others, with reactions that can be positive or negative. Forward prices do not anticipate spot prices; otherwise speculation would always be successful. The image of the future to which operators refer does not coincide with what actually happens in the future, but it undoubtedly influences what happens. The relationship between the financial economy and the real economy develops in this game of anticipations and answers, as well as in the event of crises and the measures taken in order to face them.

In 1929, the intervention of the central authorities finally succeeded, despite all the errors and the impression that a clear orientation was lacking, in bringing the situation under control, especially with the state's direct purchase of loans and troubled enterprises. Today's situation is even more complicated, due to the financial innovations already discussed. Assets have been cut and packed in various forms of bonds and derivatives, making it very difficult to assess the extent of the manoeuvre. It is also much harder to achieve the transparency necessary to restore markets' confidence. Protecting the real economy, paradoxically, is particularly difficult because the crisis has developed only as a financial crisis and, therefore, depends entirely on the mutual relationships of future projections that are chasing each other. It did not originate from of concrete problems, from an actual fall in the general price index or the panic of consumers, who were rushing to withdraw deposits, but only from the fear that these may occur. The crisis is internal to the financial system and relates to expectations, not to actual data.[2] What drives it is not so much the actual value of existing loans or the present rate of defaults, but the expectation of what these will be worth in the future, when the feared effects of the crisis will be transformed into a recession. The yields of bonds collapse with the discounting of an expected increase in default rates in the present, even before it has occurred. Recession matters even before its realization.

Those who have to face the crisis and decide upon the measures for regulation are, therefore, confronted with a very elusive situation, where the only thing they know is that they are trying to prevent a future that depends on their own regulating measures.[3] This was the enigma of the Paulson plan (Troubled Assets Relief Program – TARP), which aimed to capture the 'toxic' assets and clean the budgets of the banks in order to restore markets' confidence.[4] At what price should these be purchased?

Should they be purchased at a price close to the market price, in accordance with mark-to-market, which had become very low (not very 'fair') and would not solve the problems of banks, or at a higher price, one that corresponds to the price at expiry (the future value of houses in the case of mortgages)? This would have helped banks, but it also would have transferred all the risk to the taxpayer. Also, no one knows how to calculate the price, given that mark-to-model would be translated into an arbitrary 'mark-to-Paulson'. The issue would not have been arbitrary if it were possible to know the future price, in which case the intervention would have come about as a bargain for taxpayers and a benefit for the economy as a whole. The Treasury acquires assets at a price higher than the current one but lower than the future price, solves the crisis and then sells them later for a profit. However, this future predicted by state intervention does not occur if the state does not intervene, and intervention changes the situation.

2. HOW TO GOVERN THE ECONOMY THAT GOVERNS POLITICS?

The basic problem is a condition of circularity. This put the rescue plan of the US Treasury into the uncomfortable position of a 'prophecy forced to fulfill itself',[5] which is unfortunately incompatible with an open future. In any case, a policy of market regulation should not have this result, a result that increases uncertainty rather than reducing it.

If one listens to financial operators, then public interventions in markets seem to increase forecasting difficulties. According to Marc Faber, the 'manipulation' of markets by politics does not produce the desired effects, but instead produces a large mass of 'unintended consequences'. This increases volatility and makes it more difficult for operators to obtain information from the ongoing movements.[6] While the main 'perfection' of free markets is more the capacity to make observations observable or to produce information[7] than the ability to reach an equilibrium (which is not there and would not even be desirable), a market 'regulated' by politics becomes obscure and difficult to interpret. However, markets that are abandoned to themselves have no references to rely on in order to produce expectations. What can be done?

The basic constellation is always that described by moral hazard, the situation where an unknown future is structured by present decisions, which are immediately 'metabolized' by expectations in order to produce new possibilities. One needs to take into account that any action to change the future produces a different future than the one it intended to change.

As the financial crisis ruthlessly revealed, public interventions must always face this condition. The issue does not so much involve alternative state control or a free market, as discussed in newspapers, but the complex relationship between politics and economics, which becomes circular because neither can determine the other, while at the same time needing the other. For example, we can think of the relationship between monetary policy and market development (another issue intensely discussed during the crisis), where central banks fixed the cost of money and then markets had to adapt. The movements of the stock market, however, force central banks to react and to intervene on rates. The central banks ran to help markets after they fell. Markets seemed to be aware of this and, in fact, relied on this help, anticipating it in a perverse dynamic where the interventions to control financial risks contributed to an increase in the propensity to risk. One risked more because one knew that politics would come to one's aid.

With regard to the massive public measures to save troubled firms and stop the crisis, there has been a great deal of talk about the end of capitalism and a return to a market governed by politics. Is it true that politics dictated the rules and times of the market? Is it not equally true that politics was forced to pursue the markets, making decisions that had been imposed by the development of the economy and suited step by step to its reactions, and, in some cases, even anticipated by the economy itself (as in the case of the banks that were 'too big to fail', which had relied on this prerogative for some time)?[8] Markets collapsed and politics came to the rescue, just as it was expected to. Politics ruled markets, but, at the same time, markets dictated the political agenda.

The actual situation is more complex than this and based on relations between contingencies. Markets can expect politics to act, but it cannot know how, nor can it make the decisions itself. Politics can establish the rules and decide upon the measures, but it cannot determine how markets will take them or what the consequences will be. Politics can spend money and issue currency, but it cannot create wealth. It is a delicate weave of influences and counter-influences, one planned and exploited by both sides, making the future increasingly unpredictable, and yet giving it a structure. How does this work?

Politics cannot determine the economy, because the economy is not determined. It is not an orderly system, hierarchically organized in such a way that the directions of the top are imposed at all lower levels. Financial markets are not the top, but only the centre, of the economy,[9] where the trends of money are established, which are (as we always hear) the lubricant that flows through all the intricacies of economic activity and necessary for their smooth functioning. Money, more or less available and more or less expensive, then flows into other markets, those that constitute the real economy – markets of labour, raw materials, production – and allows them to work. However, it does not determine what they will make of it. More money means more available future, the perception of which remains to be seen. This depends on the level and form of confidence. Under conditions of optimism, the future is seen as an opportunity. If pessimism prevails, it is seen as a risk. If there were a hierarchical organization, it would be enough to act at the highest level (the financial markets) in order to govern the economy as a whole. As we have seen, however, injections of liquidity and decreases in the cost of money can produce wealth *or* inflation. Politics is not able to determine what will happen. Finance uses and anticipates political actions in order to shape the future in its own way.

Must we refrain from any action and leave the economy to follow its own course, an attitude that still has many supporters, behind the somehow worn-out flag of liberalism? This solution seems unsatisfactory, given that it does not seem to lead to any balance, and certainly does not lead to optimal conditions. Instead, it leads to an exposure to the future that has no constraints or structure, one prey to the always changing present future. The limited balance that markets were able to reach had been realized with, not in spite of, the intervention of politics. The goal should not be, since it cannot be, to determine the future, but to create the conditions that the economy must take as its starting point in order to create what will become its future, to offer more alternatives in the face of unknown possibilities. The goal should be to structure the uncertainty of the future, to prepare and learn how to react to surprises when they occur. Only politics can do this, because it is an external operator able to set constraints that hold for everyone, by broadening the horizon of possibilities to which the economy is able to react, to broaden its future rather than de-futurize it.

3. CONTROLLING THE LACK OF CONTROL

What does this mean in terms of concrete measures? First, since we must give up any idea of determination, it could be useful to revise the concept of *control*. The 'control' of the economy by politics should not refer to cause–effect relationships, where a given measure aims to achieve a given effect. This aim produces a symbolic effect at most. We need a more open and complex idea of control, one that has been available for a few decades, and has been successfully applied in a very technical field. I refer to the cybernetic notion of control, as formulated by Norbert Wiener in 1948[10] and applied (consciously or not) by information technology over the following decades.

Wiener explicitly addressed the issue of prediction and the need for a criterion for judging its success (the 'goodness' of prediction). He maintained that the criterion should be different when dealing with linear or non-linear processes. In the latter, which are those concerning the social sciences, including the economy and quantum mechanics, the past of a system is never sufficient to determine its future. One can collect all the possible information about the past, but it will not be enough to know the future. The future cannot be reduced to a range of temporal sequences – that is, it cannot be de-futurized. What one gets to know, according to Wiener, is only a statistical future, the distribution of possible futures of the system (the present future), but not the real future.[11] Under these conditions, technique, and the accumulation of techniques, involving a strict coupling of causes and effects, increases the difficulty of control, given that they multiply the factors of unpredictability. Too many determinations produce indeterminacy.

Nevertheless, one can exert a form of control, provided that it refers to the past and not to the future, which remains undetermined. What is important is to have a non-random criterion that is able to lead behaviour and direct choices. This is how computers were built. Wiener's example is a computer playing chess, which does not have a goal to attain, but only a structure. Its behaviour is controlled, in so far as it has a memory of past games with the relative courses and can use these in order to evaluate the present state of the game and the open opportunities after any given number of moves. The computer does not follow a strategy, but rewrites its projection of the future in each present, on the basis of comparison with past data and with the corresponding future developments. In its memory, it has not only facts, but also horizons (the past futures). It is, therefore, able to learn, not only from its own mistakes, but also from the successes of the opponent.[12] The great advantage is that it can refrain from specifying all possible situations and corresponding behaviours in advance, building machines capable of solving problems that were not planned in advance.[13]

Control, in this case, is achieved not by comparing the input (the present) with a goal (the future), but by comparing the input with memory (the past), in order to draw an always renewed and always open projection of possibilities. The future is rewritten again in each present, but in such a way that it depends on precise constraints and allows for indications in order to decide. This future is open without being indeterminate, and uses the past to multiply the available possibilities. On this basis, Luhmann proposes a concept of control as 'steering' (*Steuerung*). This differs from the causal notion, aimed at achieving a purpose and defined by the management of certain differences (to reduce or increase them).[14] For example, the state can decide to save a troubled bank in order to curb panic and stabilize finance. Its intervention, however, is 'steering', and not only control, so long as it is not fixed to a particular future state (the recovery of stock markets), but is meant to learn from the dynamics that it sets in motion in the financial world, changing some of its conditions and waiting to see what happens. When the state notes that finance reacts by increasing risk perception, given that it interprets the intervention as a signal that failures will multiply, it should be ready to restructure its projection of the future by taking the new possibilities and the new constraints into account. One carries on a self-fulfilling or self-defeating prophecy, but does not remain bound to it.[15] Indeed, the measure is meant to try to teach what one should have done from what one has done. This can be done only by putting the future into motion in order to understand the meaning of the present (which it did not have before).

The rationality of the procedure has nothing to do with goal attainment, which is not necessarily achieved or encouraged, but with risk rationality, with an increase in sensitivity to unexpected and even unpredictable events, which results at least in part from the 'steering' itself. It means trying to increase possibilities precisely when one is inevitably forced to reduce them with a decision. The procedure makes sense only if one stops to think of possibilities as a finite (however indefinite) set, where removing some of them reduces the range of still available possibilities. Possibilities do not exist in this way, as a set of options, but are generated out of the possibilities that become realized. The future must not be thought of as a decision tree, where from each node (from each future present) sprout already foreseeable decisions. The future is not made up of possibilities, but of possibilities of possibilities, because it generates a completely new possibility horizon at each point. In the present future, one can refer only to the possibilities that are conceivable today, but these give rise to other totally unpredictable spaces of possibilities, those of the future presents. This is the great resource of the future, to which programming and control should refer.

'Steering' lies in orienting the production of possibilities, in making decisions by referring to the future that one can imagine at any given time, and regarding those decisions as premises for other decisions, unable to be envisaged today, to be made in the future. Although the future is, and remains, unknown, if one has steering, then one is not simply exposed to the future without direction. One knows that the future still depends on what one does today, which can be controlled. One builds the future on the basis of current conditions, creating constraints and knowing they will have consequences that will bring about other conditions, which are completely open at present. One decides in order to be able to decide in the future (presumably differently). When this unpredictable future then comes about, if there was steering, one can evaluate it and learn from the events, even if new and surprising. One can observe the consequences of steering attempts, whether they were successful or not. Examples might include how the world reacts to control as such (as in school classes) or when finance reacts with concern to public interventions aimed at reproducing confidence, interpreting them as confirmation that there are grounds for concern – that is, increasing the lack of confidence.

In this sense, we can recover the notion of control by revising it. One who tries to steer exercises control over the course of things (over the production of the future), not because they can determine what happens, but because they can establish a link between different presents and sees what is happening as a result of earlier decisions, learning and correcting.[16] One can also learn from surprises, if one has learned to expect them. In such cases, the disappointment is also a confirmation of one's own expectation – that is, things have not gone as expected, but this was also expected. One faces an open, yet non-arbitrary, future, which is more open the less arbitrary its course appears. It is less de-futurized the more it is constrained by present decisions.

4.   THE MANAGEMENT OF CHANGE

Can we interpret the measures that were taken in order to face the crisis in this sense? Can we see if they were attempts at causal control or whether they were aimed at cybernetic control, at a steering of the ongoing processes? With what consequences? In this case, the situation was particularly sensitive because it was a matter of directing the orientation of the future of the same markets that were handling the future. It was a matter of governing the riskiness of risk markets, with all its circularity and paradoxes. The control of risk is clearly nonsense. If it were controlled, it would not be risky any more. Nobody can plausibly ask for measures that would lead to a condition of security. This would be like claiming to give up the future. It has been generally recognized that financial instability, as disturbing and destabilizing as it is, cannot be denied. In fact, it has an indispensable role in market economy – that is, in the economic form of second-order observation. What is required is the ability to govern risk, to avoid being exposed to its turmoil and its excesses without criteria or guidelines.[17] Crises, people say, should not be occasions for shying away from risk, but for reconsidering and improving the way in which it is managed, thereby avoiding arbitrariness and lack of direction.[18]

What does this mean in practice? There are different opinions. There are those who, much like Robert Shiller, maintain confidence in rationality and the power of information. They consider undeniably irrational behaviours as nothing more than deviations from fundamental principles, which remain untouched. The results of behavioural finance have a similar role as friction did for Newtonian mechanics. We must take them into account in order to avoid distorting the results. In this sense, we must simply introduce 'adjustments', without changing the basic model. In our terms, we can still think abstractly about achieving control, even though it becomes more complicated when we have to consider all the circumstances that may influence its success. One should then minimize 'friction' by diffusing the competent financial information as much as possible. Economic instability, according to Shiller, could then be avoided, much like an effective preventive healthcare succeeds in avoiding the spread of epidemics.[19]

There are, on the other side, those who think far more radically, like George Soros. They believe that market imperfections are not deviations from an abstract model, but correspond to the nature and 'physiological' functioning of markets, because the future and expectations are governed by reflective patterns that are constantly affecting themselves and cannot be achieved. At most, they can be irritated. Irrationality is irreducible. The task of governors cannot be control because it is not possible. Transparency cannot be achieved. However, one must not give up on intervention, which is essential. One must manage expectations with all the available instruments[20] – that is, one must govern the conditions of the construction of possibilities, whatever they are and however they evolve. One must provide steering.

During the crisis, outside intervention was essential, because the market was not working and it became necessary to rebuild it or, at least, replace it, for limited periods. The main problem was uncertainty, which spread to the point of blocking any action. The market seemed frozen in the literal sense of an absolute lack of liquidity. Nothing circulated because nobody knew how to assess the price of structured assets. At the heart of the crisis were not the movements of the stock markets or the cost of money, which were only symptoms, but the widespread crisis of confidence that paralysed credit – that is, the lack of future. There was no horizon of possibilities to which to refer when making present decisions. Hence one did not decide at all. However, without a future, the economy, which deals with the management of time, cannot go on.

Under these conditions, even the supporters of market efficiency are inevitably perplexed. If markets do nothing, it is difficult to envisage that they ever reach equilibrium.[21] An outside intervention, therefore, becomes necessary. All are in agreement that this is up to the state. When it comes to confidence, only the state seems able to act as a stabilizer, reversing expectations and retrieving a horizon of future. Markets based on imperfect knowledge require external regulation on the basis of equally imperfect knowledge, because they need a pivot for building expectations. This cannot come from the circularity of the mutual observation of observers. The state, which does not dismiss or fail, fixes constraints from which everyone must start, even if it is not always public measures that achieve the desired goals. Without a shared reference, it is not even possible to deviate. In this sense, public adjustment is important for giving observation a structure (that which is made unmanageable by opacity and insecurity).

Even if markets do what they want upon state intervention, it is important that this take place and that it is not random. The regulation is more efficient the more it is able to open up a horizon of future for the markets (which no longer have one), from which they can start to build a (presumably different) future.[22] How can one succeed in this? Here lies the conceptual and strategic difference between the first version of the Paulson plan and its subsequent revisions. In its original formulation, the TARP provided for the direct acquisition of 'troubled' (or 'toxic') assets by the state – that is, it basically maintained confidence in the ability of markets to self-regulate. The meaning of the manoeuvre was to heal the market, to let it then work by itself. The state acted directly on the market, with a precise purpose and aimed at achieving a given result. The state aimed at a kind of causal control meant to obtain effects. In this case, it failed.

The problem is that, at this level, the state becomes an operator no different from others, investing directly in bank assets. Therefore (as we have seen) it also has the problem of respecting the dynamics of the market, of setting a price that does not alter these excessively (avoiding a 'mark-to-Paulson'). However, as a direct economic operator, the issue for the state is a purely economic one. How much money does it have to act on market movements? Although astronomical, the figure of US$700 billion for the Paulson plan was only a drop in the ocean of a global derivatives traffic of US$1 400 000 billion.

The reaction to the European measures was different. It was driven by English economic politics and eventually followed by the USA. Instead of buying, the state intervened in order to allow others to buy. What they wanted remained irrelevant, the state did not decide. The choice was to intervene directly on confidence, without leaving the task of restoring it to the market. Confidence was lacking in the relations between banks, fearing that they were not solvent, and authorities decided to operate on this level. The ECB introduced a public guarantee for interbank loans, in addition to launching a series of measures designed to persuade banks to start to lend money to each other again. European governments could provide warranties on new issues of bonds by banks or buy them directly, and could recapitalize banks at risk. The intervention of the state in the economy, however, is more hypothetical than real. It is not an immediate spending of public money, but a use of public money in order to guarantee investments, in the event that this is needed. Theoretically, it could also cost nothing. If it succeeded in restoring confidence, no rescue would be necessary. In any case, the impact of the investment would be far larger. In a financial world that is ruled by leverage, the same amount of US$700 billion that gets lost in the sea of financial assets represents 60 per cent of the capital of all US banks (and indeed the Paulson plan was then redirected in this sense, in order to recapitalize banks).

This kind of action seemed to work. Markets reacted more consistently to measures that were acting directly on confidence. Even if they maintained the high volatility of those who did not know in which direction the future would go, they could at least think they would have a future, because the state had warranted the conditions to project possibilities. The state does not build the future of the economy, but provides the conditions for it to build one for itself – that is, it 'steers' the economy's evolution without pretending to control it.

Steering actions are located at the level of second-order observations. One operates by observing how observers observe and not by acting on the world they must observe. If, as we have seen, the market is the place where the mutual observation of observers develops, this kind of intervention profoundly changes the way in which to see it. One moves to a model that does not deal with market prices (actual or hypothetical) as an independent variable, as the ultimate reference that supports the whole construction of finance. In cases of bubbles, we know that prices do not give reliable indications, if only on the erratic orientation of operators. They are dependent variables, on which the state can act, not as a trader (buying assets), but as 'market maker of last resort',[23] which warrants the value of assets that the market does not want to deal with (or cannot deal with), but that have a value. Credit risk – that is, the responsibility for investments – remains with the banks, which must decide whether and how to buy and sell. The state, however, warrants liquidity – that is, it warrants future possibilities.

This type of action is just the beginning from which the economic and financial politics for managing markets and their trends must develop. If it is true, as many say, that we need a new Bretton Wood system to ground international financial institutions in a different way, one more suited to the situation of the markets of the twenty-first century, then the process will be a long and delicate one. The awareness is now widespread that current risk markets are different from traditional finance and that regulatory measures must take this into account. It is no longer a matter of managing the uncertainty of the future in the present, but of actively building the future from which this uncertainty will come. This undertaking opens an indeterminate range of possibilities, and requires precise constraints and a new awareness of circularity and connected risks. If nothing else, the crisis has shown that the current regulation and risk management procedures were insufficient at this level. They did not consider the possibilities that arose when one bound possibilities, the risks of risk management and the future resulting from de-futurization techniques.

The circulating proposals (for example, the indications that emerged from the G20 Summit of 13–14 November 2008) seem to be moving in this direction. Faced with the dilemma of deregulation and overregulation, the authorities seem to prefer moving to a higher level, where they can achieve both, where they can impose rules that allow operators to regulate themselves – that is, to establish conditions for developing open possibilities. All the measures that have been mentioned share this tendency: increasing transparency – that is, increasing the availability of information on complex financial products; supervising rating agencies (without overruling these agencies, which still have the task of the self-evaluation of finance); ensuring solid capital relationships in derivatives and securitization (avoiding excessive de-futurization); verifying banks' risk management procedures (the riskiness of risk); and strengthening the integration among the authorities at a global level. The more operational measures are also directed to manage risk management. These include reducing pro-cyclical aspects, restricting incentives, regulating the OTC market, introducing a clearing house for CDS – not to reduce risks, but to constrain the conditions under which they are produced.

One can also risk more without excessively reducing the possibilities that the future will have available to face the consequences of current decisions. One should risk in a less dangerous way, and equip oneself to manage the risks produced by risk management. The regulator should be equipped to learn from the consequences of its intervention, modifying and modulating it according to markets' reactions. If their task is to safeguard confidence and provide a stable reference in the continuous variation, this task can (paradoxically) be carried out only by changing. In the face of an open future, confidence does not rely on constancy, but on the ability to keep on steering ahead even in the face of surprises that result from steering itself. Markets should perceive that change is not only a reaction to the unexpected, but the result of a politics of management of possibilities.

NOTES

1. In *La Repubblica*, 11 July 2008.
2. I am referring to the situation of autumn–winter 2008.
3. Or can also exploit it: Tommaso Monacelli, 'Se il banchiere centrale mette mano ai suoi attrezzi', *Lavoce.info*, 5 December 2008, proposes very explicitly to manipulate the future in order to manage the present. He suggests that the American Central Bank, under conditions where it cannot lower the interest rate because it is already close to zero, acts directly on expectations. It should commit itself to keep low interest rates even in the future, when the economy will be out of deflation and the recovery will start – it should reduce the (future) long-term rates today to stimulate today's demand, even if now they are close to zero: 'Monetary policy can be effective today if it "borrows" future monetary expansions'.
4. Later progressively modified in more and more radical ways – what is left is the appropriation of US$700 billion in support of the financial market.
5. Thus Federico Rampini in *La Repubblica*, 28 September 2008.
6. Marc Faber, 'Market Commentary November 2008'.
7. Not to transmit them, because there is no autonomous information to be transmitted: see Chapter 5, section 2 above.
8. Not always rightly, as Lehman Brothers case showed in a dramatic way.
9. See Luhmann (1996b).
10. See Wiener (1948).
11. Ibid., pp. 37 and 92–3.
12. Ibid., p. 172.
13. This is more or less the approach underlying genetic algorithms: see, for example, Holland (1992), p. 50.
14. See Luhmann (2000), §13.VI; (1989c), (1986a).
15. The accusation against the Paulson plan, which has indeed been changed, but following the events that disconfirmed it: in that case the change of the project was a failure, not the explicit intention of 'steering' projects that prepare their own revision.
16. This achieves what Luhmann calls a 'temporal self-integration of the system' (zeitliche Selbstintegration des Systems: 1996a, p. 18).
17. So, for example, Marco Vitale in *Il Sole 24 ore*, 5 October 2008.
18. Shiller (2008), p. 23.
19. Ibid., pp. 148ff.
20. 'Managing expectations': Soros (2008), p. 144.
21. Unless one thinks of a motionless equilibrium in the sense of physics, where a minimal variation suffices to move to an unstable condition – but it would have nothing to do with efficiency, and this is not the meaning of equilibrium in economics.
22. In presenting his big plan of public investment to oppose the crisis in December 2008, Barack Obama said that its purpose was 'to act now, so that all Americans who lost their future know that they still have one'. The stock market reacted with a strong rise.
23. See Luigi Spaventa, 'Avoiding Disorderly Deleveraging', *CEPR Policy Insight*, no. 22, May 2008. The formula refers to the discussions of economic politics on the role of the state as 'lender of last resort'.

References

Abolafia, M.Y. (1998), 'Markets as cultures: an ethnographic approach', in M. Callon (ed.), *The Laws of the Market*, Oxford: Blackwell, pp. 1–57.

Aglietta, M. and Orléan, A. (1982), *La violence de la monnaie*, Paris: Presses Universitaires de France.

Agnew, J.-C. (1986), *Worlds Apart. The Market and the Theater in Anglo-American Thought 1550–1750*, Cambridge: Cambridge University Press.

Akerlof, G.A. (1970), 'The market for "lemons": quality uncertainty and the market mechanism', *The Quarterly Journal of Economics*, **84**, 488–500. (Reprinted in *An Economic Theorist's Book of Tales*, Cambridge: Cambridge University Press, 1984, pp. 7–22.)

Akerlof, G.A. (1984), *An Economic Theorist's Book of Tales*, Cambridge: Cambridge University Press.

Allen, F. and Gale, D. (2003), 'Capital adequacy regulation: in search of a rationale', in R. Arnott et al. (eds), *Economics in an Imperfect World. Essays in Honor of Joseph E. Stiglitz*, Cambridge, MA: MIT Press, pp. 83–109.

Appleby, J.O. (1978), *Economic Thought and Ideology in Seventeenth-Century England*, Princeton, NJ: Princeton University Press.

Arnoldi, J. (2004), 'Derivatives: virtual values and real risks', *Theory, Culture & Society*, **21**(6), 23–42.

Austin, J.L. (1962), *How to Do Things with Words*, London: Oxford University Press.

Bachelier, L. (1900), 'Théorie de la speculation', *Annales Scientifiques de l'Ecole Normale Supérieure*, 3rd series, **17**, 21–86 (Eng. trans. *The Random Character of Stock Market Prices*, Cambridge, MA: Cootner, 1964, pp. 17–79).

Baecker, D. (1988), *Information und Risiko in der Marktwirtschaft*, Frankfurt a.M.: Suhrkamp.

Barnes, B. (1983), 'Social life as bootstrapped induction', *Sociology*, **17**, 524–45.

Barnes, B. and Edge, D. (eds) (1982), *Science in Context: Readings in the Sociology of Science*, Milton Keynes: Open University Press.

Betti, F. (2000), 'Value at risk. La gestione dei rischi finanziari e la creazione di valore', *Il Sole 24 Ore*, Milan.

Black, F. and Scholes, M. (1981), 'The pricing of options and corporate liabilities', *Journal of Political Economy*, **81**(3), 637–54.

Bloch, M. (1954), *Lineamenti di una storia monetaria d'Europa*, Turin: Einaudi, 1981 (original *Esquisse d'une histoire monétaire de l'Europe*, Paris: Colin, 1954).

Bougen, P. (2003), 'Catastrophe risk', *Economy and Society*, **32**(2), 253–74.

Braudel, F. (1967), *Civilisation matérielle et capitalisme (XVᵉ–XVIIIᵉ siècle)*, Paris: Colin (It. edn *Capitalismo e cività materiale (secoli XV–XVIII)*, Turin: Einaudi, 1977).

Brunschvig, Léon (1949), *L'expérience humaine et la causalité physique*, Paris: Presses Univeritaires de France.

Bryan, D. and Rafferty, M. (2007), 'Financial derivatives and the theory of money', *Economy and Society*, **36**(1), 134–58.

Burke, K. (1969), *A Grammar of Motives*, Berkeley, Los Angeles and London: University of California Press.

Callon, M. (ed.) (1998), *The Laws of the Market*, Oxford: Blackwell.

Caranti, F. (2003), *Guida pratica al trading con le opzioni. Dominare i mercati controllando il rischio*, Milan: Trading Library.

Cesarini, F. and Gualtieri, P. (2000), *La borsa*, Bologna: Il Mulino.

Chancellor, E. (2000), *Un mondo di bolle. La speculazione finanziaria dalle origini alla new economy*, Rome: Carocci (original 1999).

Cipolla, C.M. (1989), 'La svalutazione della moneta nell'Europa medievale', in *Le tre rivoluzioni e altri saggi di storia economia e sociale*, Bologna: Il Mulino, pp. 145–56.

Clark, N. and Juma, C. (1987), *Long-Run Economics*, London: Pinter.

Collier, S.J. (2008), 'Enacting catastrophe: preparedness, insurance, budgetary rationalization', *Economy and Society*, **37**(2), 224–50.

Colombo, A. et al. (2006), 'Investire con le opzioni', *Il Sole 24 Ore*, Milan.

Coumet, E. (1970), 'La théorie du hasard est-elle née par hasard?', *Annales Économies, Sociétés, Civilisations*, **XXV**(1), 574–98.

Davidson, P. (1978), *Money and the Real World*, London: Macmillan.

Davidson, P. (1996), 'Some misunderstandings on uncertainty in modern classical economics', in C. Schmidt (ed.), *Uncertainty in Economic Thought*, Cheltenham, UK and Brookfield, USA: Edward Elgar, pp. 21–37.

Demange, G. and Laroque, G. (2006), *Finance and the Economics of Uncertainty*, Oxford: Blackwell.

Dickson, P.G.M. (1967), *The Financial Revolution in England. A Study in the Development of Public Credit 1688–1756*, London: Macmillan.

DiMaggio, P. and Powell, W.W. (1983), 'The iron cage revisited: institutional isomorphism and collective rationality in organizational fields', *American Sociological Review*, **48**, 147–60.

Dumont, L. (1977), *Homo aequalis. Genèse et épanouissement de l'idéologie économique*, Paris: Gallimard (It. edn *Homo aequalis. 1. Genesi e trionfo dell'ideologia economica*, Milan: Adelphi, 1984).

Eatwell, J. and Taylor, L. (2000), *Global Finance at Risk. The Case for International Regulation*, Cambridge: Polity.

Ericson, R.V. and Doyle, A. (2004), 'Catastrophe risk, insurance and terrorism', *Economy and Society*, **33**(2), 135–73.

Esposito, E. (2002), *Soziales Vergessen*, Frankfurt a.M.: Suhrkamp.

Esposito, E. (2004), *Die Verbindlichkeit des Vorübergehenden. Paradoxien der Mode*, Frankfurt a.M.: Suhrkamp.

Esposito, E. (2005), 'Meccanismi divinatori nei mercati finanziari', *Rassegna Italiana di Sociologia*, **1**, 95–123.

Esposito, E. (2007), *Die Fiktion der wahrscheinlichen Realität*, Frankfurt a.M.: Suhrkamp.

Fama, E.F. (1970), 'Efficient capital markets: a review of theory and empirical work', *Journal of Finance*, **25**, 383–417.

Fini, M. (1998), *Il denaro 'sterco del demonio'. Storia di un'affascinante scommessa sul nulla*, Venice: Marsilio.

Finley, M.I. (1973), *The Ancient Economy*, Berkeley and Los Angeles: University of California Press (It. edn *L'economia degli antichi e dei moderni*, Milan: Mondadori, 1995).

Fligstein, N. (2001), *The Architecture of Markets: An Economic Sociology of Twenty-First-Century Capitalist Societies*, Princeton, NJ and Oxford: Princeton University Press.

Fligstein, N. and Dauter, L. (2007), 'The sociology of markets', *Annual Review of Sociology*, **33**, 105–28.

Foerster, H. von (1970), 'Thoughts and notes on cognition', in P. Gavin (ed.), *Cognition: A Multiple View*, New York: Spartan Books, pp. 25–48. (Also in *Understanding Understanding. Essays on Cybernetics and Cognition*, New York, Berlin and Heidelberg: Springer, 2003, pp. 169–89.)

Foerster, H. von (1981), *Observing Systems*, Seaside, CA: Intersystems Publications.

Friedman, M. (1953), 'The methodology of positive economics', in *Essays in Positive Economics*, Chicago, IL: University of Chicago Press, pp. 3–43.

Galbraith, J.K. (1991), *A Short History of Financial Euphoria. Financial Genius is Before the Fall*, Knoxville, TN: Whittle Direct Books.

Goede, M. de (2004), 'Repoliticizing financial risk', *Economy and Society*, **33**(21), 197–217.

Goodhart, C.A.E. (1989), *Money, Information and Uncertainty*, London: Macmillan (It. edn *Moneta, Informazione e incertezza*, Bologna: Il Mulino, 1994).

Granovetter, M. (1985), 'Economic action and social structure: the problem of embeddedness', *American Journal of Sociology*, **9**(13), 481–510.

Grossi, P. and Kunreuther, H. (eds) (2005), *Catastrophe Modeling, A New Approach to Managing Risk*, New York: Springer.

Grossman, S.J. (1976), 'On the efficiency of competitive stock markets where traders have diverse information', *Journal of Finance*, **31**, 573–85.

Grossman, S.J. (1977), 'The existence of future markets, noisy rational expectations, and informational externalities', *Review of Economic Studies*, **44**, 431–44; also in Grossman (1989), pp. 62–90.

Grossman, S.J. (1989), *The Informational Role of Prices*, Cambridge, MA: MIT Press.

Grossman, S.J. and Stiglitz, J.E. (1980), 'On the impossibility of informationally efficient markets', *American Economic Review*, **70**, 393–408; also in Grossman (1989), pp. 91–116.

Hafner, W. and Zimmermann, H. (eds) (2009), *Vinzenz Bronzin's Option Pricing Models: Exposition and Appraisal*, Berlin and Heidelberg: Springer.

Hayek, F.A. von (1937), 'Economics and knowledge', *Economica*, **IV**, 33–54; also in *Individualism and Economic Order*, Chicago, IL: The University of Chicago Press, 1948 (reprint 1980), pp. 33–56.

Hayek, F.A. von (1948), 'The meaning of competition', in *Individualism and Economic Order*, Chicago, IL: The University of Chicago Press (reprint 1980).

Hayek, F.A. von (1978), 'Competition as a discovery procedure', in *New Studies in Philosophy, Politics, Economics and the History of Ideas*, Chicago, IL: The University of Chicago Press (It. edn *Nuovi studi di filosofia, politica, economia e storia delle idee*, Rome: Armando, 1988).

Hayek, F.A. von (1988), *Conoscenza, mercato, pianificazione. Saggi di economia e di epistemologia*, Bologna: Il Mulino.

Hicks, J. (1967), *Critical Essays in Monetary Theory*, Oxford: Clarendon Press.

Hicks, J. (1979), *Causality in Economics*, Oxford: Basil Blackwell.

Holland, J.H. (1992), 'Algoritmi genetici', *Le Scienze*, **289**, 50–57.

Hull, J.C. (1991), *Introduction to Futures and Options Markets*, Upper Saddle River, NJ: Prentice-Hall.

Hull, J.C. (1997), *Options, Futures and Other Derivatives*, Englewood Cliffs, NJ: Prentice-Hall.

Ingham, G. (2000), '"Babylonian madness". On the historical and sociological origins of money', in John Smithin (ed.), *What is Money?*, London: Routledge, pp. 16–41.

Ingham, G. (2004), *The Nature of Money*, Cambridge: Polity.

Kahneman, D., Slovic, P. and Tversky, A. (eds) (1982), *Judgement under Uncertainty: Heuristics and Biases*, Cambridge and New York: Cambridge University Press.

Kapferer, J.-N. (1987), *Rumeurs*, Paris: Seuil (It. edn *Le voci che corrono*, Milan: Longanesi, 1988).

Kaye, J. (1998), *Economy and Nature in the Fourteenth Century. Money, Market Exchage, and the Emergence of Scientific Thought*, Cambridge: Cambridge University Press.

Keynes, J.M. (1936), *The General Theory of Employment, Interest and Money*, London: Macmillan.

Kindleberger, C.P. (1978), *Manias, Panic and Crushes. A History of Financial Crisis*, New York: Basic Books (It. edn *Euforia e panico. Storia delle crisi finanziarie*, Rome and Bari: Laterza, 1981).

Knight, F.H. (1921), *Risk, Uncertainty and Profit*, Boston, MA: Houghton Mifflin (It. edn. *Rischio, incertezza e profitto*, Florence: La Nuova Italia, 1960).

Knorr Cetina, K. (2005), 'How are global markets global? The architecture of a flow world', in K. Knorr Cetina and A. Preda (eds), *The Sociology of Financial Markets*, Oxford: Oxford University Press, pp. 38–61.

Knorr Cetina, K. and Bruegger, U. (2002), 'Global microstructures: the virtual societies of financial markets', *American Journal of Sociology*, **107**(4), 905–50.

Korzybski, A. (1953), *Science and Sanity. An Introduction to Non-Aristotelian Systems and General Semantics*, Lakeville, CT: The International Non-Aristotelian Library Publishing Company.

Koselleck, R. (1979), *Vergangene Zukunft. Zur Semantik geschichtlicher Zeiten*, Frankfurt a.M.: Suhrkamp.

Lachmann, L.M. (1977), *Capital, Expectations and the Market Process. Essays in the Theory of the Market Economy*, Kansas City, MO: Sheed Andrews and McMeel.

Langley, P. (2008), 'Sub-prime mortgage lending: a cultural economy', *Economy and Society*, **37**(4), 469–94.

Le Goff, J. (1960), 'Au Moyen Age: temps de l'Eglise et temps du marchand', in *Annales ESC*, pp. 417–33 (It. edn *Tempo della chiesa e tempo del mercante*, Turin: Einaudi, 1977).

Le Goff, J. (1986), *La bourse et la vie. Economie et religion au Moyen Age*, Paris: Hachette (It. edn. *La borsa e la vita, Dall'usuraio al banchiere*, Rome and Bari: Laterza, 1987).

LiPuma, E. and Lee, Benjamin (2005), 'Financial derivatives and the rise of circulation', *Economy and Society*, **34**(3), 404–27.

Lo, A.W. and MacKinlay, Craig (1999), *A Non-Random Walk Down Wall Street*, Princeton, NJ: Princeton University Press.

Loasby, B.J. (1999), *Knowledge, Institutions and Evolution in Economics*, London and New York: Routledge.

Luhmann, N. (1976), 'The future cannot begin: temporal structures in modern society', *Social Research*, **43**, 130–52.

Luhmann, N. (1980), 'Temporalisierung von Komplexität: Zur Semantik neuzeitlicher Zeitbegriffe', in *Gesellschaftsstruktur und Semantik. Studien zur Wissenssoziologie der modernen Gesellschaft*, vol. 1, Frankfurt a.M.: Suhrkamp, pp. 235–300.

Luhmann, N. (1984), *Soziale Systeme. Grundriß einer allgemeinen Theorie*, Frankfurt a.M.: Suhrkamp.

Luhmann, N. (1988a), *Die Wirtschaft der Gesellschaft*, Frankfurt a.M.: Suhrkamp.

Luhmann, N. (1988b), *Erkenntnis als Konstruktion*, Bern: Benteli.

Luhmann, N. (1989a), 'Staat und Staatsraison im Übergang von traditionaler Herrschaft zu moderner Politik', in N. Luhmann, *Gesellschaftsstruktur und Semantik. Studien zur Wissenssoziologie der modernen Gesellschaft*, vol. 3, Frankfurt a.M.: Suhrkamp, pp. 65–148.

Luhmann, N. (1989b), 'Die Ausdifferenzierung der Religion', in N. Luhmann, *Gesellschaftsstruktur und Semantik. Studien zur Wissenssoziologie der modernen Gesellschaft*, vol. 3, Frankfurt a.M.: Suhrkamp, pp. 259–357.

Luhmann, N. (1989c), 'Kommunikationsweisen und Gesellschaft', in Werner Rammert (ed.), *Computer, Medien, Gesellschaft*, Frankfurt a.M.: Campus, pp. 11–18.

Luhmann, N. (1990a), *Die Wissenschaft der Gesellschaft*, Frankfurt a.M.: Suhrkamp.

Luhmann, N. (1990b), 'Gleichzeitigkeit und Synchronisation', in *Soziologische Aufklärung 5. Konstruktivistische Perspektiven*, Opladen: Westdeutscher Verlag, pp. 95–130.

Luhmann, N. (1991), *Soziologie des Risikos*, Berlin and New York: de Gruyter.

Luhmann, N. (1992), *Beobachtungen der Moderne*, Opladen: Westdeutscher Verlag.

Luhmann, N. (1995), *Die Realität der Massenmedien*, Opladen: Westdeutscher Verlag.

Luhmann, N. (1996a), 'Die Kontrolle von Intransparenz', unpublished manuscript, Bielefeld.

Luhmann, N. (1996b), 'Die Unbestimmtheit der Wirtschaft', unpublished manuscript, Bielefeld.

Luhmann, N. (1997), *Die Gesellschaft der Gesellschaft*, Frankfurt a.M.: Suhrkamp.

Luhmann, N. (2000), *Organisation und Entscheidung*, Opladen: Westdeutscher Verlag.

Luther, M. (1883), *Tischreden*, in *Werke*, vol. I, Weimar: Böhlhaus.

MacKenzie, D. (2005a), 'Opening the black boxes of global finance', *Review of International Political Economy*, **12**(4), 555–76.

MacKenzie, D. (2005b), 'How a superportfolio emerges: long-term capital management and the sociology of arbitrage', in K. Knorr Cetina and A. Preda (eds), *The Sociology of Financial Markets*, Oxford: Oxford University Press, pp. 62–83.

MacKenzie, D. (2006), *An Engine, Not a Camera. How Financial Models Shape Markets*, Cambridge, MA: MIT Press.

MacKenzie, D. (2007), 'The material production of virtuality: innovation, cultural geography and facticity in derivative markets', *Economy and Society*, **36**(3), 355–76.

MacKenzie, D. and Millo, Y. (2003), 'Constructing a market, performing theory: the historical sociology of a financial derivatives exchange', *American Journal of Sociology*, **109**(1), 107–45.

Malkiel, B. (1999), *A Random Walk Down Wall Street*, New York: Norton.

Mandelbrot, B. and Hudson, R.L. (2004), *The (Mis)Behavior of Markets. A Fractal View of Risk, Ruin, and Reward*, New York: Basic Books (It. edn *Il disordine dei mercati. Una visione frattale di rischio, rovina e redditività*, Turin: Einaudi, 2005).

Manuli, A. and Manuli, E. (1999), *Hedge Funds. I vantaggi di una forma di investimento alternativa*, Milan: Jackson Libri.

Marron, D. (2007), '"Leading by numbers": credit scoring and the constitution of risk within American consumer credit', *Economy and Society*, **36**(1), 103–33.

Maurer, B. (2002), 'Repressed futures: financial derivatives theological unconscious', *Economy and Society*, **31**(1), 15–36.

Millman, G.J. (1995), *The Vandals' Crown*, New York: Free Press (It. edn *Finanza barbara*, Milan: Garzanti 1996).

Miyazaki, H. (2007), 'Between arbitrage and speculation: an economy of belief and doubt', *Economy and Society*, **36**(3), 396–415.

Moore, B.J. (1979), 'Monetary factors', in Alfred S. Eichner (ed.), *A Guide to Post-Keynesian Economics*, London: Macmillan, pp. 120–38.

Motterlini, M. (2006), *Economia emotiva: che cosa si nasconde dietro i nostri conti quotidiani*, Milan: Rizzoli.

Motterlini, M. and Piattelli Palmarini, M. (eds) (2005), *Critica della ragione economica*, Milan: Il Saggiatore.

Nicholson, C. (1994), *Writing and the Rise of Finance. Capital Satire of the Early Eighteenth Century*, Cambridge: Cambridge University Press.

O'Driscoll, G. and Rizzo, M.J. (1996), *The Economics of Time and Ignorance*, London and New York: Routledge (It. edn *L'economia del tempo e dell'ignoranza*, Rubbettino, 2002).

Parsons, T. and Smelser, N.J. (1956), *Economy and Society: A Study in the Integration of Economic Social Theory*, London: Routledge & Kegan Paul.

Pascal B. (1670), *Pensées*, in Jean Lafond (ed.), *Moralistes du XVIIᵉ Siècle*, Paris: Laffont, 1992, pp. 321–604.

Piel, K. (2003), *Ökonomie des Nichtwissens. Aktienhype und Vertrauenskrise im Neuen Markt*, Frankfurt a.M.: Campus.

Polanyi, K. (ed.) (1957), *Trade and Market in the Early Empires. Economies in History and Theory*, New York: The Free Press (It. edn. *Traffici e mercati negli antichi imperi. Le economie nella storia e nella teoria*, Turin: Einaudi, 1978).

Pribram, K. (1983), *A History of Economic Reasoning. I. The Development of Economics into an Independent Discipline. Thirteenth through Eighteenth Centuries*, Baltimore, MD and London: The Johns Hopkins University Press (It. edn *Storia del pensiero economico. Volume primo. Nascita di una disciplina 1200–1800*, Turin: Einaudi, 1988).

Prigogine, I. (1985a), 'L'esplorazione della complessità', in G. Bocchi and M. Ceruti (eds), *La sfida della complessità*, Milan: Feltrinelli, pp. 179–93.

Prigogine, I. (1985b), *Dall'essere al divenire. Tempo e complessità nelle scienze fisiche*, Turin: Einaudi.

Pryke, M. and Allen, J. (2000), 'Monetized time-space: derivatives – money's "new imaginary"?', *Economy and Society*, **29**(2), 264–84.

Pryke, M. and Du Gay, P. (2007), 'Take an issue: cultural economy of finance', *Economy and Society*, **36**(3), 339–54.

Rebonato, R. (1999), *Volatility and Correlation in the Pricing of Equity, FX and Interest-rate Options*, Chichester: Wiley.

Rizzo, M.J. (1979), 'Disequilibrium and all that: an introductory essay', in Mario J. Rizzo (ed.), *Time, Uncertainty and Disequilibrium*, Lexington, KY: Lexington Books, D.C. Heath and Company, pp. 1–18.

Robinson, J. (1971), *Economic Heresies. Some Old-Fashioned Questions in Economic Theory*, London: Macmillan.

Ross, S. (1987), 'Finance', in J. Eatwell, M. Milgate and P. Newman (eds), *The New Palgrave Dictionary of Economics*, vol. 2, London: Macmillan.

Rotman, B. (1987), *Signifying Nothing. The Semiotics of Zero*, London: Macmillan (Ger. edn *Die Null und das Nichts. Eine Semiotik des Nullpunkts*, Berlin: Kadmos, 2000).

Sarcinelli, M. (2000), 'Introduzione', in M. Tivegna and G. Chiofi, *News e dinamica dei tassi di cambio*, Bologna: Il Mulino, pp. 13–19.

Sassen, S. (1996), *Losing Control?, Sovereignty in an Age of Globalization*, New York: Columbia University Press (It. trans. *Fuori controllo*, Milan: Il Saggiatore, 1998).

Sassen, S. (2005), 'The embeddedness of electronic markets: the case of global capital markets', in K. Knorr Cetina and A. Preda (eds), *The Sociology of Financial Markets*, Oxford: Oxford University Press, pp. 17–37.

Schoffeniels, E. (1975), *L'Anti-Hasard*, Paris: Gauthers-Villars.

Shackle, G.L.S. (1955), *Uncertainty in Economics and other Reflections*, Cambridge: Cambridge University Press (reprint 1968).

Shackle, G.L.S. (1967), *The Years of High Theory. Invention and Tradition in Economic Thought. 1926–1939*, Cambridge: Cambridge University Press.

Shackle, G.L.S. (1972), *Epistemic & Economics. A Critique of Economic Doctrine*, Cambridge: Cambridge University Press.

Shackle, G.L.S. (1988), *Business, Time and Thought*, London: Macmillan.

Shackle, G.L.S. (1990a), *Time, Expectations and Uncertainty in Economics*, ed. J.L. Ford, Aldershot, UK and Brookfield, USA: Edward Elgar.

Shackle, G.L.S. (1990b), 'General thought-schemes and the economist', in 1990a, pp. 179–94.

Shackle, G.L.S. (1990c), 'Evolutions of thought in economics', in 1990a, pp. 207–19.

Shiller, R.J. (2000), *Irrational Exuberance*, Princeton, NJ: Princeton University Press (It. edn *Euforia irrazionale, Analisi dei boom di borsa*, Bologna: Il Mulino, 2000).

Shiller, R.J. (2003), *The New Financial Order*, Princeton, NJ: Princeton University Press.

Shiller, R.J. (2008), *The Subprime Solution. How Today's Global Financial Crisis Happened, and What to Do about It*, Princeton and Oxford: Princeton University Press.

Shleifer, A. (2000), *Inefficient Markets. An Introduction to Behavioral Finance*, Oxford: Oxford University Press.

Simmel, G. (1889), 'Psychologie des Geldes', *Jahrbuch für Gesetzgebung, Verwaltung und Volkswirtschaft im Deutschen Reich*, **13**, pp. 1251–64 (It. edn in G. Simmel, *Il denaro nella cultura moderna*, Rome: Armando, 1998).

Simmel, G. (1900), *Philosophie des Geldes*, Leipzig (It. edn *Filosofia del denaro*, Turin: UTET, 1984).

Smith, V. (2002), 'Constructivist and ecological rationality in economics', Nobel Lecture (It. edn 'Razionalità costruttivista e razionalità ecologica' in M. Motterlini and M. Piattelli Palmarini (eds), *Critica della ragione economica*, Milan: Il Saggiatore, pp. 141–220).

Smithin, J. (ed.) (2000), *What is Money?*, London: Routledge.

Sohn-Rethel, A. (1990), *Das Geld, die bare Münze des Apriori*, Berlin: Wagenbach.

Soros, G. (1987), *The Alchemy of Finance. Reading the Mind of the Market*, Chichester: Wiley (It. edn *L'alchimia della finanza. La logica, le tecniche e i segreti del mercato*, Florence: Ponte alle Grazie, 1995).

Soros, G. (1995), *Soros on Soros: Staying Ahead of the Curve*, Chichester: Wiley (It. edn *Soros su Soros*, Florence: Ponte alle Grazie, 1995).

Soros, G. (2008), *The New Paradigm for Financial Markets: The Credit Crisis of 2008 and What it Means*, New York: Public Affairs.

Stiglitz, J.E. (1985), 'Information and economic analysis: a perspective', *Economic Journal*, **95**, 21–41.

Stiglitz, J.E. (1986), 'Theory of competition, incentives and risk', in J.E. Stiglitz and G.F. Mathewson (eds), *New Developments in the Analysis of Market Structure*, Basingstoke: Macmillan, pp. 399–446.

Stiglitz, J.E. (1992), 'Methodological issues and the new Keynesian economics', in A. Vercelli and N. Dimitri (eds), *Macroeconomics. A Survey of Research Strategies*, Oxford and New York: Oxford University Press, pp. 38–86.

Stiglitz, J.E. (2003), 'Information and the change in the paradigm in economics', in R. Arnott, B. Greenwald, R. Kanbur and B. Nalebuff (eds), *Economics in an Imperfect World. Essays in Honor of Joseph E. Stiglitz*, Cambridge, MA: The MIT Press, pp. 569–639.

Strange, S. (1986), *Casino Capitalism*, Oxford: Basil Blackwell (It. edn *Capitalismo d'azzardo*, Rome and Bari: Laterza, 1988).

Strange, S. (1998), *Mad Money*, Manchester: Manchester University Press (It. edn *Denaro impazzito. I mercati finanziari: presente e futuro*, Turin: Edizioni di Comunità, 1999).

Swan, E.J. (2000), *Building the Global Market. A 4000 Year History of Derivatives*, The Hague, London and Boston, MA: Kluwer.

Swedberg, R. (1990), *Economics and Sociology*, Princeton, NJ: Princeton University Press.

Swedberg, R. (1994), 'Markets as social structures', in N.J. Smelser and R. Swedberg (eds), *The Handbook of Economic Sociology*, Princeton, NJ: Princeton University Press, pp. 255–82.

Swedberg, R. (2003), *Principles of Economic Sociology*, Princeton, NJ: Princeton University Press.

Taleb, N.N. (2001), *Fooled by Randomness. The Hidden Role of Chance in the Markets and in Life*, New York and London: Texere LLC.

Tivegna M. and Chiofi, G. (2000), *News e dinamica dei tassi di cambio*, Bologna: Il Mulino.

Voegelin, E. (1925), 'Die Zeit in der Wirtschaft', *Archiv für Sozialwissenschaft und Sozialpolitik*, **53**, 186–211.

Weber, M. (1922), *Wirtschaft und Gesellschaft*, Tübingen: Mohr (It. edn *Economia e società*, Milan: Edizioni di Comunità, 1995).

White, H.C. (1981), 'Where do markets come from?', *American Journal of Sociology*, **87**(3), 517–47.

White, H.C. (2002), *Markets from Networks: Socioeconomic Models of Production*, Princeton, NJ and Oxford: Princeton University Press.

Wiener, N. (1948), *Cybernetics, or Control and Communication in the Animal and the Machine*, Cambridge, MA: MIT Press.

Wolf, M. (1985), *Teoria delle comunicazioni di massa*, Milan: Bompiani.

Zelizer, V.A. (1983), *Moral and Markets. The Development of Life Insurance in the United States*, New Brunswick, NJ and London: Transaction.

Zelizer, V.A. (1997), *The Social Meaning of Money*, Princeton, NJ: Princeton University Press.

Zelizer, V.A. (1998), 'The proliferation of social currencies', in M. Callon (ed.), *The Laws of the Market*, Oxford: Blackwell, pp. 1–57.

Index